Unless Recal

Verstehen

The Uses of Understanding
in Social Science

Verstehen

Michael Martin

Transaction Publishers
New Brunswick (U.S.A.) and London (U.K.)

Library of Congress Catalog Number: 99-040104
ISBN: 0-7658-0003-9
Printed in the United States of America

Library of Congress Cataloging-in-Publication Data

Martin, Michael, 1932 Feb. 3-
    Verstehen : the uses of understanding in social science / Michael Martin.
        p. cm.
    Includes bibliographical references and index.
    ISBN 0-7658-0003-9 (alk. paper)
    1. Social sciences—Philosophy. I. Title.
H61.M4246 1999
300'.1 21—dc21   99-040104

To Maxwell Oliver Martin

Contents

Preface

My interest in Verstehen goes back at least thirty years. Over the decades, I have developed my ideas on this topic in journal articles, book reviews, and book chapters.

There are several people who helped me along the way and whom I wish to thank. My wife, Jane Roland Martin, read and edited the entire manuscript; in addition, her own work on Verstehen has greatly influenced my own. Lee McIntyre read the manuscript and made important suggestions for its improvement. I am grateful also to Robert Cohen and the late Marx Wartofsky for their encouragement and their invitation in the late 1960s to speak at the Boston Colloquium for the Philosophy of Science. The paper I gave there touched on many of the themes I argue for in this book. Daniel Little invited me to present an earlier version of chapter 2 to a discussion group he organized at Harvard University and I wish to thank him for that opportunity. I am also indebted to Dagfinn Føllesdal of the University of Oslo for inviting me to present my ideas on methodological pluralism to the Philosophy of Science Colloquium, University of Oslo, and to the members of that colloquium for their constructive comments. Abner Shimony has been a constant source of support with respect to all my research and especially with regard to my work on Verstehen. Jane Cullen, my former editor at Temple University Press, has also been a steady source of encouragement. Finally, I would like to thank Irving Horowitz, my editor at Transaction Publishers, for his wise counsel and guidance.

I would like to express my gratitude to those editors and publishers who have granted me permission to incorporate into this book the following previously published material:

Taylor on "Interpretation and the Sciences of Man," in *Readings in the Philosophy of Social Science*, ed. Michael Martin and Lee McIntyre

(The MIT Press, 1994), chapter 17; reprinted by permission of The MIT Press.

"Geertz and the Interpretative Approach in Anthropology," *Synthèse*, 97; 1993, pp. 269-86; reprinted by permission of Kluwer Academic Publishers.

"Winch on Philosophy, Social Science, and Explanation," *Philosophical Forum*, 23, 1966, pp. 29-41; reprinted by permission of the *Philosophical Forum*.

"Justification by Verstehen," in Michael Martin, *Social Science and Philosophical Analysis* (University Press of America, 1978), pp. 355-68; reprinted by permission of the University Press of America.

"Popperian Anthropology," *Methodology and Science*, 4, 1971, pp. 41-79; reprinted by permission of Uitgeversmaatschappij J H Kok.

Cambridge, Massachusetts, 1999

Introduction

In this book, I will critically evaluate the method of Verstehen, a doctrine of long standing that has generated great controversies and bitter disputes in the social sciences. As we shall see, it has meant different things to different people. Even some methodologists who do not explicitly advocate the use of Verstehen have argued for a position in the social sciences that is similar to those who do.

In its strongest forms, Verstehen entails reliving the experience of the actor or at least rethinking the actor's thoughts, while in its weaker forms it only involves reconstructing the actor's rationale for acting. Some methodologists have argued that Verstehen is a method of verification; others have said that it is only a method of discovery; still others have argued that it is neither and is best construed as a requirement for understanding. The doctrine has been embraced in one form or another by such thinkers as Wilhem Dilthey, Max Weber, R. G. Collingwood, Peter Winch, William Dray, Karl Popper, Michael Scriven, Alfred Schutz, Charles Taylor, Clifford Geertz, and Jürgen Habermas. Its best-known critics have been the positivists such as Carl Hempel, Ernest Nagel, Richard Rudner, and Theodore Abel.

In this book, I analyze the arguments of both the advocates of Verstehen and its critics. I will reject *both* the Verstehen position as well as the positivistic critique of it on the ground that both views fail to appreciate the pluralistic nature of social scientific inquiry. On the one hand, I will argue that both the classical Verstehen theorists and recent proponents presume too narrow and restricted a view of the social sciences. On the other hand, I will argue that the most famous positivistic critique that Verstehen is not a method of verification misses the point, whereas a lesser-known positivist critique of Hempel and Nagel that Verstehen is not necessary for scientific understanding is on target but for the wrong reasons.

A Preliminary Account of Verstehen

"Verstehen" is a German term meaning "understanding," or "comprehension." However, in late-nineteenth-century German academic circles it came to be associated with the view that social phenomena have to be understood "from within." This approach to social inquiry tended to be qualitative rather than quantitative and was opposed by positivists who stressed external, experimental, and quantitative knowledge. Although the positions have been modified over time, this dispute between the positivists and the antipositivists—nowadays called the naturalists and antinaturalists—has persisted and still defines many of the debates in the field. Although positivism is no longer a popular view—indeed, many contemporary philosophers of social science believe it is not a viable position—this controversy has persisted into contemporary times albeit sometimes under different labels. Instead of appealing to "Verstehen" in describing their preferred approach, antipositivists today speak about the interpretation of meaning, or of hermeneutical understanding.[1] The underlying hostility remains, and the wide gap between positivism and antipositivism continues.

Briefly stated, the positivists maintained that the social sciences should approach the study of social phenomena in the same way that the natural sciences have approached the study of natural phenomena—in other words, that the social sciences should have as their goals prediction and nomological explanation. Advocates of this approach, of course, admitted that the search for laws may be more difficult in the social than in the natural sciences (due to certain allegedly unique obstacles faced in the study of human behavior), and that the laws produced may be less precise, statistical, or less well-supported than they are in the natural sciences. Nonetheless, they denied that such differences represent any fundamental difference in kind between the natural and the social sciences. Making no sharp separation between explaining and understanding, positivists argued that to understand a social phenomenon, for example, some social action, one explained it by subsuming it under a causal law. Understanding an agent's actions in terms of his or her reasons was assimilated to explaining the action causally by laws since having a reason for an action was a type of cause. Explanation was not necessarily tied to understanding the action from the point of view of the actor, and Verstehen was at best a heuristic device in suggesting hypotheses.

Antipositivists, on the other hand, deny what the positivists assert. They hold that the study of social phenomena should not be approached in the same way as the study of nature, due to basic differences in the subject matter at hand, as well as differences in what we want to know about the phenomena. In particular, they maintain that the social sciences should use the method of "Verstehen"—that they should attempt to understand social phenomena from the point of view of the social agent. Instead of focusing on the causes, social inquiry should concentrate on the agent's reasons which, according to the antipositivists, are not causes. Advocates of this view typically claim that there are no laws in the social sciences; and even if there were, the laws would be impractical or irrelevant, given what it is that we seek to understand about social phenomena. Thus, in their view, there is not just a difference in degree concerning the methodology appropriate to the study of natural and social phenomena, but rather an unbridgeable gulf.

The Structure of the Book

In the first three chapters, I consider the classical debate between Verstehen theorists and positivists. In chapter 1, I consider the classical position on Verstehen: the views of Wilhelm Dilthey, Max Weber, and R. G. Collingwood. I show that the classical theory puts unacceptable a priori limits on social scientific inquiry and allows social phenomena to be understood in only one way, thus setting the stage for later Verstehen theory to fall into the same trap. In chapter 2, I consider the best-known critique of the best-known critics of Verstehen—the positivists—that Verstehen is not a method of verification. Since, however, the classical Verstehen theorists did not say that it was, I show that the positivists were talking past them. Moreover, despite Peter Munch's and Scriven's arguments to the contrary, I show that Verstehen is not a method of verification. In chapter 3, I consider a lesser-known criticism of the positivists. Hempel and Nagel argue that Verstehen is not a necessary condition for social scientific understanding. This criticism is correct, but was offered for the wrong reasons.

In the next seven chapters, I consider contemporary varieties of the Verstehen position that have limitations similar to the classical position and argue that all of these conflict with the pluralistic nature of social science. In chapter 4, Peter Winch's and William Dray's variants of Verstehen are considered and shown to set unacceptable restrictions to understanding. In chapters 5 through 9, I consider other recent

Verstehen theorists and argue that they, like Winch and Dray, have too limited a view of what constitutes understanding in the social sciences. It should be noted that, although some of the theorists I consider in the chapters that follow—Popper, Taylor, and Geertz— do not use the term "Verstehen" to describe their own views, their views can be fairly characterized in Verstehenist terms. While Popper's situational logic involves explaining human behavior in terms of the actors' beliefs, goals, and rationality, Taylor and Geertz advocate interpreting social action in terms of the social meaning of the actors. However, such approaches would be congenial, not only to classical, Verstehenists such as Dilthey and Weber, but to more recent advocates of Verstehen such as Winch, Dray, and Schutz.

In the Conclusion, I maintain that neither the classical Verstehen position nor more recent interpretivists' variations of it are defensible because they presuppose a much too narrow view of the social sciences. Verstehen interpretation in terms of the actor's meaning is necessary to scientific understanding only in certain contexts and for certain purposes. The methodological pluralism advocated in this book is contrasted and compared with three other types.

Definitions and Theses

The following definitions and theses concerning Verstehen will set the stage for the discussion that follows.

Verstehen can be defined as taking the subjective standpoint of the social actors. In some versions of Verstehen taking this standpoint would involve reliving the experiences or rethinking the thoughts of the social actors, while in other versions it would involve merely using their subjective categories in formulating hypotheses or in interpreting social action.

Classical Verstehen theorists claimed:

(1) Verstehen is necessary for social scientific understanding.

Positivists famously claimed:

(2) Verstehen (a) could be a method of discovery but (b) could not be a method of verification.

However, (2a) and (2b) are irrelevant to (1). Although a lesser-known relevant and correct positivistic critique of Verstehen denied (1), it was based on questionable assumptions. Although some more recent Verstehen theorists explicitly argue for (1), others—interpretivists— do not use the term "Verstehen" and advocate a closely related thesis:

(3) Interpretation of human action in terms of the meaning of the social actors is necessary for social scientific understanding.

I reject (1), (2b)—unless it is severely qualified— and (3), and accept

(4) A methodological pluralism in which different approaches to social scientific understanding are justified relative to the purposes and the context of inquiry.

Note

1.   See Paul Rabinow and William M. Sullivan, *Interpretive Social Science: A Second Look* (Berkeley: University of California Press, 1987).

1

The Classical Verstehen Position

In this chapter, the views of Wilhelm Dilthey (1833-1911), Max Weber (1864 -1920), and R. G. Collingwood (1889-1943) will be examined. A main point of contention in late-nineteenth-century German academic circles was the status of the human sciences. Should they be assimilated to the natural sciences as positivists such as Auguste Comte and John Stuart Mill maintained or should they be regarded as autonomous? Two of the most important theorists who advocated an autonomous approach to the social sciences were Wilhelm Dilthey and Max Weber.[1] Both Dilthey and Weber argued that the separation was based on a difference in subject matter. They maintained that, unlike purely physical phenomena, social behavior has an inner dimension. In one standard interpretation of Dilthey, understanding social behavior involves reliving the subjective experience of the actor. For Weber, in contrast, understanding social behavior requires giving causal explanations that are subjectively meaningful, that is, comprehensible in terms of the actor's point of view.

Collingwood is the prime representative of the Verstehen approach in the English-speaking world before the middle of the twentieth century. Although he seldom used the term "Verstehen" in his writings, his basic approach to the study of history could be embraced by the most radical Verstehenist, for he held that historical events must be understood from the inside, and that in order to understand the action of historical agents, historians must rethink the agents' thoughts. Although Collingwood worked in virtual isolation at Oxford between the two wars, the posthumous publication of his *The Idea of History* in 1946 influenced a new generation of philosophers of history.[2]

In this chapter, I will show that these three classical Verstehen theorists placed unacceptable limitations on social science.

7

Wilhelm Dilthey

A historian of ideas and culture, Dilthey wrote extensively on the Renaissance, Reformation, and German Enlightenment as well as on the history of German idealism. He made contributions to metaphysics, the theory of knowledge, psychology, and moral philosophy. Dilthey's philosophy of the social sciences can be understood in part as a reaction to the positivism of Auguste Comte and especially to the naturalistic view of the social sciences of John Stuart Mill. As Mill put it: "If we are to escape from the inevitable failure of social science when compared with the steady progress of the natural science, our only hope lies in generalizing the methods which have proved so fruitful in the natural sciences so as to fit them to the uses of the social sciences."[3] According to Dilthey, the philosophy of Comte and Mill "seemed to me to mutilate the historical reality in order to adapt to the idea and methods of the natural sciences."[4]

Influenced by Kant and the idealists, and the romantic philosophies of Hegel, Schelling, and Schleiermacher, as well as by British empiricism, Dilthey argued that the methodology of the human sciences could not be reduced to that of the natural sciences.[5] The proper object of philosophy, Dilthey maintained, is life in all its unique cultural and historical complexity. Social and historical reality are an accumulation of numerous individual human lives. Dilthey called the sciences that enable us to understand social, cultural, and historical reality Geisteswissenschaften (human studies). He argued that these sciences (psychology, history, philology, literary criticism, economics, comparative religion, and jurisprudence) are different from the natural sciences in that they require that the knower know the inner life of his or her subjects.[6]

According to Dilthey, a crucial difference between the natural and the human sciences prevents the reduction of social science methodology to natural science methodology. Although both the natural and human sciences are based on experience, the experience is different. The human sciences are based on inner experience and the natural sciences on outer experience. Dilthey maintained:

> The motivation behind the habit of seeing these [human] sciences as a unity in contrast with those of nature derives from the depth and fullness of human self-consciousness. Even when unaffected by investigation into the origins of the mind, a man finds in this self-consciousness a sovereign of will, a responsibility of action, a capacity of subordinating everything to thought and for resisting any for-

eign element in the citadel of freedom in his person: by these things he distinguishes himself from all of nature.[7]

This difference leads to different results. In the natural sciences we unify the elements of experience by construction, that is, by inference and hypothesis. However, in the human sciences, Dilthey alleged, unity and coherence are not imposed but are found in their own inherent structure.[8]

This basic difference between the human and natural sciences leads to further differences between their subject matters. First, human beings are purposeful and nature is not. Second, the human sciences are not value-free whereas the natural sciences are. Third, the human sciences rely on rules, norms, and principles but the natural sciences do not. Fourth, humans are conscious of their history and shape their actions in light of this knowledge; the objects studied by the natural sciences do not.[9]

Dilthey's view of the unique aspects of the human sciences was part of his "critique of historical understanding" in which he used Kant's *Critique of Pure Reason, Critique of Practical Reason,* and *Critique of Judgment* as models. Dilthey based his own critique on the following three principles:

1. The manifestations of human life are part of a historical process and should be explained historically. The state, the family, even human beings cannot be satisfactorily characterized abstractly because they are different in different ages.
2. Different times and different human beings can only be understood by projecting oneself imaginatively into their specific points of view. Thus, what was thought during a particular time or what ideas an individual had must be taken into account by the historian.
3. The historian is restricted by the perspective of his or her own times. How the past manifests itself to a historian in light of his or her own concerns becomes a justifiable aspect of the meaning of that past.[10]

These principles formed an important aspect of what has come to be known as historicism, that is, the view that all human behavior must be understood historically. Dilthey, himself, thought that this historicism was liberating because it delivered us from illusions and superstition.[11]

For Dilthey, the differences he perceived between the human and the natural sciences on his analysis of historical understanding necessitated a special methodology for the human sciences. In brief, he held that although the human sciences as well as the natural sciences employ methods such as observation, description, classification, induction, deduction, the testing of hypotheses, and so on, they also used the method of Verstehen.

For Dilthey "Verstehen" had a technical meaning that was not to be confused with the ordinary meaning of the German term—to understand or comprehend—although it was continuous with this meaning. According to H. P. Rickman, a Dilthey scholar writing in the 1960s, Verstehen is "the comprehension of some mental content—an idea, an intention, or feeling—manifested in empirically given expressions such as words or gestures."[12] The use of this method, Dilthey argued, enabled social scientists and historians to arrive at more reliable results and more intelligible findings than the natural sciences since, in his words, "only what the mind has produced, the mind can fully understand."[13] Natural phenomena are relatively opaque and can be explained only by abstract theoretical models that postulate general laws and causal relations. As Dilthey put it: "Nature we explain, psychic life we understand."[14]

But what this comprehension of mental content includes is not completely clear. The most common and widely accepted interpretation is that empathy is the reliving of the mental content of the social actors. Dilthey said: "On the basis of this empathy or transportation there arises the highest form of understanding in which the totality of mental life is active—recreating or re-living."[15] Dilthey says that although most people today could not live through a religious experience such as Martin Luther's, they can empathize with Luther. By using historical documents and cultural records "I can re-live it. I transpose myself into" Luther's circumstances and relive his experience. "Thus, inner-directed man can experience many other existences in his imagination."[16]

This reliving is not an inferential process. When one sees a person stricken with grief one does not first see that the person's expression is that of grief, and then infer from this that the person whom one is observing is experiencing grief. The sight of the expression induces in the observer an immediate emotional response. Dilthey maintains that what happens to the observer when a grief stricken-figure is seen is the reverse of what happens to the figure. In the figure, the experience of grief has manifested itself in an external expression. In the observer, the perceived experience of grief has internalized itself in what Dilthey calls a reproduction [Nachbild] of the experience expressed by the grief stricken-person.[17]

Although the intellectual activity of constructing a coherent picture by fitting the evidence together and filling in the gaps plays a large role in understanding a complex historical period, reliving the events is still essential. H. A. Hodges, another Dilthey scholar writing in the 1960s, puts Dilthey's position this way: "This process of assembling the evidence and filling in the gaps includes, of course, a great deal of reasoning on the lines made familiar to us by formal logic; but it is wholly misconceived if it is thought of as entirely or even primarily that. It is based on the thought processes of imaginative amplification whose nature we shall understand if we go back to the root from which understanding grows—the mirroring in one mind of experiences taking place in another."[18]

Positivist critics of Verstehen have supposed that classical Verstehenists have assumed that Verstehen helps confirm hypotheses about a social actor's inner life. But Dilthey scholars do not interpret his view of Verstehen in this way and this interpretation is not the most convincing reading of Dilthey's intentions. A more plausible construal is that he considered Verstehen to be a necessary condition for understanding. Unless one relives a person's experience one does not really understand him or her. How one verifies the hypothesis about the person's inner life is an independent issue. Although this reading of Dilthey is hardly new among Dilthey scholars, it is in conflict with a popular and widely shared construction of his views.

In any case, on the basis of the above exposition one can formulate *the reliving interpretation* of Dilthey's position as follows:

(1) In order to understand human beings it is necessary to empathize with them.

(2) In order to empathize with them it is necessary to relive their experience.

However, not everyone agrees with this interpretation. Passages in his later writings have suggested to some scholars that Dilthey held the view that in order to understand human beings it was not necessary to relive their experience but only to know what these experiences were. For example, Dilthey distinguished a reconstruction of the thoughts and feelings of another person from the thoughts and feelings manifested in his or her actions and the reliving of this person's experience, and argued that it is possible to understand this person *via* a reconstruction of these thoughts and feelings.[19] On *the reconstruction interpretation* of Dilthey, it is crucial to understanding human beings that one must know what their thoughts and feelings are; but it is not necessary to actually empathize with them in the sense of reliving their experiences.[20] On this interpretation, Verstehen is also not a method of verification. Rather it is a necessary condition for understanding human beings. Let us state the position as follows:

> (3) In order to understand human beings it is necessary to reconstruct the inner life of these human beings from its manifestation in their actions.
>
> (4) This reconstructing involves knowing what the inner lives of these human beings are.

According to some scholars other passages in Dilthey's later work suggest a still different interpretation.[21] As they treat him, Dilthey gave up the psychological view of understanding and maintained that one understands a human action by situating it in a larger cultural whole which gives it its significance.[22] Let us call this *the cultural context interpretation* of Dilthey and formulate it as follows:[23]

> (5) In order to understand human beings it is necessary to relate their actions to the cultural contexts in which the actions take place.

Dilthey's justification of the theory of Verstehen was based on the alleged differences between the human and natural sciences. However, the difference Dilthey finds between the human and natural sciences is questionable. There is no good reason to suppose that the unity of natural phenomena is any more imposed and constructed than the unity of human phenomena. Psychologists, anthropologists, and sociologists, no less than physicists, astronomers, and chemists produce theories that attempt to make sense of their data. To suppose that social scientists in their theorizing are simply tracing the unity that is already there while natural scientists in their theorizing are creating a unity that was not there before finds little support in the actual working of science and begs the question of whether there is a fundamental difference between the human and natural sciences.

Furthermore, the other differences Dilthey finds between the human sciences and natural sciences are either nonexistent or of dubious significance in drawing a methodological distinction between them. The purposeful nature of human behavior can hardly be denied but this does not show that a positivistic social science is impossible. One obvious strategy a positivist could take would be to assimilate purpose to cause and argue that purposeful explanation is simply a species of causal explanation.[24] Dilthey was correct in that social scientists make value judgments concerning their subject matter. However, whether they *must* make these is another matter. In any case, natural scientists also make value judgments about their subject matter and the necessity or lack of necessity in doing so seems no different from that of social scientists.[25] There is no doubt that human society is governed by rules, norms, and principles whereas nature is not. But what exactly is supposed to follow from this about the methodology of the social sciences? Understanding social action need not be in terms of rules, norms, and principles.[26] Finally, it is true that humans are conscious of their history and act accordingly. However, a positivist would say that this only means that people's knowledge of their history will be an important causal factor in explaining their action.

Are one or more of these three interpretations—the reliving, the reconstruction, the cultural context—justified on methodological grounds? The answer is negative because Dilthey has restricted the meaning of understanding so as to rule out legitimate modes of understanding.

The reliving account of understanding specified in (1) and (2) entails that in order to understand, someone must relive their experience. However, this is not true. Understanding someone might simply involve knowing certain facts about the person.[27] Of course, which sort of facts these are will be relative usually to the context.[28] Sometimes the facts will concern the person's motivation, her purposes, her character; at other times they will pertain to her social or cultural background and their relation to her present behavior. But these facts can be known without reliving the person's experience; indeed, reliving the person's experience might not provide the facts necessary for this kind of understanding.[29]

Something similar can be said about understanding a community or society. Understanding a community or a society can consist in having certain propositional knowledge about the community or society. Again just what this knowledge will consist of will depend on the context of the inquiry. Thus, to say that John Beattie understands Bunyoro[30] may mean only that Beattie knows that certain social institutions in Bunyoro are related to each other in ways that form a functional system. In other contexts, understanding a community may consist in knowing about the community's historical development.

Of course, Dilthey might object that factual understanding may not be the primary goal of social science. But then the onus was surely on him to say why reliving the experience of the social actor is so essential to the social sciences. Once it is seen that understanding is possible without empathy in Dilthey's sense, the plausibility of his view is significantly diminished. Dilthey gave Verstehen a special meaning that has little to do with most of the ordinary or scientific senses of the term "understanding."

Further, the point that understanding sometimes simply involves having certain factual understanding tends to undermine Dilthey's contrast between the social and the natural sciences. To say, for example, that someone understands a cold front is usually to say that the person has some particular kind of factual knowledge. Again the context will usually make clear what this factual knowledge will be. It might consist in knowing that a cold front has certain important structural properties or that crucial aspects of the front are causally related; or it might consist of knowing certain facts about the historical dynamics of this cold front or about how this cold fronts functions in the overall weather pattern.

Although Dilthey was mistaken to maintain that Verstehen in the sense of reliving is necessary to understanding, could reliving have other uses? Critics of Verstehen as a way of understanding have allowed that attempting to relive, others experiences might be a useful way of generating hypotheses. As far as I can tell, Dilthey did not argue that reliving others' experience served this function. However, he did believe that reliving served other useful functions. For example, he argued reliving the experiences of others broadens and deepens human experience, thus widening our horizons.[31] However, one could well grant this yet object that this humanizing effect of the use of Verstehen in the human sciences shows nothing about whether it is relevant to factual understanding.

What about the reconstruction sense of understanding specified in (3) and (4)? Certainly Dilthey's view of Verstehen is made more plausible if we take away the reliving aspect of Dilthey's theory and substitute the reconstruction idea. On the reconstruction account, an action is a manifestation of an underlying idea, intention, or feeling. These are reconstructed by the social scientist, not relived. Some commentators have argued that this conception of Verstehen was Dilthey's most mature conception. So interpreted, Dilthey's Verstehen is a form of factual understanding: One knows facts about how one part of an action—the ideas, intentions, and feelings—relates to the other part—the overt manifestation of the underlying idea, intention, and feeling. As we shall see, when it is interpreted in this way, Dilthey's view of Verstehen is probably close to Weber's notion of Verstehen.

However, the reconstructive view also presupposes a limited view of understanding in the social sciences—a form of what Jane Roland Martin has called *internal* in contrast to *external* understanding. When understanding is internal some entity is taken in isolation and some parts or aspects of it are seen in relation to one another.[32] For example, a person who sees how a poem's style, meter, and content are related to one another has internal understanding of the poem. Now one who sees how the goals, beliefs, attitudes, and actual physical movements are connected will have internal understanding of human action. But this is only one type of internal understanding. Dilthey's approach to understanding restricts the use of the descriptive terms to those of the actor—to the terms of folk psychology. However, an action could be described in technical terms, for example, of cognitive psychology, or sociobiology, or psychoanalysis.

Moreover, there are all sorts of phenomena that need to be understood that cannot be fitted into this model of understanding. For example, how can we understand why people have certain ideas, intentions, and feelings? Obviously, this sort of question cannot be answered by understanding human behavior as a manifestation of some mental content for the question concerns the mental content itself and not its manifestation or expression. One also might want to understand why the same sort of mental content gives rise to different manifestations in different situations or perhaps one manifestation in one situation and none in another. Again this cannot be understood in terms of mental content since by hypothesis this remains the same in different manifestations.

In contrast to internal understanding there is what Martin calls *external* understanding. In external understanding a given thing is treated as a whole and understanding involves relating it to something apart from it. For example, a revolution can be understood in terms of the historical causes that have produced it or its consequences for the future of the country; a poem can be understood in terms of its psychological origins or its effects on future poetry; a person's action can be understood in terms of some historical trend and the precedent it sets for the future; marijuana can be understood in terms of the history of the legal sanctions against it or the prospects for legal reform. In short, in the constructive sense of Verstehen, Dilthey wrongly restricts understanding to one type of internal understanding, thus neglecting other kinds of internal understanding as well as all external understanding.[33]

What about the cultural context sense of understanding specified in (5)? Here Dilthey shifts from a type of internal understanding to a type of external understanding. Rather than taking a human action as a whole and understanding how the goals, beliefs, attitudes, and actual physical movements are connected, one understands by relating it to the culture of which it is a part. However, there is no more reason to restrict understanding to external understanding than to restrict it to internal understanding. So (5) also is too restrictive. Moreover, every action can be placed in an indefinite number of contexts, including ones that would not normally be considered cultural, for example, geographic, political, or economic contexts. So (5) is also restricted in this way.

In conclusion, the most common and widely accepted interpretation of Dilthey's notion of Verstehen is the reliving sense. Interpreted in this way, Dilthey maintained that reliving the experience of a social actor was necessary for understanding her action. There is no reason to suppose, however, that social scientific understanding should be so restricted. Understanding can be based on factual knowledge. Other interpretations of Dilthey's notion of Verstehen were also too restricted for social scientific understanding. On the reconstruction sense of Verstehen, understanding is restricted to one type of internal understanding. But external understanding and other types of internal understanding are also possible. The cultural context sense of Verstehen is also too restricted, since on this interpretation social scientific understanding is restricted to one type of external understanding. But internal understanding and other types of external understanding are also possible.

Max Weber

Max Weber, a German social scientist, historian, philosopher, and one of the founders of modern sociology, also advocated a Verstehen approach to social phenomena. Whether or not Dilthey's philosophy of the social sciences influenced Weber is difficult to say. Although Dilthey's work was either unpublished or buried in obscure periodicals when Weber produced his work, Weber could have been exposed to Dilthey's views in two different ways. As a young man he probably heard Dilthey lecture in Berlin. Moreover, in Heidelburg, Troeltsch, who was influenced by Dilthey, was a close friend of Weber. In any case, there are interesting parallels between Dilthey's and Weber's thought. Both of them were concerned with the problem of how subjective understanding could become subject to test and verification. In addition, although Dilthey did not use the term "ideal type" in his work, he, like Weber, referred to the need for typologies. According to Rickman, "It was the best that could be achieved in a field in which the importance and uniqueness of individual cases made generalization and establishment of general laws impossible."[34] Moreover, both men stressed the importance of history and were concerned with understanding society as a whole.

Like Dilthey, Weber used the term "Verstehen" in his methodological writings and it has been translated as "understanding."[35] But translators have also used other expressions to convey the meaning of "Verstehen," for instance, "subjectively understandable," "interpretation in subjective terms," "comprehension."[36] Weber's position on Verstehen was closely connected with his views on the objectivity of sociology. The goal of sociology Weber said is to arrive at subjectively meaningful causal explanations of social behavior.

> Sociology . . . is a science which attempts the interpretive understanding of social action in order thereby to arrive at a causal explanation of its course and effects. In "action" is included all human behavior when and in so far as the acting individual attaches a subjective meaning to it. . . . Action is social in so far as, by virtue of the subjective meaning attached to it by the acting individual (or individuals), it takes account of the behavior of others and is thereby oriented in its course.[37]

Thus, sociology is subjective in the sense that its causal explanations are in terms of the subjective categories of the actors but it is objective in the sense that it uses causal explanations.[38]

Weber's position on subjective understanding of the status of the human sciences, generally, was a judicious compromise mediating between the two extremes. On the one hand, he rejected the view that subjective understanding comprises the entire method of the social sciences while at the same time arguing that this method is essential. On the other hand, he rejected the position that simply obtaining causal explanations of social phenomena embraces the whole of social scientific tasks while he acknowledged the necessity of obtaining causal explanations.

Thus, the natural sciences do not deal with subjectively meaningful phenomena while the social sciences do. In this respect they are fundamentally different. But both the natural sciences and the social sciences understand phenomena by using causal explanations. In this respect they have important similarities. Since the subject matter of the social sciences is basically different, the causal explanations of the social sciences must reflect this difference and be couched in subjectively meaningful terms. This is where Verstehen comes into Weber's theory. Although Weber distinguishes several different types of Verstehen, the most important sense of Verstehen for his general theory is rational explanatory Verstehen, that is, the explanation of human action in terms of the subjective categories of the actor—the actor's beliefs, goals, and intentions.

How did rational explanatory Verstehen function in this theory? Suppose we have a statement of a causal relation between two social events in the following form: If A, then B.[39] Now, suppose some belief, feeling, or purpose of the actors is associated with A. Let us call this A^l. And suppose some belief, feeling, or purpose of the actors is associated with B. Let us call this B^l. Now, suppose A^l and B^l are intuitively closely connected. This close connection between the beliefs, emotions, and goal of the actors makes the causal relation meaningful; one understands the causal link between A and B because of the close link between A^l and B^l.

An example should make this point clear. Suppose there is a causal relation between being the inhabitant of a city that has been devastated by bombs (A) and the lack of resistance to aggression (B). Suppose the feeling of terror and dread (A^l) is associated with A and the feeling of helplessness (B^l) is associated with B. Now, one can argue that there is strong, intuitive connection between A^l and B^l and consequently one understands the causal relation between A and B in terms of this subjectively meaningful connection.

Rational explanatory Verstehen is closely associated in Weber's thought with his notion of ideal types. Weber argued that for scientific purposes it is convenient to treat irrational behavior as departure from pure rational behavior. Pure rational behavior serves as a base line for social scientists from which deviations can be explained. For example,

A panic on the stock exchange can be most conveniently analyzed by attempting to determine first what the course of action would have been if it had not been influenced by irrational affects; it is then possible to introduce the irrational components as accounting for the observed deviations from the hypothetical course. . . . Only in this way is it possible to assess the causal significance of irrational behavior as accounting for the deviations from this type. The construction of a purely rational course of action in such cases serves the sociologists as a type ("ideal type") which has the merit of clear understandability and lack of ambiguity. By comparison with this it is possible to understand the ways in which actual action is influenced by irrational factors as affects and errors, in that they account for the deviations from the line of conduct which would be expected on the hypothesis that the action were purely rational. [40]

Weber stresses that this does not introduce a rational basis into sociology since there is no supposition that people's actual behavior is rational. This "ideal type" of rational behavior has methodological convenience only.[41]

Weber cautions that, in order to accept a meaningful causal relation in sociology as a true account more than rational explanatory Verstehen is needed, that is, more is needed than understanding the actor's behavior in terms of the actor's purposes and motives. Without empirical verification by statistical methods, statements of such causal relations are only plausible hypotheses; they should not be accepted as true.

> Every interpretation attempts to attain clarity and certainty, but no matter how clear an interpretation as such appears to be from the point of view of meaning, it cannot on this account alone claim to be the causally valid interpretation. On this level it must remain only a peculiarly plausible hypothesis. . . .More generally, verification of subjective interpretations by comparison with a concrete course of events is, as in the case of all hypotheses, indispensable.[42]

In contrast to rational explanatory Verstehen, Weber distinguished another type of rational Verstehen: direct observational Verstehen. In this type of Verstehen one immediately categorizes some piece of behavior as an action in terms which the actor uses to categorize it.[43] For example, one has observational Verstehen when one immediately sees the arm-moving behavior of a man as chopping wood and this is indeed how the man categorizes his own behavior. Direct observational Verstehen can best be understood as the preliminary stage of explanatory Verstehen which involves attributing a motive to the agent.[44] However, there is no sharp line between the two different kinds of Verstehen. Direct observational Verstehen involves a description of the action in the agent's terms. However, this description will sometimes constitute an explanation of the behavior depending on what question is being asked. If the question is "why is that man swinging his arms?" this is answered by saying he is chopping wood. One can go on and ask the further question, "why is that man chopping wood?" This also can be answered by a description that the man might give of his own action, namely, that he is making money for his family.

In contrast to both types of rational Verstehen, Weber distinguishes emotional empathetic Verstehen. This type of Verstehen is achieved "when we can adequately grasp the emotional context in which the action took place." This is obtained through "sympathetic participation" in the action.[45] This type of Verstehen seems to be somewhat related to Dilthey's reliving sense of "Verstehen." However, there seem to be some differences. For Dilthey, Verstehen in the sense of reliving seemed to involve all aspects of experience not just the emotional.

Weber argues that, although it is a great help to be able to put oneself imaginatively in the place of the actor and thus sympathetically participate in his experience, this is not an essential condition of meaningful interpretations.[46] For example, Weber says that one need not have been Caesar in order to understand Caesar.[47] One plausible way of understanding Weber is that emotional empathetic participation is helpful but not essential for rational Verstehen. In what way emotional empathetic Verstehen is supposed to be helpful is unclear. One way sometimes suggested by positivists' critics is that empathetic participation may be useful in generating hypotheses. Whether this is what Weber had in mind is not certain.[48] But by and large, Weber says very little about emotional empathetic Verstehen and concentrates his discussion on rational Verstehen.

Weber did believe that emotional empathetic Verstehen was sometimes impossible since it was impossible to participate imaginatively in the emotional content connected with other people's ultimate values when they were radically different from one's own.[49] However, this possibility need not, he thought, exclude the possibility of rational explanatory Verstehen. Although one might not be able to emotionally participate in X's ultimate ends, one could rationally understand X's actions in terms of X's pursuit of their ultimate value. Sometimes Weber seemed to suppose that even rational explanatory Verstehen was impossible. It is not completely clear why Weber thought this was so. There is some indication that he thought rational explanatory Verstehen was impossible when the goals are pursued irrationally, that is, when inappropriate means are taken. But it is unclear why this should prevent rational explanatory Verstehen, for Weber also admitted that we are able to understand, that is, have rational explanatory Verstehen of, error and confusion in the pursuit of ends.[50]

Weber's ideas can be stated more formally and precisely and this construal will clarify the relation between them. Thus the rational explanatory Verstehen can be defined as follows:

(1) S_1 has explanatory Verstehen of act A of S_2 if and only if S_1 comprehends why S_2 does act A in terms of S_2's beliefs, purposes, motives, or feelings.

Weber seemed to believe that in order for rational explanatory Verstehen to be scientifically acceptable it must be in terms of subjectively meaningful causal relations. A subjectively meaningful causal relation can be analyzed as follows:

(2) A causal relation R between A and B is subjectively meaningful if and only if R is understood in terms of some intuitively plausible relation R^1 holding between A^1 (some subjective state of the actors associated with A) and B^1 (some subjective state of the actors associated with B).

To interpret (2) in terms of the account of factual understanding introduced earlier, Weber can be said to have required that the understanding-appropriate sociology be a species of factual understanding known as causal understanding. But not any causal understanding would do. The causal relation he postulated must be subjectively meaningful. Thus, one understands a causal relation in the appropriate sense only if one knows that there is a meaningful causal relation holding between the cause and effect and one knows what this meaningful relation is. Thus, explanatory Verstehen is scientifically acceptable only if it is in terms of subjective meaningful causal relation. The following definitions capture three crucial and related ideas.

(3) S_1 has explanatory Verstehen of a causal relation R between A and B about social behavior if and only if S_1 understands R in terms of some intuitively plausible relation R^1 holding between A^1 (some subjective state of the actors associated with A) and B^1 (some subjective state of the actors associated with B).

(4) A causal relation R between A and B about social behavior is subjectively meaningful for S only if S has explanatory rational Verstehen of R.

(5) H is an acceptable sociological causal hypothesis for S if and only if (a) H states some causal relations R between A and B, (b) S has rational explanatory Verstehen of H, (c) S has adequate statistical evidence for H, and (d) S has adequate evidence that A^1 (some subjective state of the actors) is associated with A and B^1 (some subjective state of the actors) is associated with B.

The other type of rational Verstehen—direct observational Verstehen—can be defined in this way:

(6) S_1 has direct observational Verstehen of behavior B of S_2 if and only if (a) S_1 sees B as some action A and (b) S_2 intends B as A.

Observational Verstehen is a type of factual understanding that is not causal: one understands that p when one knows that p where p is a description of some action under a description that is used by the actor.
Emotional empathetic Verstehen can be defined in this way:

(7) S_1 has emotional empathetic Verstehen of act A of S_2 if and only S_1 has emotion E by empathetic participation in A and S_2 had E while doing A.

There are two basic problems in Weber's methodology of the social sciences and, in particular, in his doctrine of Verstehen.

1. The Limitations on Sociology

Weber limits the task of sociology to establishing subjectively meaningful causal explanations of social phenomena, and one important question is whether this limitation is justified. He admits that the "line between meaningful and merely reactive behavior to which subjective meaning is not attached, cannot be sharply drawn empirically. A very considerable part of all sociological relevant behavior, especially purely traditional behavior, is marginal between the two."[51] According to Weber, traditional behavior "is very often a matter of almost automatic reaction to habitual stimuli which guide behavior in a course which has been repeatedly followed."[52] Moreover, according to Weber, a "considerable part of all sociological relevant data" is of apparently dubious importance according to the goal of sociology set out by him, namely, obtaining meaningful causal explanations.

The paradoxical nature of what Weber is saying can be brought out in the following way. Weber seems to be holding at the same time the following proposition:

(1) The subject matter of sociology should be limited to subjectively meaningful action.

(2) Traditional behavior is not clearly subjectively meaningful.

(3) Traditional behavior is sociologically relevant.

(1) and (2) together imply:

(4) Traditional behavior is not clearly part of the subject matter of sociology.

But (4) combined with (3) implies:

(5) What is sociologically relevant is not clearly part of the subject matter of sociology.

However, (5) combined with what seems like the truism:

(6) What is sociologically relevant is clearly part of the subject matter of sociology,

yields a contraction. This certainly seems to suggest that there is something seriously wrong with Weber's goal.

Putting this contradiction aside, it seems obvious that sociology should attempt to causally explain traditional behavior—after all, by Weber's own admission it is "sociologically relevant"—despite the fact that such behavior would have at best an uncertain subjective meaning. For example, driving on the right side of the road seems to be habitual for people in the United States and would probably be classified as traditional behavior on Weber's scheme and thus would be dubiously meaningful from a subjective point of view. However, there seems to be no good reason why sociologists could not scientifically investigate such behavior, and explain it in terms of other social and historical factors. However, if Weber's standard of adequacy is accepted, these explanations might well be ruled out as not meeting the condition of subjective understandability.

Weber also says: "In the case of many psychophysical processes, meaningful, i.e., subjectively understandable, action is not found at all. . . ."[53] Consequently, psychological explanations are excluded by Weber from the purview of sociology. In general, Weber argued that psychology is no more relevant to sociology than other sciences such as geology and chemistry which study conditions that influence human behavior.[54] Again, this seems to be an unnecessary limit on the scope of sociology. Although Talcott Parsons in his commentary on Weber's methodology suggests that Weber's rejection of psychology was understandable in terms of the limitations of the psychology of his day, he argued that Weber "went too far" and "in some sense, a 'psychology' is an essential *part of* . . . a theory of social action."[55] Be that as it may, there seems be no a priori reason why psychological factors, for example, cognitive progresses and structures should not be used to explain social phenomena. However, these explanations would normally not be subjectively meaningful in Weber's terms.[56]

2. Limitations on Observational and Explanatory Verstehen

Weber seems to have believed that only an agent's purposes or goals can provide meaningful causal explanation. Unless an arbitrary sense is given to the term "meaningful," this thesis certainly seems to be false. One first must distinguish between something being linguistically meaningful and something being intellectually meaningful. A postulated causal relation is linguistically meaningful if the language in which the causal relation is stated meets certain syntactic, semantic, and pragmatic rules of language. If a statement does not meet these rules, one says the language used in the stating of the postulated causal relation is unintelligible. Weber does not seem to be talking about this sort of meaningfulness.

A causal relation is intellectually meaningful only if one understands why the causal relation holds. And one can understand why a relation holds in social behavior in many ways. One can comprehend some causal regularity found in people's social behavior in terms of the social conditions prevailing at a particular time, in terms of people's psychosexual development, in terms of reinforcers and operants, and in many other ways. Weber's theory seems to exclude all those as legitimate ways of making causal relations intellectually meaningful.

This criticism, of course, is closely related to my first. Regularities holding between what Weber called traditional behavior—that is, behavior which has dubious subjective meaning—may not be intellectually comprehensible in terms of the purposes of the agents, but may be comprehensible in some other ways, e.g., in terms of the historical development of traditions in society. A historical trend, rather than the agent's goal or purpose, would make certain causal relations connected with traditional behavior intellectually meaningful. So sociology need not be restricted to establishing intellectually meaningful causal explanations just in terms of the purposes of the actors.

Closely tied to the above two critical points is another. Sometimes in order to comprehend a piece of behavior it may not be necessary to use action language at all. Thus, exclusive use of what Weber calls direct observational Verstehen in one's description of the data to be explained would be too restrictive. That Jones may indeed be chopping is an action description but in some theoretical frameworks, e.g., Skinnerian behaviorism, Jones' behavior may be described not in action terms at all but in terms of schedules of reinforcement.

Even if one uses an action description of behavior, it does not seem to be necessary to use the action description of the agent as observational Verstehen requires. Recall that Weber speaks of the "actually intended meaning of concrete individual action." To be sure, Weber allows for rational explanatory Verstehen explanations in terms of ideal types. Still Weber does not seem to contemplate the possibility of action descriptions which are not of the ideal-type variety and yet depart from the intended meaning of the actor. Under his own description, Jones may be chopping wood. Under some ideal-type description, Jones may be maximizing profits. However, Jones also may be acting in the role of a member of an exploited class in some theoretical framework he is not even aware of. Weber's construal of observational Verstehen would seem to exclude this sort of description and the explanation that is associated with it. But there is no reason why it should be excluded.

These criticisms suggest that Weber's doctrine of Verstehen must be rejected. Weber's theory, like Dilthey's, puts unwarranted restrictions on social inquiry. Perhaps the main difference between Dilthey and Weber is that, in the usual interpretation of Dilthey (what I called the reliving interpretation), a necessary condition of understanding social phenomena is reliving the experience of the actors. Reliving plays little importance in Weber's scheme and his theory of Verstehen is closer to the reconstruction interpretation of Dilthey. However, Weber's theory of Verstehen interpreted as rational explanatory Verstehen is more restrictive than Dilthey's on the reconstruction interpretation since it requires explanatory Verstehen to be in terms of subjectively meaningful causal relations. Dilthey's reconstruction sense of Verstehen, although restricted to one type of internal understanding, was not restricted to causal understanding.

R. G. Collingwood

Coming from the idealistic background—a philosophical background that assumed that reality is in some way mental—of the 1920s and 1930s, Collingwood advocated the view that all history was the history of thought, which historians knew by reenacting the thought of past historical actors. In his most important work on historical method, *The Idea of History*,[57] Collingwood maintained that it is a serious mistake to construe the science of human nature on the model of the natural sciences, that is, to regard human beings as "mere events" that one observes from "the outside." We must understand human nature historically from "the inside," he says.[58] By this he meant that to understand human nature we must know people's thoughts:

> By the inside of the event I mean that in it which can only be described in terms of thought: Caesar's defiance of Republican law, or the clash of constitutional policy between himself and his assassins. The historian is never concerned with these to the exclusion of the other. He is investigating not mere events (where by a mere event I mean one which has only an outside and no inside) but action, and an action is the unity of the outside and inside of an event. He is interested in the crossing of the Rubicon only in relation to Republican law, and in the spilling of Caesar's blood only in its relation to a constitutional conflict. [59]

Collingwood maintained that one discerns an actor's thoughts by rethinking them in one's own mind.

> But how does the historian discern the thoughts which he is trying to discover? There is only one way in which it can be done: by re-thinking them in his own mind. The historian of philosophy, reading Plato, is trying to know what Plato thought when he expressed himself in certain words. The only way in which he can do this is by thinking it for himself. . . . So the historian of politics or warfare, presented with an account of certain action done by Julius Caesar, tries to understand these actions, that is, to discover what thoughts in Caesar's mind determined him to do them. This implies envisaging for himself what Caesar thought about the situation and the possible ways of dealing with it. The history of thought, and therefore, all history, is the re-enactment of past thought in the historian's own mind.[60]

However, Collingwood stressed that this reenactment is "not a passive surrender to the spell of another's mind; it is a labor of active and therefore critical thinking. The historian not only re-enacts past thought, he re-enacts it in the context of his own knowledge and therefore, in re-enacting it, criticizes it, forms his own judgment of its value, corrects whatever errors he can discern in it."[61] This criticism, Collingwood said, is an indispensable condition of historical knowledge itself.

Offhand, this approach seems close to Dilthey's idea of reliving the experience of historical agents. However, although Collingwood acknowledged Dilthey's contribution, he saw a crucial difference between his position and Dilthey's. According to Collingwood, for Dilthey reliving the experience of a historical agent meant reliving the immediate experience as distinct from reflection and knowledge. He objected: "It is not enough for the historian to *be* Julius Caesar or Napoleon, since that does not constitute a knowledge of Julius Caesar or Napoleon any more than the obvious fact that he *is* himself constitutes knowledge of himself."[62]

Indeed, Collingwood held that rethinking the actor's thoughts in his sense is neither necessary nor sufficient for Verstehen in Dilthey's reliving sense. It is not sufficient since on a hypothetical interpretation of rethinking—an interpretation we will consider later—the actor might not have actually thought about the rationale for action. Consequently, a social scientist could in this sense rethink what a social actor thought without reliving any of the actor's actual life. It is not necessary since one can relive an actor's life without actually rethinking what the actor thought, for the actor might not have thought about what he or she was doing. Weber's rational explanatory Verstehen comes closer to Collingwood's view than does Dilthey's but it seems much less extreme in its requirements. Weber required not that the historian actually rethink the thought of the actor but that he or she interpret the actor's action in terms of the actor's subjective categories.

Although Collingwood did not rule out causal concepts in history, he argued that "cause" has different meanings in history and the natural sciences. "When a scientist asks 'Why did that piece of litmus paper turn pink?' he means 'On what kinds of occasions do pieces of litmus paper turn pink?' When an historian asks 'Why did Brutus stab Caesar?' he means 'What did Brutus think, which made him decide to stab Caesar?'"[63] Thus, for Collingwood the cause of an historical event is a thought in the mind of the actor "by whose agency the event came about: and this is not something other than the event, it is the inside of the event itself."[64] Given this understanding of cause, Collingwood could argue: "After the historian has ascertained the facts, there is no further process of inquiring into their causes. When he knows what happened, he already knows why it happened."[65] Thus, knowing the facts entails knowing the inside of the event and this involves knowing the thought behind the outside of the event. But in knowing this, Collingwood said, one knows the cause and thus why the event occurred.

In view of this conception of historical explanation Collingwood saw no need for general laws. To be sure, natural science has a need for such laws since its data are "mere particulars" that are unintelligible in their particularity:

> A science which generalizes from historical facts is in a very different position. Here the facts, in order to serve as data, must first be historically known; and historical knowledge is not perception, it is the discerning of the thought which is the inner side of the event. The historian, when he is ready to hand over such a fact

to the mental scientists as a datum for generalization, has already understood it in this way from within. If he has not done so, the fact is being used as a datum for generalization before it has been properly "ascertained."But if he has done so, nothing of value is left for generalization to do. If by historical thinking, we already understand how and why Napoleon established his ascendancy in revolutionary France, nothing is added to our understanding of that process by the statement (however true) that similar things have happened elsewhere.[66]

With respect to causality Collingwood's view contrasts in interesting ways with Weber's. Weber's account assumed that causal laws about social phenomena are possible but that these are acceptable only if they are explained by the subjective mental states of the actors. Such states provide a meaningful link between causal factors that otherwise have no meaningful connection between them. Collingwood's view, on the other hand, seems to have been that causal relations in history can only be in terms of the actors' thoughts.

According to Collingwood, what place does the science of psychology have in historical inquiry? It might seem that it should have an important role to play since on his theory historical understanding involves rethinking the thoughts of historical actors and psychology studies thinking. However, Collingwood rejected the idea that psychology has any role to play, on the grounds that its subject matter is either a branch of physiology or else deals with the nonrational part of the mind, for example, sensations, feelings, appetite. But neither physiological processes nor the nonrational aspects of the mind, Collingwood said, are parts of the historical process:

They are the basis of our rational life, though no part of it. Our reason discovers them, but in studying them it is not studying itself. By learning to know them, it finds out how it can help them live in health, so that they can feed and support it while it pursues it own proper task, the self-conscious creation of its own historical life.[67]

Again Collingwood's rejection of psychology bears similarities to Weber's position. The latter rejected psychology as irrelevant to sociology because it does not provide subjectively meaningful explanations and causal explanations must be causally meaningful. Collingwood rejected psychology as inapplicable to history since it only deals with the irrational part of thought and history deals only with rational thought.

Although Collingwood believed that scientific and historical explanations are very different, he also thought that they are in some respects alike. Science as well as history is based on knowledge of individuals, he said, for science is based on perception and perception has as its proper object something individual—for example, an atom, a cell, a falling object. History, in turn, is based on thought and this also has as its proper object something individual, for example, the Peloponnesian wars or Queen Elizabeth. Of course, perception is always of the here and now, while history never is. Second, both science and history are reasoned and inferential: "But whereas science lives in the world of abstract universals. . .things which the historian reasons with are not abstract but concrete."[68] Third, both science and history use the Baconian method, that is, they both put questions to the evidence:[69]

> As natural science finds its proper method when the scientist, in Bacon's metaphor, puts Nature to the question, tortures her by experiment in order to wring from her answers to his own questions, so history finds its proper method when the historian puts his authorities in the witness-box, and by cross-questioning extorts from them information which in their original statements they have withheld.[70]

There are three related questions that one needs to ask about Collingwood's theory: (1) Is his theory of historical understanding adequate? (2) Is all history the history of thought? (3) Does his theory neglect objective factors, for example, external factors?

(1) Although Collingwood did not use the term "Verstehen," it seems clear that his theory of historical understanding is closely related to that of Dilthey and Weber and that it has similar problems. He seems to have made the following assumption concerning historical understanding:

> (HU) Only by rethinking the thoughts of the historical agent can one understand the agent's action.

This does not mean that historians discover what is in the mind of the historical actors by putting themselves in the place of the actors but that historical understanding is constituted by this rethinking.[71]

Although neither Dilthey nor Weber made an assumption exactly like HU, HU is too restrictive, very much as their theories are. Like them, Collingwood limited historical understanding to internal understanding of a particular type: to understanding an action in terms of the relationship between the overt behavioral manifestation and the rational thought behind this manifestation and also in terms of the basic descriptive language of the actor. But other types of internal understanding are possible and external understanding is also possible.

Further related problems come to light in answering questions (1) and (2).

(2) Collingwood's theory does not simply hold that intellectual history is the history of thought; he maintains that all history is. Furthermore, by "thought" Collingwood means "rational thought." Some historians have argued that this thesis is an exaggeration of the importance of thought in historical understanding. They have argued that what is often behind a historical agent's actions is not thoughts but feelings, emotions, reflexes, instincts, and habits.[72]

There seem to be three ways to meet this criticism. One might restrict the range of historical inquiry to actions based on rational thought and exclude as historical actions that are based on nonrational elements. However, this restriction seems arbitrary and out of keeping with historical practice.

A second and more interesting way to meet the criticism is to deny that when Collingwood's talks about thought he is always referring to thoughts of which the actor is aware at the time of the action. It is possible to understand the thought behind a person's action, not as the actual conscious calculation formed in someone's mind before he or she acts, but as the calculation the person would have made *if,* for example, he or she had time to reflect before acting or *if* the actor had thought about what he or she did. Interpreted in this dispositional way, it might be argued that Collingwood can claim that there is thought behind all historical action even in cases in which there does not seem to be.[73]

There are at least two problems with this dispositional interpretation of the thesis that all history is the history of thought, however. One is that there is good reason in some cases to suppose that if a historical actor had had time to reflect before acting he or she would have done something different. If so, what was behind the actor's actual action can hardly be the calculation the actor would have gone through if he or she had reflected. A second shortcoming is that in many other cases, we simply do not know what an agent who did not consciously think before acting would have done if he or she had thought. In addition to this, even if the agent's action would have been the same with or without reflection, historians are typically interested in the *actual* basis for a historical action, not the basis had the actor been articulate and self-aware. Moreover, the actual basis for a historical action might well be habit or reflex.

A third way to meet the problem is to argue that by "thought" Collingwood meant something very broad; that he included feelings, desire, etc., so long as these are raised to a certain level of consciousness. For example, Louis Mink argued that Collingwood distinguished four levels of consciousness and that "thought" referred to all except the lowest level of the "undifferentiated sensuous-emotional flux." The historian who deals with Caesar's ambition is still dealing with his thought and need not confine his inquiry to his policies. Mink said,

> *Ambitiousness* belongs to the second level of appetite (vague hunger for something); *ambition* belongs to the third level of desire (hunger for a specific object); *ambitious decision* belongs to the fourth level of *will*. In re-enacting the latter the historian can and must re-enact ambitiousness and ambition as far as they survive in it.[74]

Given this broad meaning of "thought," Mink said that one performs an act of reflective thought "when one orders from a menu, punishes a child, argues about politics, or climbs a mountain."[75] Mink admitted that Collingwood's language "transforms ordinary meanings"[76] and that for Collingwood "thought" was "a quasi-technical term."[77] If Mink is correct, then Collingwood's claim that history is the history of thought is not very controversial and perhaps not very interesting. Moreover, it is misleading.

But let us suppose that Collingwood did not hold such a broad view of thought. Given the above considerations, his rejection of the relevance of psychology to historical inquiry is still unacceptable. Even if we agree with Collingwood that psychology is limited to studying nonrational elements of the mind, psychology becomes relevant to historical inquiry. For so long as one grants that historical actors sometimes act on the basis of nonrational elements such as emotions, not thought, and that psychology studies these, then psychology is germane to historical inquiry.

But even in cases where a historical agent acts on the basis of thought alone, psychology is relevant. In the first place, a historical actor sometimes makes mistakes in reasoning and psychology can be relevant in explaining the error. This is not to say that psychology can explain *why* it was a mistake, that is, provide criteria by which to judge that it was a mistake. This is a task for philosophy: for example, for logic, epistemology, action theory. But psychology could perhaps explain why the mistake was made: for example, because of the emotionally charged subject matter of the calculation.[78] Moreover, even if there is no mistake, psychology might still have a role to play, for, given that some action is rational from a historical agent's point of view, there is still the question of why the agent had the goals and beliefs that he or she did.

Collingwood said that nonrational aspects of the mind "are the basis of our rational life, though not part of it." However, he failed to see that historians often want to know what this basis is and use this in their explanations. They not only want to know why Caesar crossed the Rubicon (because he wanted to remove Pompey from the capital) but why he wanted to remove Pompey. Caesar's emotional attitude toward Pompey—for example, his hatred or envy—might well provide a partial answer to this question, and for the understanding of these emotions psychology is relevant. This is not to deny that emotions have a cognitive dimension; on the contrary, someone usually has reasons for hating or envying someone else, and psychology, especially clinical psychology, would be relevant in understanding these.

There is another reason to be skeptical of Collingwood's thesis that all history is the history of thought. Whatever its plausibility, this theory stems from our tendency to think that all of history consists of the actions of individual people. But some kinds of history—economic history or the history of language—focus on immense social interactions. In this sort of history rational thought seems to play a minor role.[79] For example, historians of language who trace the long-range drift of phonetic changes seem to be little concerned with rational thought. Thus, Patrick Gardiner has said of Collingwood's theory that "the behavior of human beings *en masse* rather than *qua* individuals is not easily covered by it,"[80] and Morton White has maintained that insofar as Collingwood "deals with social behavior, with social events, with group actions, the historian can hardly be described as someone who seeks the thoughts in the mind of *society*."[81]

To be sure, defenders of Collingwood, such as Alan Donagan,[82] have argued that Collingwood was a methodological individualist who maintained that group and social behavior are in principle analyzable in terms of individuals and the relations between them. But although in some cases—for example, in a run on a bank when all of the members of a group are doing the same thing for the same reason—such an analysis seems plausible enough, in more complex cases, belief in an in-principle-reduction seems a leap of faith. To make use of Donagan's example:

> Thus, a given depression might be explained in terms of different common actions by bankers, farmers, industrial firms, and wage-earners, the members of each group doing something different from those of the other groups, and in all probability none of them foreseeing or desiring what their interactions would bring upon them.[83]

But why should one believe that in such a case an individualistic explanation is possible? Credibility is stretched to the breaking point when one recalls that Collingwood rejected historical laws. For what this rejection means is that the reduction to individuals is supposed to be achieved *without* recourse to so-called bridge or composition laws that might link social wholes to individual behavior. Since empirical laws are ruled out by fiat, the only other possible linkage between descriptions of individual actions and group actions would seem to be via definitions or analytic statements. But neither Collingwood nor Donagan suggests what forms such statements might take or provides any actual examples of such statements.

In his *Autobiography,* Collingwood brushed aside a hypothetical request for a demonstration of such reduction. Collingwood said he would not offer "to help a reader who replies 'ah, you are making it easy for yourself by taking an example where history really is the history of thought; you couldn't explain the history of a battle or a political campaign in this way.' I could, and so could you, Reader, if you tried."[84] Donagan's comment on Collingwood's reply is interesting. "It may be so. That a perceptive and intelligent reader, with leisure to spare, could do so, I do not doubt; but it was not an unreasonable burden to lay on even the most willing of them."[85] One wonders on what Donagan's confidence is based since even Collingwood himself did not offer such an account.

(3) Collingwood's position regarding the influence of environmental factors on historical action is completely consistent with his theory that all history is the history of thought. Thus he maintained that natural factors such as weather and geographical conditions and natural disasters such as flood, fires, and tidal waves never in themselves influence human action. They only influence it through the way they are interpreted by human thought. For example, the eruption of Vesuvius in A.D. 79, Collingwood said, did not affect human history directly but only in terms of how humans reacted to it and this depended on how they interpreted the event.[86]

What precisely did Collingwood mean by this? If he meant that historians can explain all human action without reference to actual natural conditions and can rely completely on what historical actors think about the situation, he was surely mistaken. Human actions that have an intended goal can be described as successes or failures, that is, they do or do not succeed in their purpose. But the success or failure of an action surely cannot always be explained by the thoughts of the actor.

Sometimes the result is directly due to natural conditions and whether or not the actor expected success is irrelevant.

A doctor may fail to cure a patient by bleeding him, a farmer may fail to increase his yield by using manure as a fertilizer, a general may fail to achieve victory by attacking over the mountains, a sailor may fail to reach a destination by going directly west. All of these failures might be explained by existing natural conditions of which the agent either has no knowledge or possesses misinformation. Suppose a general tried to attack a mountain fort by going over unclimbable mountains mistakenly thinking that they are climbable.[87] The action of *attempting* to attack the fort by going over the mountains may be explainable in terms of his thought and even rational in the light of his beliefs, but his *failure* to achieve his goal in this way cannot be so explained. To explain why he did not succeed in attacking the mountain fort by approaching it over the mountains can only be explained by knowing not what the general's interpretation of the natural conditions was, but by knowing what the natural conditions really were. Indeed, it would seem that his interpretation is irrelevant. The objective facts, let us suppose, indicate that a direct overland attack must have ended in failure.

Another example of the same pattern is Columbus's failure to discover India by sailing west. Let us grant that Columbus's attempting to sail west to reach India can be explained entirely by his thoughts. But to explain the failure of his attempt, his actual geographic situation must be known, not his interpretation of it. Indeed, Columbus's interpretation seems irrelevant to this, for sailing directly west in order to reach India is impossible, no matter what he thought.[88]

This point can be put in another way, namely, that historians are interested not only in why historical agents perform certain actions but in whether beliefs held by the agents are either true or false. Knowledge of the truth value of the agents' beliefs will in turn help historians to know why the agents' actions were successful or not. Again in order to know this, historians must know what the objective facts are. Knowing only the agents' interpretations of the situation will not enable them to know the truth value of the agents' beliefs.

Now Collingwood said that the historian must exercise critical thinking, that he or she must not only reenact the thoughts of the historical agents but correct "whatever errors he can discern in it." Can this idea save Collingwood? Unfortunately, it is unclear what Collingwood meant. Did he mean, for example, that historians should correct false beliefs about the natural events held by historical actors? If so, this sits uneasily with his point that the interpretation of natural events by historical actors, and not the natural events themselves, are what is crucial for historical understanding. If, on the other hand, Collingwood meant only that historians correct formal mistakes in the reasoning of historical agents, and not the content of their beliefs, this would normally not be enough to account for all unsuccessful action. Often action is unsuccessful, not because of a mistake in the reasoning of the actor, but because of a mistaken belief that could not have been corrected by simply correcting the reasoning.

Conclusion

Although the Verstehen doctrines of Dilthey and Weber are strikingly different, the restrictions they put on social science are similar. The reliving interpretation of Dilthey's Verstehen required social scientists to relive the experience of the social actor while Weber's rational explanatory Verstehen required only that causal explanations be meaningful in terms of the subjective categories of the actor. No reliving was necessary. Although Weber allowed for emotional empathetic Verstehen, this played an unimportant role in his general scheme. But in both the case of Dilthey and the case of Weber, social scientific understanding was restricted in unacceptable ways.

Although he did not use the term "Verstehen," Collingwood's theory of historical understanding was also too restrictive in that it was limited to one type of internal understanding. Related to this was Collingwood's thesis that all history is the history of thought. However, depending on how one interprets it, this thesis is either false, or unwarranted, or misleading and uninteresting. In addition, Collingwood's thesis that environmental factors do not directly influence the historical actor is often interpreted to mean that the historian can rely completely on what historical actors think about the situation. However, so construed, Collingwood's position is problematic. In order to explain the success or failure of historical actions, the thoughts of the actors are not enough.

As I will show in later chapters, although the limitations placed on social science by the classical Verstehen theorists were correctly pointed out by positivists in a relatively unknown critique, the basis of their criticisms was misconceived. Moreover, as I will also show, unacceptable limitations were placed on social science by later theorists who followed in their footsteps. So, in an important sense, later Verstehen theories inherited the problems of earlier ones and failed to meet positivists' objections.

Notes

1. Don Martindale, "Verstehen," *International Encyclopedia of the Social Sciences*, ed. David L. Sills (New York: Macmillan Pub. Co. Inc., and The Free Press, 1968), p. 308.
2. W. J. Van Der Dussen, *History as a Science: The Philosophy of R. G. Collingwood* (The Hague: Marinus Nijhoff Publishers, 1981), pp. 1-2.
3. John Stuart Mill, *Logic*, II, Book VI, i quoted by Marcello Truzzi, (ed.) *Verstehen* (Reading, MA: Addison-Wesley Publishing Co. 1974), p. 8.
4. Wilhelm Dilthey, *Introduction to the Human Sciences*, translated with an introductory essay by Ramon J. Betanzos (Detroit, MI: Wayne State University Press, 1988), p. 72.
5. Ibid., pp. 77-88. See also H. P. Rickman, "Wilhelm Dilthey," *Encyclopedia of Philosophy*, ed. Paul Edwards (New York: Macmillan Pub. Co. Inc., and The Free Press, 1967) vol. 2, p. 403.
6. Pete A. Y. Gunter, "Wilhelm Dilthey," *The Grolier Multimedia Encyclopedia*, 1995.
7. Wilhelm Dilthey, *Introduction to the Human Sciences*, p. 79.
8. Ibid., pp. 147-48, 206-7, 214-15, 326-28. See also Theodore Plantinga, *Historical Understanding in the Thought of Wilhelm Dilthey* (Toronto: University of Toronto Press, 1980), pp. 32-34, and H. A. Hodges, *Wilhelm Dilthey: An Introduction* (New York: Horward Fertig, 1969), p. 17.
9. H. P. Rickman, *Wilhelm Dilthey: Pioneer of the Human Studies* (Berkeley: University of California Press, 1979), pp. 63-65.
10. Wilhelm Dilthey, *Patterns and Meaning in History*, edited by H. P. Rickman (New York: Harper and Row, 1961), chapter 3; Rickman, "Wilhelm Dilthey," p. 405.
11. Hodges, *Wilhelm Dilthey: An Introduction*, p. 33. There are, however, some serious problems associated with historicism. For example, historical skepticism and relativism, and whether in assuming these principles Dilthey committed himself to them is unclear. Apparently, Dilthey thought it did not. According to Theodore Plantinga, *Historical Understanding in the Thought of Wilhelm Dilthey*, p. 135, Dilthey distinguished between inquiry into the origins and conditions of knowledge and inquiry into the validity of knowledge and denied that the later resulted in skepticism. Rickman in *Wilhelm Dilthey: Pioneer of the Human Studies*, p. 141, suggests that Dilthey escaped from the problem of relativism by "putting his own demarcation line – fluid thought it is – between what is due to a common human nature and what to historical forces." Thus, knowledge of human nature would provide a bulwark against relativism. Hodges *op. cit.*, p.33 argues that Dilthey sees historicism "as a revelation of the manifold capacities of human life" and argues that, according to Dilthey, "the more we learn that every particular set of principles is the mind's reaction to a particular set of circumstances, the more it appears that even historicism has to admit one absolute after all, viz. the marvelously adaptable human mind itself."
12. Rickman, "Wilhelm Dilthey," p. 405.

13. Quoted in Fred R. Dallmayr and Thomas A. McCarthy, (eds.) *Understanding and Social Inquiry* (Notre Dame, IN: University of Notre Dame Press, 1977), p. 4.
14. Wilhem Dilthey, *Gesammelte Schriften* (Stuttgart: B. G. Teubner, and Göttingen: Vandenhoeck & Ruprecht, 1914-77), vol. 5, p.144. Quoted in Michael Ermarth, *Wilhelm Dilthey: The Critique of Historical Reason* (Chicago: The University of Chicago Press, 1978), p. 246.
15. Wilhelm Dilthey, *Selected Writings,* edited, translated, and introduced by H. P. Rickman (Cambridge: Cambridge University Press, 1976), p. 226.
16. Ibid., p.228.
17. Hodges, *Wilhelm Dilthey: An Introduction*, p. 15.
18. Ibid., pp. 17-18.
19. Dilthey, *Gesammelte Schriften*, vol. 6, p. 134.
20. For this interpretation, see Ermarth, *Wilhelm Dilthey*, pp. 245-67.
21. Dilthey, *Gesammelte Schriften*, vol. 7, p. 146f.
22. For this reading of the later work of Dilthey, see William Outwaite, *Understanding Social Life: The Method Called Verstehen* (London: George Allen & Unwin, Ltd., 1975), chapter 3. See also David Copper, "Verstehen, Holism and Fascism," *Verstehen and Humane Understanding*, ed. Anthony O'Hear, (Cambridge: Cambridge University Press, 1996), pp. 95-109 who considers no other reading than a contextual holistic one. Indeed, Copper finds in Dilthey some of the seeds of Nazism with his emphasis on context and the whole.
23. Outwaite (p. 36) calls this sort of understanding "hermeneutic understanding" and Copper (pp. 98-99) refers to it as understanding based on "deep holism."
24. See for example, Kathleen Lenin, *Explaining Human Action* (La Salle, IL: Open Court, 1990), Fred Dretske, *Explaining Behavior* (Cambridge, MA: The MIT Press, 1988).
25. See Ernest Nagel, *The Structure of Science* (New York: Harcourt, Brace and World, Inc., 1961), pp. 485-502.
26. See the critique of Winch in chapter 4.
27. See Michael Martin, "Understanding and Participant Observation in Cultural and Social Anthropology," *Social Science and Philosophical Analysis: Essays in the Philosophy of the Social Sciences* (Washington, DC: University Press of America, 1978), pp. 327-54.
28. The contextual nature of explanation which is closely related to understanding is worked out in detail by Achinstein. See Peter Achinstein, *The Nature of Explanation* (New York: Oxford University Press, 1983). I interpret the term 'fact' quite broadly here. One fact about Smith that Jones might have to know in some contexts to understand Smith is that Smith's behavior is subsumable under certain laws. The present analysis remains neutral with respect to the question of whether knowledge of such facts would be necessary. Cf. C. G. Hempel, *Aspects of Scientific Explanation* (New York: The Free Press, 1965), p. 488. According to Hempel, to understand a phenomena is to show that it fits "into a nomic nexus." According to present analysis, Hempel's view would be a special case of factual understanding.
29. Cf. Brian Fay, *Contemporary Philosophy of Social Science* (Cambridge, MA: Blackwell, 1996), chapter 1.
30. See John Beattie, *Understanding an African Community: Bunyoro* (New York: Holt, Rinehart and Winston, 1965).
31. Hodges, *Wilhelm Dilthey: An Introduction*, p. 124.
32. For the distinction between internal and external understanding, see Jane Roland Martin, "Another Look at the Doctrine of Verstehen," *Readings in the Philoso-*

phy of Social Sciences, eds. Michael Martin and Lee C. McIntyre (Cambridge, MA: The MIT Press, 1994), pp. 247-58. This was first published in *The British Journal for the Philosophy of Science*, 20, 1969, pp. 53-67. This distinction will be utilized again in chapter 4 when I consider William Dray's version of Verstehen.

33. For a critique of this position along somewhat different lines, see Brian Fay, *Contemporary Philosophy of Social Science,* chapter 6.

34. Ibid.

35. Max Weber, "The Fundamental Concepts of Sociology," in *The Theory of Social and Economic Organization,* trans. A. M. Henderson and Talcott Parsons (London: The Free Press of Glencoe, 1947), p. 87.

36. Ibid., pp. 87-88, n. 2.

37. Ibid., p. 88.

38. But it is also both subjective and objective in another sense. Weber maintained that on the one hand there cannot be an objective analysis of social phenomena since our values influence which problems are selected for social scientific investigation and how general laws are applied in explaining concrete social reality. All knowledge of concrete social reality, Weber says, is from "particular points of view." Maintaining on the other hand that a social scientist's values influence the construction of the conceptual scheme that is used in an investigation but not its truth, Weber nevertheless holds that the results of social research are valid not just for one person and that scientific truth is valid for all who pursue the truth. With respect to the goal of sociology this means the choice of what meaningful causal relations one investigates and how they are conceptualized is determined by one's values, but that the truth of the outcome of the investigation into meaningful causal relations is not determined by one's values.

39. See Theodore Abel, "The Operation Called *Verstehen,*" *Understanding and Social Inquiry*, eds. Fred. R. Dallmayr and Thomas A. McCarthy (Notre Dame: University of Notre Dame Press, 1977), p. 84.

40. Weber,n "The Fundamental Concepts of Sociology," p. 92.

41. See Friedel Weinert, "Weber's Ideal Types as Models in the Social Sciences," *Verstehen and Humane Understanding*, ed. Anthony O'Hear (Cambridge: Cambaridge University Press, 1996), pp. 73-94.

42. Weber, "The Fundamental Concepts of Sociology," pp. 96-97.

43. Ibid., p. 94.

44. See W. G. Runciman, *A Critique of Max Weber's Philosophy of Social Science* (Cambridge: Cambridge University Press, 1972), pp. 42-43.

45. Weber, "The Fundamental Concepts of Sociology," p.91.

46. Ibid., p. 90.

47. See William T. Tucker, "Max Weber's *Verstehen,*" *The Sociological Quarterly*, 6, 1965, pp. 158.

48. Carl Baar argues that Weber did use Verstehen to generate hypotheses but he cites no reference and says that "the process by which motives and meanings are utilized to generate hypotheses is not spelled out in any of Weber's work thus far translated." See Carl Baar, "Max Weber and the Process of Social Understanding," *Sociology and Social Research*, 51, 1967, p. 338.

49. See Weber, "The Fundamental Concepts of Sociology," p. 91.

50. Ibid.

51. Ibid., p. 90.

52. Ibid., p. 116.

53. Talcott Parson, "Weber's Methodology of Social Sciences," in Max Weber, *The Theory of Economic and Social Organization* (London: The Free Press of Glencoe, 1947), p. 25.

54. Ibid.
55. Ibid., p. 26.
56. See Michael Martin, "Are Cognitive Processes and Structures a Myth?" in *Social Science and Philosophical Analysis* (Washington, D.C.: University Press of America, 1978), pp. 95-100.
57. R. G. Collingwood, *The Idea of History* (New York: Oxford University Press, 1956).
58. Ibid., p. 213.
59. Ibid.
60. Ibid.
61. Ibid.
62. Ibid. , p. 172.
63. Ibid., p. 214.
64. Ibid., p. 215.
65. Ibid., p. 214.
66. Ibid., pp. 222-23.
67. Ibid., p. 231.
68. Ibid., p. 234.
69. See Alan Donagan, "Robin George Collingwood," *Encyclopedia of Philosophy*, ed. Paul Edwards (New York: Macmillan Pub. Co. Inc., and The Free Press, 1967) vol. 2, p. 142.
70. Collingwood, *The Idea of History*, p. 237
71. Patrick Gardiner, "Interpretation in History: Collingwood and Historical Understanding," *Verstehen and Humane Understanding*, ed. Anthony O'Hear, (Cambridge: Cambridge University Press, 1996), p. 114.
72. Van Der Dussen, *History as a Science*, pp. 81-88.
73. Cf. Ibid., pp. 86-87.
74. L. O. Mink, "Collingwood's Dialectic of History," *History and Theory* 7, 1968, p. 14.
75. L. O. Mink, "Collingwood's Historicism: A Dialectic of Process," M. Krausz, *Critical Essays on R.G. Collingwood* (Oxford: Oxford University Press, 1972) p. 167.
76. Ibid.
77. Ibid., p. 165
78. Cf. Alan Donagan, *The Later Philosophy of Collingwood* (Chicago: The University of Chicago Press, 1985), p. 167.
79. Van Der Dussen, *History as a Science,* p. 84.
80. Patrick Gardiner, *The Nature of Historical Explanation*, (Oxford: Oxford University Press, 1952), p. 49 quoted in Van Der Dussen, *History as a Science,* p. 386.
81. Morton White, *Foundations of Historical Knowledge* (New York: Harper and Row, 1965) p. 148 quoted in Van Der Dussen, *History as a Science,* p. 386.
82. See Donagan, *The Later Philosophy of Collingwood,* pp. 206-209.
83. Ibid., pp. 207-208.
84. R. G. Collingwood, *An Autobiography* (London: Oxford University Press, 1939), pp. 111-112 quoted by Donagan, *The Later Philosophy of Collingwood,* p. 209.
85. Donagan, *The Later Philosophy of Collingwood,* p. 209.
86. Collingwood, *An Autobiography*, p. 128, cited by Van Der Dussen, *History as a Science,* p. 90.
87. My example is borrowed from R. F. Atkinson, *Knowledge and Explanation in History* (London: 1974), pp. 26-27 quoted by Van Der Dussen, *History as a Science,* pp. 90-91.

88. In chapter 3 we will see Ernest Nagel make a similar criticism against one aspect of the Verstehen doctrine when he discussed the question, "Are the distinctions required for exploring the subject matter exclusively 'subjective'?" Nagel argues that explanations of social behavior may use assumptions that do not refer to the subjective states of the actors. For example, cotton planters in the United States before the Civil War mistakenly believed that the use of animal manure would preserve indefinitely the fertility of the soil. In order to explain why under this mistaken belief in cotton production gradually deteriorated and why as a result there was an increased need for virgin land to raise cotton if the normal cotton crop was not to decrease, social scientists had to go beyond the subjective categories of the actors and appeal to modern laws of soil chemistry. Notice again in order to explain the failure of using manure in order to preserve the fertility of the soil natural conditions must be known. The farmers' interpretation of the natural conditions might explain why they tried to preserve fertility by using manure but it does not explain why this method was unsuccessful.

2

The Positivists' Critique I:
Not a Method of Verification

Background

The classical Verstehen approach to social science and history was not accepted by everyone. The most famous critics of the classical Verstehen position were the positivists. But what is positivism and what was the positivist charge against Verstehen?

The term "positivism" has been used in many ways in the history of philosophy.[1] Indeed, it has been suggested that the term "now functions more as a polemical epithet than as a designation for a distinct philosophical movement."[2] Nevertheless, the term was first used by Saint-Simon to refer to the extension of the scientific method to philosophy. It was then appropriated by Auguste Comte to designate what in his system of thought was to be the last and highest stage of knowledge—the stage of science: descriptions of sensory experience formulated in terms of mathematical formulas.[3] In this positivistic stage both explanations in terms of supernatural and metaphysical entities were rejected, explanations that were accepted in earlier stages. In the theological stage the actions of gods were used to explain natural events while in the metaphysical stage these actions were depersonalized and became forces and essences. Comte called his own position "positivism" since he eschewed theological and metaphysical explanations and advocated the kind of explanations that characterized the last stage. In addition to Comte, those philosophers identified with positivism in the history of philosophy include John Stuart Mill, Ernst Mach, and Herbert Spencer.

In the early and middle parts of the twentieth century, the term positivism was usually associated with logical positivism—sometimes referred to as logical empiricism or scientific empiricism—the philosophical movement that advocated the theory that only statements of mathematics and logic, on the one hand, and statements of empirical science, on the other, are cognitively meaningful. The logical positivists' theory of meaning was based on the verifiability theory of meaning, which held that meaningful nontautogical statements had to be capable in principle of empirical verification. Using this theory logical positivists argued that metaphysical claims were neither true nor false, that is, factually meaningless, and that ethical language did not have cognitive status. Rudolf Carnap, Herbert Feigl, Hans Reichenbach, and Carl Hempel were all logical positivists.

Despite their differences, positivists have tended to embrace three related doctrines.[4] One is that science is the only source of valid knowledge. In so doing, they had rejected, for example, theology, mysticism, and poetry as sources of valid knowledge A second doctrine, that any kind of metaphysics and metaphysical speculation whether by Plato, Hegel, Aristotle, or Whitehead must be rejected. Third, that only procedures for verification that are reducible to scientific verification are acceptable. In particular, revelation, intuition, rational insight, poetic inspiration, and similar approaches are ruled out as procedures of verification, while admitting these procedures might have other uses. For example, positivists would maintain that intuition might be useful in the context of discovery, that is, in generating a hypothesis. What they denied was that it had any relevance in the context of justification, that is, in the verification of hypotheses.

With respect to the social sciences, positivism is the position that the methodology of the social sciences is not fundamentally different from that of the natural sciences. Here it is closely identified with what has been called naturalism.[5] Starkly stated, the naturalist approach maintains that the social sciences should approach social phenomena in the same way the natural sciences approach natural phenomena: In other words, the social sciences should attempt to explain and predict. Further, according to naturalism, the explanation and prediction of social phenomena typically involves either general or statistical laws. Thus, naturalism in the social sciences is committed to a nomological model of explanation, the view that an event is explained when it is subsumed under a law or laws. Advocates of this approach, of course, admit that laws are more difficult to discover in the social sciences than in the natural sciences and that they might be looser and less well supported than the former. However, naturalism maintains that the difference is merely one of degree.

The Anti-Verification Criticism

Although the criticism that Verstehen is not a method of verifying hypotheses but is a heuristic device for generating them is not the most important one offered by logical positivists, it is the criticism most commonly associated with logical positivism. The Anti-Verification Criticism (AVC) is an application of the positivists' rejection of any procedures for verification that are not reducible to scientific verification. Since Verstehen was not a procedure reducible to scientific verification it was not acceptable. To be sure, it could have other uses. In particular, it might be useful in the context of discovery. Using Verstehen could generate hypotheses. However, these hypotheses would have to be tested in other ways.

Although the AVC of Verstehen was historically associated with logical positivism, it could be given by those who did not embrace all or even most aspects of the positivist program. For example, a philosopher who rejected its dismissal of metaphysics could still embrace AVC and so could a methodologist of the social sciences who did not accept the nomological model of explanation. Conversely, a defender of Verstehen as method of verification—a defender of the Verification Thesis (VT)—need not reject all or even most of the positivistic program or, on the other hand, embrace all or even most aspects of the Verstehen approach. Thus, a philosopher who accepted VT might also accept the nomological model of explanation; a methodologist of the social sciences sympathetic with VT might reject Dilthey's thesis that understanding involves reliving the experience of the actor.

These cautionary remarks should prevent us from making unwarranted inferences about the overall positions of the thinkers discussed in this chapter. In the first part of this chapter two purported refutations of Verstehen based primarily on the AVC, one by Theodore Abel and one by Richard Rudner, will be considered.[6] Later two defenses of VT, one by Peter Munch and one by Michael Scriven will be criticized. To what extent these methodologists are committed to a Verstehen approach to understanding or to the positivist program cannot be inferred from their advocacy of either VT or AVC.

Two Criticisms of Verification Thesis

A paper entitled "The Operation Called *Verstehen*"[7] by Theodore Abel, a sociologist, is perhaps the best known and most widely cited and reprinted example of AVC. Although sociologists have long discussed the method of Verstehen, Abel says, its exact nature has not been clarified. According to Abel "*Verstehen* is the postulation of an intervening process 'located' inside the human organism, by means of which we recognize an observed—or assumed—connection as relevant or meaningful. *Verstehen*, then, consists of bringing to the foreground the inner-organic sequence intervening between a stimulus and a response."[8]

Consider two examples used by Abel to illustrate his thesis.

In his first example, during an April cold snap, one sees one's neighbor rise from his desk, go to the shed, and chop wood. One then observes him carry the wood back to house and place it the fireplace. He then lights it, sits down at his desk, and resumes his daily task of writing. How does one understand this sequence of behavior?

According to Abel, one concludes that while working one's neighbor felt chilly and, in order to get warm, lighted a fire. There are, Abel says, three items of information that are used in reaching this conclusion: (1) low temperature (A) reduces the temperature of the body (B); (2) heat is produced (C) by making a fire (D); (3) a person "feeling cold" (B^1) will "seek warmth"(C^1).

> We immediately recognize the third item as the significant element of the interpretation. The two conditions (A-B), together with the known consequences (C-D), are disparate facts. We link them into a sequence and state that C-D is the consequence of A-B by "translating" B and C into feeling-states of a human organism, namely, B^1 and C^1. Introducing these intervening factors enables us to apply a generalization concerning the function of the organism (behavior maxim), from which we deduce the drop in temperature as possible "cause" of the neighbor's behavior.[9]

In Abel's second example, that statistical research has established a high correlation between the annual rate of crop production and the rate of marriage, we understand this connection in the following way:

> We use as items of information the fact that the failure of crops (A) materially lowers the farmer's income (B) and the fact that one is making a new commitment (C) when one marries (D). We then

internalize B into "feeling of anxiety" (B^l) and C—since the behavior is "postponement of marriage"—into "fear of new commitments"(C^l). We are now able to apply the behavior maxim: "People who experience anxiety will fear new commitments" (B^l-C^l). Since we can fit the fact of fewer marriages when crops fail into this rule, we say we "understand" the correlation.[10]

Thus, according to Abel, Verstehen involves three steps: (1) internalizing the stimulus, (2) internalizing the response, and (3) applying the behavior maxims.

(1) To internalize a stimulus we imagine "what emotions may have been aroused by the impact of a given situation or event."[11] In doing so we might employ behavior clues or, in the absence of these, simply imagine how we would have been affected by the situation or event.

(2) To internalize a response we also use our imagination to infer a motive from observed behavior. We can "utilize our personal experience with motives or feelings we had when we ourselves acted in order to produce a similar result."[12] Abel says that when both stimulus and response are given, our imagination "is facilitated by the fact that both can be viewed as part of a complete situation." Presumably, Abel means that in such cases we can imagine some subjectively meaningful relation linking the internalized stimulus to the internalized response.

(3) This meaningful relation linking "two feeling states together in a uniform sequence" Abel calls a behavior maxim.[13] We apply these maxims to understand the connection between stimulus and responses. According to Abel these are not recorded in any textbook on human behavior; they can be constructed *ad hoc*, and are accepted as true propositions even though they have not been established experimentally. Appearing self-evident to us, "they are generalizations of direct personal experiences from introspection and self-observation."[14]

Abel's basic criticism of Verstehen is that "it does not add to our store of knowledge."[15] Although Verstehen "gives us 'hunches' and points out the general character of possible factors," it "does not enable us to evaluate probabilities"[16] since the "probability of a connection can be ascertained only by means of objective, experimental, and statistical tests."[17] In short, the operation of Verstehen is "*not a method of verification*"[18] and is at best a method of generating hypotheses.

Several comments are relevant to Abel's account of Verstehen. First, it is unclear exactly whom Abel is arguing against. It is true that he cited Max Weber, as well as many others, in a footnote,[19] but Weber did not advocate VT and would have, in fact, agreed with the main thrust of Abel's criticism. Moreover, although on the standard interpretation of Dilthey, he maintained that empathy was essential for understanding social phenomena, it is not clear that Dilthey embraced VT either.

Second, it is not immediately obvious that Abel would disagree with one of the main points of Weber's doctrine of explanatory Verstehen, namely, that acceptable causal explanations must be understood in terms of the subjectively meaningful categories of the actors. Abel certainly allows that a causal connection can be true and yet not be subjectively understandable. However, Weber would allow this too. The question remains of whether in Abel's eyes the social sciences must aim at finding true causal connections that are subjectively meaningful. At one point he seems to suggest that they must for he says that Verstehen implies "that our curiosity concerning human behavior does not rest until we have in some way been able to relate it to our personal experience."[20] This is compatible with Weber's theory that explanatory Verstehen is necessary for acceptable causal explanations as well as his rejection of Verstehen as a method of verification. However, this interpretation of Abel as accepting Weber's restrictions on causal explanations results from taking his words out of context. After the sentence just quoted, Abel says: "The satisfaction of curiosity produces subjective increment but adds nothing to the objective validity of the proposition. . . . These limitations virtually preclude the use of the operation of Verstehen as a scientific tool of analysis."[21] This combined with Abel's belief that Verstehen cannot be used to validate the assumption of a dichotomy between the physical and the social sciences, indicates that he probably would not have accepted Weber's restrictions.

Third, at one point Abel comes close to saying that, depending on the training and experience of the empathizer, Verstehen can be used as a method of verification:

> The ability to define behavior will vary with the amount and quality of the personal experience and the introspective capacity of the interpreter. It will also depend upon his ability to generalize his experience. In some cases it may be possible to secure objective data on the basis of which the verification of an interpretation is approximated.[22]

This remark is not developed further by Abel and it is not clear exactly what he means. The possibility of using the Verstehen of experts as a method of verification was explored by Michael Scriven and will be discussed in detail later in this chapter.

Abel was not alone in advocating AVC. The philosopher of the social sciences, Richard Rudner, in his book, *Philosophy of Social Science*, construes the question of Verstehen as "whether empathetic understanding constitutes an indispensable method for the validation of hypotheses about social phenomena."[23] Rudner considers the question in two stages. First, he asks in what sense, if any, Verstehen is a method of validation and, second, he considers whether it is an indispensable methodological resource of the social sciences alone.

Rudner argues that some "influential students of the methodology of the social sciences"—in which category he includes Weber—have argued that the aim of social inquiry is "a kind of *understanding* of the phenomena to be investigated, which can be gained or validated *by* the empathetic, or empathy like, or other participatory acts of the investigator."[24] Rudner says that for "Weber and others, not only is this empathy method a means for the social scientist to 'capture' the significance of" a social phenomenon such as Christian martyrdom, "but it is the only, and, hence, indispensable, means of doing so. It is, moreover, peculiar to social science by its very nature."[25]

Arguing that empathy can be a method of validation only if there is an independent way of validating that the empathizer's empathetic state is veridical, Rudner raises the following questions:

> But how can we establish independently the reliability of such an empathetic act without having had previous knowledge of . . . the very psychological state that is the object of empathy? And if we do have this presupposed knowledge. . . what more could be methodologically required? If further confirmation of the investigator's hypotheses about the character of the target psychological state is in order, then the logic of the situation just outlined entails that some means are available, independent of empathy, for acquiring it.[26]

According to Rudner, the first question is now answered. Verstehen can be a method of validation only when empathy's reliability has been independently established in "such a way as to make it redundant." The second question is also answered. Empathy is not an indispensable methodological device of the social sciences since the "very logic of its methodological employment precludes this by guaranteeing that there will be independent means for validating the hypothesis its use is intended to validate."[27]

Two critical comments concerning Rudner's critique are in order here. One is that Rudner has badly misunderstood Weber. Whether or not Weber would allow, as the positivists did, that empathetic understanding could be a useful method for generating hypotheses is not completely clear, but he certainly did not suppose that empathetic Verstehen is a means of validation. Nor did he think that rational explanatory Verstehen was a method of validation. In Weber's view rational explanatory Verstehen was a requirement of subjectively meaningful causal explanations of human action and achieving such explanations was the major goal of the social sciences. Objective statistical evidence, Weber thought, was necessary for validating hypotheses about subjectively meaningful causal explanations.

Rudner might ultimately have criticized Weber's assumption that social science must seek subjectively meaningful causal explanations, but he did not. To be sure, he criticized the idea that he seems to have attributed to Weber as well as to Peter Winch, that understanding involves a direct experience of the phenomenon to be understood.[28] But Weber did not require this. He did not suppose that it is necessary to experience certain subjective states directly in order to impute them to social actors. Weber did believe that this imputation is essential for having acceptable causal explanations. However, although Rudner does not explicitly reject Weber's requirement for scientific understanding, there is reason to suppose that he would do so. Rudner distinguishes between understanding based on direct experience and understanding provided by theoretical science. He gives no indication, however, that if the scientific understanding of social phenomena is not based on direct experience, then it must be based on the subjective categories of the actor. Moreover, insofar as Rudner mistakenly thinks that imputations of subjective states to social actors are based on direct experience of these states, he is at pains to argue that scientific understanding of social phenomena need not involve this direct experience.

Second, there is much more to be said about VT than Rudner says.[29] In particular, although Rudner is correct to maintain that the reliability of empathetic participation needs to be independently validated, he is mistaken in that it is redundant as a method of validation. For example, once the reliability of X's empathetic judgments is established on independent grounds, X's empathetic judgments can function as independent sources of validation in the future. An analogy should make this clear. Once a method M_1 of archaeology dating is validated by an independent method M_2 that is known to be reliable, M_1 can function as a reliable dating method in future cases without recourse to M_2. A similar point holds for empathizers.

This does not show, of course, that Verstehen is an indispensable methodological resource of the social sciences. But it is compatible with Verstehen being not merely nonredundant but even extremely useful as a method of validation.

Defenses of Verstehen as a Method of Verification

The conflict between Verstehen critics such as Abel and Rudner and classical Verstehenists such as Dilthey and Weber suggests that they were talking past one another. For the critics the main problem with Verstehen was as a method of verification. But for the Verstehen theorists verification was not the issue at all. Rejecting the view that Verstehen was a method of verification but accepting the thesis that it was a heuristic tool used in the context of discovery, some of the best-known critics failed to realize that Verstehenists rejected it as either a method of discovery or a method of verification.

The issue of Verstehen as a method of verification is not dead, however. It is well to remember that VT has had its champions. As far back as 1957, the sociologist Peter Munch challenged this rejection, arguing that Verstehen could be construed as an analogical argument that is used to verify hypotheses.[30] In 1969, Michael Scriven[31] argued a similar thesis but in a much more detailed and sophisticated way, and Howard Cohen[32] had challenged some aspects of Scriven's thesis with respect to historical inquiry. Munch's, Scriven's, and Cohen's arguments concerning VT will now be considered.

Three Defenses of Verstehen as a Method of Verstehen

Munch argues in "Empirical Science and Max Weber's *Verstehende Soziologie*," published in *American Sociological Review*, that Verstehen can be considered as a way of validating hypotheses. Thus, Munch's argument can be interpreted as a direct challenge to Abel's analysis. Munch argues that if Verstehen is understood as an inference based on an analogy, it "is a *legitimate* procedure in an empirical study of human behavior."[33] With respect to social action one sees a person behaving in a particular manner. This behavior is perceived as:

> an observable "property" of a unit event, "social action," which includes other properties, partly observable (e.g., the respondent) and partly inaccessible to immediate sensation. The crucial question here, of course, is what kind of experience the observer has had, on the basis of which he can make the inference by analogy as to presence or absence of a state of mind of the actor described as "'subjectively meaningful."[34]

According to Munch "from experience with my own person I know that my own behavior 'reflects' events in my nervous system, events that I perceive as ideas, emotions, intentions, or volitions. Observing another person's behavior I infer by analogy that similar events are taking place in the other person's nervous system, that he perceives these events as ideas, emotions, intentions, or volitions, and that this behavior 'reflects' these properties."[35]

Although Munch does not apply his ideas to the examples used by Abel, it might be instructive to do so. Consider the case of the neighbor chopping wood. Presumably, in its simplest terms, one could construe Abel's example as an argument from analogy as follows. Let B be the sequence of behavior exhibited by the neighbor—getting up from his desk, chopping wood, putting it on the fire, going back to his desk— and let B^1 be a similar sequence exhibited by the observer. Let M^1 be the subjective state of the observer—feeling cold, desiring to get warm— that motivated B^1 and that the observer has direct access to, and let M be a possible similar subjective state of the neighbor that the observer has no direct access to. Let C^1 be circumstances—physiological, educational, social, and so on—that are relevant to having M^1 given B^1, and let C be similar relevant circumstances associated with B. Then an obvious argument from analogy formulated by the observer would be this:

In my case I have observed that whenever (or with a high probability) I manifest behavior B^1 under circumstances C^1, it has been motivated by my subjective state M^1. My neighbor has manifested similar behavior B in similar circumstances C. I conclude that B is probably motivated by a similar subjective state M.

Traditionally, arguments by analogy have been judged by two criteria: the relevance of the similarities and the lack of relevance of the differences between B and B^1 and C and C^1. With respect to B and B^1, the probability of the inference would be a function of the number of relevant similarities and lack of relevant differences between B and B^1. If B^1 had been getting up from his desk, putting coal in the furnace, going back to his desk, the analogy would have been stronger and the inference more probable than if B^1 had been getting up from his desk, raising the thermostat, and going back to bed. With respect to C and C^1, the probability of the argument would be increased by such factors as the similarities between the backgrounds of the observer and the neighbor. For example, suppose that both the observer and the neighbor were raised in environments where taking swift action when one is chilly by raising the heat in one's dwelling was commonplace and acceptable. This similarity would tend to increase the strength of inference. Moreover, the probability of the argument would be decreased by the presence of relevant dissimilarities. For example, suppose that the neighbor, unlike the observer, was dressed in warm clothing. The probability that he was chilly and wanting to become warm would be diminished.[36]

Does Munch's argument as explicated here undermine Abel's thesis and reveal a serious problem with AVC? The first thing to notice is that analogical arguments are probable only under certain restricted circumstances. Munch refers at one point to "general human experience" as the basis for analogical inferences.[37] But strong analogical inferences usually rely on particular human experiences; their strength varies from context to context and is dependent on the particular background information of the persons making the inferences. Elsewhere Munch seems to admit that Verstehen is concerned with "*specific* meanings of *particular* actions."[38] But then, general human experience cannot be the basis of analogical inference insofar as these experiences are part of the method of Verstehen.

The second point to note is that Abel comes close to granting the truth of VT under restricted circumstances for he says: "In some cases it may be possible to secure objective data on the basis of which the verification of an interpretation is approximated."[39] Abel thinks this will depend on the quality of the personal experience, introspective capacity, and ability to generalize one's experience. Given his statement, it seems plausible to suppose that he would accept that Verstehen under some circumstances can be a means of verification.

The third point to note is that Abel was not assuming these restricted conditions in most of his article.[40] To internalize a stimulus, Abel says, we might employ "behavior clues" but if these are absent we "simply imagine how we would have been affected by the situation or event." To internalize a response we also use our imagination to infer a motive from observed behavior. He maintains that we can use our personal experience with the motives or feelings we acted on to produce similar results. Nothing is asserted by Abel to indicate that the inference must be a strong analogical inference by the standard criteria. Indeed, it seems clear that for Abel, the following would be a legitimate use of Verstehen: When I imagine why I would manifest behavior B[I] I imagine I would have subjective state M^l. My neighbor has manifested similar behavior B. I conclude that he has similar subjective state M.

Surely this is a rather weak analogical argument. My neighbor and I might have very different backgrounds; I might never have exhibited behavior remotely similar to B^l; my powers of imagination might be quite limited, and so on. Munch admits that "any inference by analogy is a source of error. I may be mistaken in a given instance." However, he rejects the view that error is likely. "But the likelihood that I shall always be mistaken, or even most of the time, is very small. Therefore, I accept the inference as reasonably valid on the principle of *probability*."[41] Again this would be true only for a certain restricted class of analogical inferences. There would be no reason to suppose that it is true in the majority of cases in which Verstehen is used. Indeed, error would be inclined to be more common as B^l and C^l tend to diverge more and more from B and C.

The final point to remember is that advocates of AVC were not opposed to legitimate inductive arguments. Indeed, they believed that such arguments were the basis of science. If it could be shown that in some cases Verstehen could be construed as a species of inductive argument that yielded probable conclusions, they could hardly have complained about its use in such cases. But showing this would not undermine their general criticism of Verstehen, that is, that in the vast majority of cases its use does not validate hypotheses.

However, although Munch's version of VT preceded Scriven's by over a decade, it is Scriven's arguments that are remembered today. Scriven's paper, "Logical Positivism and the Behavioral Sciences," appeared in a volume of essays by philosophers of science evaluating the contributions of logical positivism to philosophical thought. Scriven saw the task of evaluation as that of determining if the criticisms logical positivism made of pre-positivistic philosophy had been met and saw his own special task as evaluating logical positivism's contribution to the behavioral sciences and, in particular, to the analysis of understanding.

Scriven takes his position to be in sharp contrast with the traditional positivistic view of Verstehen, saying: "The positivists argued that empathy was not a reliable tool at all, and the methods of obtaining knowledge, especially in history, were just the same as those used in the physical sciences."[42] He argues instead that Verstehen does provide knowledge in history and in the natural sciences and also is a useful tool in science for verifying hypotheses. He illustrates this use by showing how experts' empathetic judgments can and should be relied on.

Interestingly enough, Scriven seems to be unaware of Munch's earlier attempt to argue something similar, and makes no attempt to relate his rather unorthodox defense of Verstehen to views of Dilthey and Weber or even to the more recent Verstehen theories of Winch and Dray. Indeed, the only traditional theorist he mentions is Collingwood, whom he misinterprets. Scriven argues that although the positivists were reacting to a school of historians who advocated the doctrine that empathic insight is a special and valuable tool for the study of the human sciences, this doctrine did not die with them, but "it is explicit in Collingwood's philosophy of history."[43] However, Collingwood did not hold that Verstehen was a valuable tool; he maintained that it was a necessary aspect of understanding. Thus, even as Scriven is critical of positivism for rejecting Verstehen, he uncritically accepts a significant and very misleading aspect of their construal of it.

Scriven speaks of Verstehen as "empathetic insight," without making clear what he means by this expression. At times he speaks of empathy in terms of "estimating our reactions and their transferability." One thinks "about the likely effect" of some event on oneself and "its likely effect" on others.[44] In this transfer sense of Verstehen, "X has empathetic insight that p" could be defined as follows: (1) X believes that p, and (2) X infers that p on the basis of X's estimate of X's reaction and X's estimate of the transferability of X's reaction to other people. Presumably in this sense p is some statement about some other person's reaction, behavioral or otherwise.

However, given this transfer sense of Verstehen, it is difficult to understand Scriven's claim that empathetic insight is a reliable tool for the natural sciences as well as social sciences and history. Since it seems to be limited to establishing hypotheses about people's reactions, it seems relevant only to the social sciences and history. But Scriven also speaks of "instant perception"[45] in connection with Verstehen, and this suggests that in relation to the natural sciences he simply means intuitive insight. In this *intuitive insight Verstehen*, "X has empathetic insight that p" means (1) X believes that p, (2) X's belief that p is not based on conscious or explicit inference, and (3) X's belief that p came to X instantly.

It is important to notice that there is a connection between transfer Verstehen and intuitive insight Verstehen. The latter sense of Verstehen leaves open the possibility that implicit inference was involved; the only thing excluded is the possibility of explicit inference. The former sense leaves open the possibility that the inference involved is implicit.

Thus an instance of transfer Verstehen where the inferences involved were implicit and instantaneous would be a special case of intuitive insight Verstehen.

In what follows, the two senses of Verstehen will be examined. However, transfer Verstehen as a case of intuitive insight Verstehen will be my main concern.

In what way does Scriven claim that Verstehen is a useful tool in the natural and social sciences? Suppose that someone X has empathetic insight that p in the intuitive insight sense of Verstehen. Scriven wants to claim that under certain conditions such insight is reliable: In other words that we have a right to believe X's judgment and X does too. Now Scriven does not hold that such empathetic insight is always free from error. People sometimes have an empathetic insight that p and p is false. However, beliefs that are based on nonempathetic methods, for example, traditional methods of verification, can also turn out to be false. Furthermore, he does not claim that empathetic insight is a more reliable method than the traditional methods of verification. Although he does not say so explicitly, his position seems to be that empathetic insight is as reliable under certain conditions as belief based on the more standard methods. The crucial question is, under what conditions is it as reliable?

One sort of condition Scriven apparently has in mind is the following: Let us suppose that a person is usually correct when he has an empathetic insight and that in the present case he has an empathetic insight that p. On inductive grounds we can then reasonably suppose that he is correct in the present case. In this sort of situation a man's intuitive insight is used as an indicator or symptom of the truth of his belief in the same way that a barometer is used as a symptom or indicator of rain.[46] Now someone who had much more reliable empathetic insight in a particular realm than the average person is considered an expert in that realm: in other words, his empathetic insight can be better trusted than that of other people.

Although Scriven presents this position as if it is in sharp contrast with that of Verstehen critics such as the positivists, it is not clear in what way his construal of Verstehen differs from their view. To be sure, traditional critics did not entertain the possibility of linking the intuitive judgments of experts with Verstehen. However, the use of the intuitive judgments of experts in prediction in the inexact sciences was explored in some detail by Helmer and Rescher in a well-known monograph[47] and there is no reason to suppose that their ideas were rejected by the critics of Verstehen.

Furthermore, it is extremely dubious that the critics, had they thought of identifying Verstehen with the use of empathetic judgments by experts, would have had any objections to it. Empathetic insight by itself provides no justification for knowledge claims. Supposing X has empathetic insight that p, this by itself gives no reason to believe that p unless we know that X's empathetic insight has been reliable in similar circumstances. However, the advocates of AVC would not have denied that someone's empathetic insight *plus* knowledge about the reliability of this person's empathetic insight established by non-Verstehen methods can provide knowledge. They argued that empathetic insight *taken by itself* provides no knowledge. Neither Rudner nor Abel would have denied the inductive strength of the following sort of argument:

(1) Jones is usually correct in his empathetic insights.

(2) Jones has an empathetic insight that p.

---

(3) Therefore, p.

Premises (1) and (2), they would surely admit, make (3) probable. (They would have required, of course, that (1) and (2) be established by standard intersubjectively testable non-Verstehen methods.)

What Abel and Rudner would deny is the inductive strength of the following argument:

(1) Jones has an empathetic insight that p.

---

(2) Therefore, p.

Thus Abel says, "from the affirmation of a possible connection we cannot conclude that it is probable. From the point of view of Verstehen alone, any connection that is possible is *equally* certain."[48] Both he and Rudner would agree with Ernest Nagel who wrote, "competent evidence for the assumptions about the attributes and action of other men is often difficult to obtain; but it is certainly not obtained merely by introspecting one's own sentiments or by examining one's own beliefs as to how some sentiments are likely to be manifested in overt action."[49] Rudner himself goes so far as to consider the possibility of Verstehen as a means of verification and argues that such a method presupposes that the empathetic act is veridical but that this must be established by nonempathetic means. He says, "We need not argue against empathy or discard it as a validation step, but clearly in order to accept some specific empathetic act as validational, we must presuppose an investigation establishing the hypothesis that this act is veridical ... we must have established independently that empathy is sufficiently like the state of which it is an empathy."[50] To be sure, Rudner fails to notice that the independent validation he requires could be achieved by showing by nonempathetic methods that a person's empathetic acts are often veridical and arguing that probably this act is as well. But it is unlikely that he would have rejected such a suggestion if he had considered it. His major point, like Abel's, seems to be that empathetic insight by itself cannot verify a hypothesis.

I think one can safely say that, although it may be true that advocates of AVC did not contemplate Scriven's particular use of intuitive insight Verstehen in science, such a use could be assimilated to the positivist program.

What is not completely clear is whether Scriven believes that statistical justification of Verstehen is essential for its defense. Here is a reconstruction of an example adduced by Scriven to illustrate the use of empathetic insight in combination with nonempathetic methods.[51]

(1) Intensive bombing of a city (C_1) is a possible cause of defeatism in the population of the city (E_2).

(2) Intensive bombing of city X occurred.

(3) Defeatism occurred in the population of city X (E_2).

(4) All other possible causes (C_2, C_3, ... C_n) were not present in this case of defeatism in city X.

(5) This case of defeatism has a cause.

---

(6) Therefore, intensive bombing (C_1) is the cause of defeatism in city X (E_2).

Now Scriven argues that premises (2)-(5) are established by non-Verstehen methods. Nevertheless, without premise (1) these do not allow us to infer (6). However, (1) is established by empathetic insight—presumably in the transfer sense and perhaps also in the intuitive insight sense. Thus he argues that empathy (premise 1) and nonempathetic methods (premises 2 and 3) combined allow us to infer the cause of some social phenomenon.

The crucial question, however, is whether empathy by itself gives any justification for believing that (1) is true. Suppose some expert has an empathetic insight that (1). Consequently, because of the high reliability of his past judgments (established by non-Verstehen methods), we have good inductive evidence that he is correct in this case as well. If this is what Scriven has in mind, empathy itself has not established premise (1). Independent knowledge about the reliability of the empathizer is also necessary.

Under this interpretation there is no clear conflict with AVC although advocates of AVC never seemed to have considered cases of this sort; however, another slightly different interpretation of Scriven is possible. Let us suppose that the person with empathetic insight in the transfer sense makes his inference explicit. He argues,

(1a) Intensive bombing could cause me to become a defeatist.

(1b) I am very similar to people in City X with respect to my reaction to bombing.

---

(1) Therefore, intensive bombing is a possible cause of defeatism in the populace of City X.

Now critics of VT would raise no objections to this as a strong inductive argument. Their question would be how (1a) and (1b) are to be established. Certainly (1b) cannot be established by empathetic insight. It might be suggested that (1a) can be established by what G.E.M. Anscombe has called "knowledge without observation." Anscombe's example[52] of knowing without observation that the bark of a crocodile caused one to be startled, it might be said, is not unlike knowledge of (1a). Furthermore, Anscombe's knowledge without observation might well be considered a special case of intuitive insight: It is direct—not based on any explicit inference and instantaneous.

However, I am dubious that (1a) could be established by knowledge without observation. First of all, if Anscombe's knowledge without observation establishes anything, it presumably would establish

(1a^l) Intensive bombing caused me to become a defeatist.

But (1a^l) is not at issue in the above argument. In (1a) one must have knowledge of what could cause one to become a defeatist, but Anscombe's knowledge without observation is not direct knowledge of psychological possibilities. To be sure (1a^l) entails (1a): given intensive bombing as the actual cause of my defeatism, one can deductively infer that intensive bombing could cause my defeatism. However, without (1a^l) how is (1a) to be established? As far as I can determine, Anscombe did not suppose one could establish (1a) independently of (1a^l).

Secondly, in the bombed city example, the empathizer may have never been in a city during a bombing. Consequently, he could not establish by knowledge without observation that bombing causes any of his psychological states. Thus, he would not be able to rely on knowledge without observation in establishing (1a') and then inferring (1a) from (1a^l).

Thirdly, even if (1a^l) is established by deduction from (1a), it is dubious that (1a) can be established by intuition alone. Our reliance on someone's judgment about the cause of his own psychological states and reactions is usually a function of his past reliability in making such judgments—the truth of which is ascertained on independent grounds. People can be mistaken in their judgments about the causes of their own psychological states and reactions, and the more mistakes they have made in the past, the more inclined one is to discount their judgment now.

On the other hand, if it is supposed that (1a) and (1b) could be established by the intuitive insights of people whose intuitive insights have been reliable in the past and that this reliability has been established on independent grounds, then critics of VT would presumably have no objections.

So I have argued that Scriven has not shown that empathy itself provides any way of confirming hypotheses either in the natural or the social sciences. What does seem to be true is that empathy plus independent knowledge about the past reliability of the empathizer provides a way of justifying belief in a hypothesis. But, as already noted, critics of VT need not deny this so long as the independent knowledge is verified by standard intersubjective methods.

What is the disagreement between Scriven and the critics of VT? Does Scriven believe that sometimes empathy by itself provides a test of hypotheses? Or does he think, rather, that although independent knowledge of the reliability of the empathizer's judgment is necessary, independent knowledge does not have to be verified in the standard independent way?

Some of Scriven's remarks suggest that he believes that empathy by itself can provide a way of testing hypotheses. Thus he says, "If empathy can in principle provide knowledge, does it in practice?. . . .To suppose that one cannot rightly be certain from empathy that an air raid is causing one's children the anxiety they are manifesting strikes me as unreasonable."[53] Although there is no mention here of the past reliability of one's empathetic insights in similar cases, some sort of assumption of past successes certainly seems to be required.

Consider the following argument where this requirement is contradicted:

(1") Jones is usually mistaken in his empathetic insight concerning the cause of children's anxiety.

(2") Jones has an empathetic insight that his children's anxiety is caused by the bombing.

(3") Therefore, his children's anxiety is caused by the bombings.

Given (1"), (2") tends to disconfirm (3") rather than support it. So unless Scriven is assuming that empathetic insight has been successful in a certain type of case it is reasonable to suppose that one cannot be certain on the basis of empathy in this case. On the other hand, if he is supposing this past success, how does his view conflict with positivist critiques of Verstehen?

Perhaps the answer is that, although Scriven assumes the past success of Verstehen, he does not believe that the evidence for past success needs to be based on standard positivistic intersubjective methods of verification. Sometimes Scriven seems to mean something different from what positivists meant. At one point he seems to identify intersubjective testability with the possibility of "inter-judge agreement,"[54] that is, the agreement between judges. However, this account of intersubjective testing would not be agreed to by positivists, for it is obvious that agreement among judges by itself gives no support to what they are agreeing to. One must have independent reason to think the judges are reliable.

The question the critics of VT would raise is how this reliability is to be established. Scriven seems to agree that this is an important question and argues that we have independent criteria for identifying experts.[55] Critics would insist that these criteria should be their past success as verified by intersubjective methods, that is, methods that could be used by nonexperts, and that the given results are open to the public scrutiny. Moreover, they would insist that even when experts need not be involved, intersubjective testing seems necessary. Although it may not take an expert to have justified empathic insight that his child's anxiety is caused by bombing, the justification, as already noted, still requires past successes of the empathizer in relevantly similar cases. And knowledge of past successes, in turn, seems to demand intersubjective verification. Now whether, according to Scriven, knowledge of such past success is intersubjectively verifiable in the sense required by the positivists is uncertain. Scriven says,

> But intersubjective testability, taken in the usual sense, is not even a necessary condition for scientific knowledge. A single witness of a unique astronomical event may be reliable enough to justify us in believing his knowledge claim although it is not testable. We'll hesitate to drop a good theory that turns out to be incompatible with his observation, but that just shows it *was* (indirectly) testable; in the absence of such conflict, we'll believe him.[56]

What is the relevance of these remarks to the intersubjective testability of Verstehen? Perhaps Scriven is suggesting in this passage that knowledge claims by experts using empathetic insight are justifiable but not intersubjectively testable in "the usual sense" (the sense required by critics such as Rudner).

But to what sense is Scriven referring? Scriven's talk about unique events and single witnesses implies that positivist critics of VT were committed to the view that a statement about an event is not intersubjectively testable unless the event is repeatable or directly observable by more than one witness. But this is not so. Positivism allowed for indirect intersubjective verification. As Scriven points out, the testimony of the witness is indirectly intersubjectively testable when it conflicts with or confirms some theory.[57] Moreover, the witness's testimony was intersubjectively testable in other ways as well. For if the witness was reliable in cases in which direct intersubjective test was possible, both his reliability in general and in the case at issue gain inductive support.

In a similar way the expertise of empathizers (in the intuitive insight sense) is indirectly intersubjectively testable. Suppose, for example, that one is considering the reliability of the empathetic insights of violin appraisers. These experts are, among other things, called upon to judge the maker of certain violins. Now although nonexperts apparently cannot intersubjectively test the judgments of these experts, those experts' judgments are accepted. This is presumably because in cases in which their intuitive insights about violins can be directly verified, they are usually correct, and by straightforward inductive argument, it is assumed that they are probably correct in cases where their judgments cannot be directly verified. The basic argument used to establish these conclusions has the following form:

Suppose our evidence is that

    (1) In most cases in which expert X's intuitive judgment could be directly intersubjectively tested it was correct.

By inductive generalization one concludes from (1)

    (2) In most cases expert X's intuitive judgment was correct.

By another inductive generalization one infers from (2)

    (3) In most cases expert X's intuitive judgment is correct.

And (3) combined with

    (4) X intuitively judges that p.

allows one by direct inference to infer

    (5) p.

Now such an argument is an inductively acceptable one. Further, there is nothing in the positivist program that would be opposed to such an argument.

In principle, it is possible to argue that Verstehen is appropriate as a way of verifying hypotheses in certain areas and not in others and just this intermediate position has been taken by Howard Cohen. Cohen argues that Scriven is correct to suppose that Verstehen is a way of verifying hypotheses, but that it is inappropriate in history although it is appropriate in violin appraising. This is because intersubjective testability is more important in history than in violin appraising.

Now Cohen presumably is using "Verstehen" in the intuitive insight sense. Thus, he introduces his discussion of Verstehen in relation to violin appraising with the following remark by Scriven:[58] "One may see (or understand) why someone or some group did some thing, and not require further testing to be justifiably confident that this really is the reason."

He then argues that the use of Verstehen in this sense is inappropriate in history. The difference between history and violin appraising, as Cohen sees it, is that in violin appraising it is of the utmost importance to settle doubtful cases, and the use of an expert violin appraiser's intuitive insight is the only available and plausible way of doing this in many cases. Furthermore, extremely precise distinctions must be drawn and they cannot be drawn on the basis of available explicitly formulated evidence. The intuitive insight of experts is the only way this can be done.

For Cohen, the need for definite and very finely drawn conclusions makes the use of Verstehen appropriate in violin appraising. In history, however, he argues that other needs are primary. In particular, objectivity, that is, intersubjective verification, is of primary importance:

> In general when a historian's explanation is challenged—when it becomes doubtful or disputed—it must survive the judgment of his peers. Other historians—if they are interested—must be in a position to examine the evidence invoked and decide whether the conclusion follows or not. . . .The class of historians is not a closed circle of experts. Nor, for that matter, is any small segment of the class—at least not in the sense that their judgments are authoritative in virtue of the proven reliability of the investigator. [59]

Furthermore in history the historian is not required to draw finer conclusions than are justified by the historical evidence. Consequently, Verstehen in history is not a provider of knowledge.

One misleading aspect of Cohen's argument is that, as we have seen, the use of experts in history does not preclude intersubjective testing. Cohen's thesis must therefore be modified to read that in history, unlike violin appraising, intersubjective verifiability of a certain kind is appropriate. Consequently, although the results of intuitive insights are verifiable in one sense, they are not intersubjectively verifiable in another sense.

Cohen argues that historians, unlike violin appraisers, are not required to make distinctions that are indeterminate in relation to the
historical evidence. However, whether or not this view is correct depends on what one takes the function of history to be. If one is talking
about the traditional view of history as a detached ethically neutral
inquiry, Cohen may be correct. But if other goals are given prominence, the restriction he places on the use of experts becomes dubious.

Howard Zinn, for example, argues that historians should not be af-
forded the luxury of detachment and aloofness traditionally associated
with historical inquiry. Indeed, he maintains that historians have an
important social function to serve. Historians, according to Zinn, can
"intensify, expand, sharpen our perceptions of how bad things are for
certain victims of the world"; they can expose "the pretensions of government to either neutrality or beneficence"; they can expose the "ideology that pervades our culture"; they can "recapture those few mo-
ments in the past which show a better way of life than that which has
dominated the earth thus far."[60] Although Zinn does not, as far as I
know, consider the possibility of using experts in history inquiry, there
is no reason to think he would be opposed to using them. For the social
function he attributes to historians requires the drawing of finer conclusions than those permitted by the historical data. In such cases, the
intuitive historian need not forsake objectivity in the sense of
intersubjective testability. If it becomes necessary to fulfill history's
social function by going beyond the historical evidence and relying on
the intuitive insights of experts, such insight would be indirectly
intersubjectively testable.

However, one need not embrace Zinn's program of radical history
to see that in some cases social goals should be given special weight.
The Warren Commission Report on the assassination of President
Kennedy is an example of historical writing motivated by special social concern. Critics as well as defenders of the Warren Commission
Report admit that many crucial points about the assassination cannot
be discerned by recourse to the available historical evidence. It seems
plausible to suppose that in a report of such crucial national interest the
use of the intuitive judgments of experts would have been quite appropriate.

It is not necessary to consider special cases like the Warren Commission Report to question Cohen's thesis, however. For Cohen argues
that although historians are not required to draw finer conclusions
than are warranted by the explicitly statable evidence, he admits that

they *may* draw such conclusions. "The historian *may* if he wishes explain details for which there is no formulatable evidence. When he does so the explanations rest on his authority as a diagnostician if they are acknowledged to be known at all." Cohen goes on to argue, "One cannot reasonably say, however, that achieving that sort of precision is such an important part of historical knowledge that intersubjective verifiability should be sacrificed to it."[61]

But if historians are permitted to use such insight, then intersubjective verifiability (in his sense) can be (although it need not be) sacrificed in order to make such fine distinctions. What he must say, I should think, in order to have a coherent thesis is that historians—unlike violin appraisers—are not even permitted to draw conclusions "for which there is no formulatable evidence."

But this thesis surely is too strong, and Cohen's apparent inconsistency suggests that he does not want to embrace it. Historians, given a traditional view of historical inquiry, should be permitted to draw conclusions that are not warranted by formulatable evidence provided that such conclusions are based on the intuitive insights of historical experts—people whose intuitive insights are shown to be reliable. Drawing historical conclusions based on such insights would not be sacrificing intersubjective verifiability in one important sense.

There is a third approach to the study of history, which suggests that the sacrifice of Cohen's type of intersubjective testability may be worth the price. Many historians have argued that history would benefit greatly from the use of social scientific techniques, and indeed there are increased use of computers, mathematical models, statistical analyses, social scientific theories in history.

From this vantage point the intuitive judgments of experts in history can be seen as just one more social scientific technique in history. Helmer and Rescher[62] have suggested using experts in the "inexact sciences," for example, in prediction, decisions making, simulation techniques, gaming techniques, and pseudoexperiments. Some of their suggestions are already being used in social science and there seems to be no good reason why certain uses of experts could not be employed in a scientifically oriented historical inquiry.

Now it might be argued that the use of experts in history would restrict the freedom of the nonexpert historians to challenge the expert findings and that this would, in effect, create a historical elite. Thus Cohen argues, "When a historian's explanation is challenged—when it becomes doubtful or disputed—it must survive the judgment of his peers." He maintains "the class of historians is not a closed circle of experts. Nor for that matter is any small segment of that class. . . . Any young or previously unacknowledged historian may dispute an old diagnostician."[63]

Would the use of experts undercut this attractive picture sketched by Cohen? I believe it would not in any objectionable way. First of all, nonexpert historians would still be needed to check the judgments of experts where these could be checked. Thus the judgments of the nonexperts would in an important sense be basic. Second, historians could challenge the judgments of accepted experts in at least two different ways. They might argue that new evidence has come to light in terms of which the intuitive judgment of an expert could be directly tested. Moreover, they could challenge the authority of an expert indirectly by showing that, in those cases where his judgment could be checked, he or she was wrong much more often than previously thought and, consequently, in those cases where the expert's insight could not be checked directly, it would become dubious.

These reasons suggest that the so-called elitism among historians, if experts are used, is something that would be tolerable. Whether there are experts in history in the sense that there are experts in violin appraising is another question. But if there are, then, it seems to me, historians should welcome their use rather than fear for the objectivity of history.

Conclusion

Abel and Rudner explicitly rejected Verstehen interpreted as empathetic understanding solely on the grounds of its not being a method of validating hypotheses. However, empathetic understanding was not thought by classical Verstehenists such as Weber to be relevant to the validation of hypotheses. It might be supposed that their criticism is, however, relevant to the reliving interpretation of Dilthey. But even here it is dubious that he considered empathy as a method of verification.

However, even though Abel and Rudner misunderstood the classical Verstehen position, VT may be correct. Verstehen can be used to validate hypotheses under restricted conditions. In such cases Verstehen can be used as part of an analogical argument that yields probable conclusions. This interpretation would probably be accepted by advocates of AVC. However, Verstehen is not commonly used under these circumstances and, insofar as it is not, it cannot be used to validate a hypothesis about a subjective motivational state.

Scriven's argument for VT is misleading. Verstehen, as Scriven seems to understand it, does not *by itself* verify hypotheses in either science or history. It is true that Verstehen combined with independent established knowledge, namely, the reliability of someone's past empathetic insights, does enable hypotheses to be verified. Although advocates of AVC did not envisage this use of Verstehen, it is doubtful they would be opposed to it as Scriven seems to suggest. Such a use of Verstehen is not incompatible with the general program of positivism or the explicit statements of the critics of Verstehen. Whether Scriven thinks the independently established knowledge of the past reliability of the empathizer is intersubjectively testable in the sense desired by positivists is unclear. But in any case such knowledge does seem to be intersubjectively testable in an indirect way that is in keeping with positivism.

Cohen is therefore incorrect to suppose that if the intuitive judgments of experts are relied on in history the intersubjective testability of their judgments would be precluded. He is correct that a certain type of intersubjective testability would be precluded by their use. However, the use of the intuitive insight of experts may be necessary for certain special historical writing dominated by practical motives, and in any case it seems in keeping with the desirability of using social science techniques in history. The use of such experts correctly understood would not preclude criticism of these experts' judgments or establish an elite of historians.

The upshot is that with suitable qualification advocates of AVC are correct. What they neglected to say was that empathetic identification combined with other knowledge could be used as a method of verification. Munch and Scriven performed a valuable service of bringing this to our attention although they were confused in their analysis in how Verstehen works as a tool of verification. The positivists who advocated AVC were not alone in neglecting this use of Verstehen. This oversight was also found in the classical Verstehen position. For example, neither Dilthey nor Weber supposed Verstehen could be used in this way. In fact, Munch, Scriven, and Cohen are unique in being concerned with this issue. As will be evident in the chapters that follow, Verstehen theorists who came after them did not consider such use of Verstehen.

Moreover, as should be clear from chapter 1 and the remaining chapters of this book, my limited defense of VT here—accepting it only under very restricted conditions—does not mean that I do not think there are serious problems with Verstehen when it is not used as a method of verification, for example, as a necessary condition for social scientific understanding.

Notes

1. See Fred R. Dallmayr and Thomas A. McCarthy, (ed.) *Understanding and Social Inquiry* (Notre Dame, IN: University of Notre Dame Press, 1977), p.77.
2. Ibid.
3. Nicola Abbagnano, "Positivism" *Encyclopedia of Philosophy*, ed. Paul Edwards, (New York: Macmillian Pub. Co. Inc., and The Free Press, 1967) vol. 6, p. 414.
4. Abbagnano, "Positivism," p. 414.
5. David Braybrooke, *Philosophy of Social Science* (Englewood Cliffs, NJ: Prentice-Hall, Inc., 1987), p. 3.
6. I do not consider in this book philosophers such as W.V.O.Quine and Alexander Rosenberg who want to eliminate social science as it is usually understood, that is, social sciences that deal with meaning. For a critique of this approach, see Harold Kincaid, *Philosophical Foundations of the Social Sciences* (New York: Cambridge University Press, 1996), pp. 194-205.
7. Theodore Abel, "The Operation Called *Verstehen,*" *Understanding and Social Inquiry*, (ed.) Dallmayr and McCarthy, pp. 81-92. Originally published in *The American Journal of Sociology*, 54, 1947, pp 211-18.
8. Ibid., p. 83-84.
9. Ibid., p. 84.
10. Ibid., p. 85.
11. Ibid., p. 87.
12. Ibid.
13. Ibid
14. Ibid., p. 88.
15. Ibid., p. 90.
16. Ibid., p. 90.
17. Ibid., p. 91.
18. Ibid., p. 89.
19. Ibid., p. 91n. 6.
20. Ibid., p. 89.
21. Ibid.
22. Ibid.
23. Richard S. Rudner, *Philosophy of Social Science* (Englewood Cliffs, NJ: Prentice-Hall, 1966), p. 72.
24. Ibid.
25. Ibid.
26. Ibid., p. 73.
27. Ibid.
28. Ibid., pp. 81-83.
29. See the discussion in chapter 4.
30. Peter A. Munch, "Empirical Science and Max Weber's *Verstehende Soziologie,*" in M. Truzzi, (ed.) *Verstehen: Subjective Understanding in the Social Sciences* (Reading, MA: Addison-Wesley Publishing Co., 1974), pp. 56-69. This article

was originally published in *American Sociological Review*, 22, 1957, pp. 26-32 and was a response to Albert Pierce's article "Empirical Science and Social Science, *American Sociological Review*, 21, 1956, pp. 135 -37.

31. Michael Scriven, "Logical Positivism and the Behavioral Sciences," in *The Legacy of Logical Positivism*, eds. Peter Achinstein and Stephen F. Barker (Baltimore: Johns Hopkins University Press, 1969), pp. 195 -210, and Michael Scriven, "Verstehen Again", *Theory and Decision*, I , 1971, pp. 382 -86

32. Howard Cohen, "*Das Verstehen* and Historical Knowledge," American *Philosophical Quarterly*, 1973, pp. 299-306.

33. Munch, op. cit., p.63.

34. Ibid., p.64.

35. Ibid., p. 65.

36. The probability of the argument could be increased by other inferences that are strictly speaking not direct analogical inferences based on the Verstehen. Suppose the observer knows that the neighbor tends to chop wood, and burn it when he is chilly. Indeed, in every case observed in the past when the neighbor's behavior was similar to what the observer had just seen, it was, according to the neighbor, because he was chilly. (The neighbor has told the observer this is what he usually does and the observer has seen him behave in ways that are compatible with what he says, and so on.) So probably this sequence of behavior is based on the same motivation. This is not an analogical inference based on Verstehen but one based on the similarity of the neighbor's past wood-chopping behavior to his present wood-chopping behavior.
In addition, suppose that the observer has made many analogical inferences about his neighbors and they have tended to be correct. Probably this analogical inference connected with this wood-chopping neighbor is correct as well. Here we do not have a direct analogical inference but an inference based on the tendency of a certain class of such inference to be correct. One might call such an inference metaanalogical.

37. Munch, op. cit., p. 64.

38. Ibid., p. 65.

39. Theodore Abel, "The Operation Called *Verstehen,*" *Understanding and Social Inquiry*, (eds.) Fred R. Dallmayr and Thomas A. McCarthy (Notre Dame, IN: University of Notre Dame Press, 1977), p. 89.

40. In fact, it seems unlikely that if Weber would have considered Verstehen under these restricted circumstances he would have argued that empathetic Verstehen was merely a means of hypotheses generation.

41. Munch, op.cit.

42. Scriven, "Logical Positivism and the Behavioral Sciences," p. 201

43. Ibid.

44. Ibid., p. 204.

45. Ibid.

46. Scriven, "Verstehen Again," p. 383.

47. O. Helmer and N. Rescher, "On the Epistemology of the Inexact Sciences," *Management Science*, 6, 1969.

48. Abel, "The Operation Called *Verstehen,*" p.89.

49. Ernest Nagel, *The Structure of Science* (New York: Harcourt, Brace and World, 1961), pp. 482-83.

50. Richard Rudner, *Philosophy of Social Science*, (Englewood Cliffs, NJ: Prentice-Hall, 1966). p. 73.

51. Scriven, "Logical Positivism," pp. 202-205.

52. G.E.M. Anscombe, *Intention*, (Oxford: Blackwell, 1957), p. 15.

53. Scriven, "Verstehen Again," p. 383.
54. Ibid.
55. Ibid.
56. Ibid., p. 384.
57. See Carl G. Hempel, *The Philosophy of Natural Science*, (Englewood Cliffs, NJ: Prentice-Hall, 1966), pp. 38-40, for a discussion of the indirect support given by a theory.
58. Cohen, op. cit., p. 300.
59. Ibid., pp. 304–305.
60. Howard Zinn, *The Politics of History* (Boston: Beacon Press, 1970), pp. 33-55.
61. Cohen, op. cit., pp. 305–306.
62. Helmer and Rescher, "On the Epistemology of the Inexact Sciences."
63. Cohen, op. cit., pp. 304–305.

3

The Positivists' Critique II: Not a Necessary Condition for Understanding

Background

The criticisms by methodologists such as Abel and Rudner missed the point and are therefore largely irrelevant to the classical view. Furthermore, defenders of VT, such as Munch and Scriven, although they seemed to think that they were defending the classical Verstehen, were not. Whatever the merits of their arguments, they have little to do with the views of Dilthey, Weber, and Collingwood.

However, not all methodologists sympathetic to positivism limited their criticisms to AVC. Another positivists' criticism was that social scientific understanding should not be restricted to the understanding provided by Verstehen, however this is construed. Social science should be free to develop explanations in any terms so long as these explanations meet various methodological criteria used in both the natural and social sciences, such as testability, simplicity, explanatory power. Let us call this the Methodological Restraint Thesis (MRT). MRT is not the criticism of Verstehen usually associated with positivism. MRT is, however, directly relevant to the classical doctrine. Dilthey, Weber, and Collingwood all seemed to be claiming that Verstehen, as they variously construed it, defined the boundary of social scientific understanding.

MRT can best be understood as being based on two theses associated with positivism. First, the positivists were committed to what came to be called the Nomological Model of Explanation (NME). First formulated with regard to the natural sciences and extended to the social sciences, on this model an event is explained when it is subsumed under a general or else a statistical law or laws. Thus, a social event such as revolution is explained when it is subsumed under some law or set of laws. The relevance of NME to MRT is that the laws in question need not be restricted in the way specified by Verstehen theorists. So, in other words, acceptable explanations on the NME are not required to rely on laws that are subjectively meaningful in Weber's terms. Similar points can be made concerning Dilthey and Collingwood. In the social sciences and history, the NME does not require reliving the experience or rethinking the thoughts of the person whose behavior is being explained.

However, acceptance of NME does not undermine the classical doctrine of Verstehen unless another assumption is made. The classical theory was intended to give an account of social scientific *understanding*. In contrast, the positivists were interested in giving an account of social scientific *explanation*. The positivists' critique is therefore only relevant to the classical Verstehen view if it is assumed that having a scientific explanation of something and having scientific understanding are basically the same. Let us call this assumption the Equivalency Thesis (ET). Without ET advocates of Verstehen could argue that although a scientific explanation does not need to be restricted in terms of Verstehen, social scientific understanding does.

Now although NME and ET are associated with positivism, advocates of NME and ET need not embrace all or even most of the positivists' program. Thus, for example, a person could consistently accept NME and ET without accepting positivism's rejection of metaphysics. Moreover, it is important to see that a critic of Verstehen who accepts MRT need not be wedded even to that part of the positivists, program most relevant to social scientific understanding. Thus, a person could consistently reject either NME or ET and yet accept MRT. For example, maintaining that laws are not needed in scientific explanations, a critic of Verstehen might reject NME. Yet it does not follow that such a person would have to suppose that scientific understanding should be in terms of Verstehen. Furthermore, a critic of Verstehen need not embrace ET. A critic could maintain that an explanation is not necessary for social scientific understanding. However, such a critic could consistently argue that social scientific understanding is not restricted to Verstehen.

In short, although the positivists had their reasons for rejecting the thesis that social understanding is not restricted to Verstehen, such rejection neither entails a commitment to all aspects of the positivist program nor precludes giving other reasons for this rejection. Indeed, as I will show, although the positivists were correct in advocating MRT, they did not need NME and ET to make their case. Rejection of the Verstehenist account of understanding does not commit one either to all aspects of positivism or even to the most relevant aspects, namely, NME and ET.

Positivists' Arguments for MRT

Carl Hempel, one of the most famous logical positivists, produced a criticism of Verstehen that went beyond Abel's and Rudner's. He maintained that Verstehen, when interpreted as empathetic understanding, is neither necessary nor sufficient for scientific explanation. Verstehen so interpreted is not necessary, according to Hempel, "for the behavior of psychotics or of people belonging to a culture very different from that of the scientist may sometimes be explainable and predictable in terms of general principles even though the scientist who establishes or applies these principles may not be able to understand his subjects empathetically."[1] Hempel goes on to say that "empathy is not sufficient to guarantee a sound scientific explanation, for a strong feeling of empathy may exist even in cases where we completely misjudge a given personality."[2] Furthermore, Hempel argues that empathetic understanding leads to incompatible results. For example, one might conclude by means of empathetic understanding that a population subject to heavy bombing attacks would have its morale broken. But one might also conclude by empathetic understanding that it should develop a defiant spirit of resistance.[3]

However, this does not mean that Hempel thought that Verstehen was useless. Hempel says that "the understanding of another person in terms of one's own psychological functioning may prove a useful heuristic device in the search for general psychological principles which might provide a theoretical explanation."[4] In other words, Hempel like Abel, argued that empathetic understanding might be useful in the context of discovery as a way of generating hypotheses. Putting oneself in the place of someone else might enable one to think of explanatory hypotheses that could be tested by the standard methods of science, for example, deducing consequences from a hypothesis and verifying these consequences.

Hempel did not limit his critique of Verstehen to a critique of empathetic understanding, however. Max Weber distinguished rational explanatory Verstehen and empathetic Verstehen. In the former, social scientists place the action to be understood in some larger context in which the motives or purposes of the actors come into play. Only in this way, Weber thought, could one have meaningful causal explanations which, according to Weber, were essential for sociology. Causal connections were meaningful, Weber argued, because they were understood in terms of the connections between subjective states of the actors. Hempel had this to say about Weber's requirement:

> Weber's limitation of the explanatory principles of sociology to "meaningful" rules of intelligible behavior . . . is untenable: many, if not all, occurrences of interest to the social scientists require for their explanation reference to factors which are "devoid of subjective meaning," and thus to "non-understandable uniformities," to use Weber's terminology. Weber acknowledges that the sociologist must accept such facts as causally significant data, but he insists that this does "not in the least alter the specific task of sociological analysis . . . , which is the interpretation of action in terms of its subjective meaning." But this conception bars from the field of sociology any theory of behavior which foregoes the use of "subjective meaningful" motivational concepts. This means either an arbitrary restriction of the concepts of sociology—which, as a result, might eventually become inapplicable to any branch of sociological research—or else it amounts to an a priori judgment as to the character of any system of concepts that can possibly yield an explanatory sociological theory. Clearly, such an a priori verdict is indefensible; and indeed, the more recent developments of psychological and social theory indicate that it is possible to formulate explanatory principles for purposive action in purely nonintrospective terms.[5]

Four points should be made regarding Hempel's critique of Verstehen. First, with respect to empathetic understanding as a sufficient condition for the scientific understanding of human action, might it not be argued that Verstehen theorists were not talking about a strong feeling of empathy that may or may not correspond to the psychological state that one is trying to understand? Were they not talking about empathetic feelings that truly corresponded to the psychological state of the person with whom one is empathetic? Given this sort of empathetic understanding, one might argue, empathetic understanding *is* a sufficient condition for scientific understanding. So, one might maintain that Hempel's characterization misrepresents the Verstehen position.

Hempel would maintain that even if one knew that the empathizer's state corresponded to the empathized person's state, this would not be sufficient for a scientific understanding of the person's behavior. After all, one might know that a person P has psychological state S and not understand why S leads to action A. Peter might know that John is angry at his boss—and by empathy have the same feeling as John—

and yet not understand why John threw a book against the wall. Being empathetic with John's feeling of anger would not answer this question. Indeed, John may not know—and, if asked, might have no idea—why he expressed his anger in this way. It is important to recall that Verstehenists such as Weber did not suppose that Verstehen interpreted as using the subjective categories of the actor in understanding human behavior was a sufficient condition for understanding. As we have seen, he believed that causal considerations were also necessary for understanding. It is also doubtful that Dilthey thought reliving an actor's experience was sufficient for understanding.

Second, Hempel takes a needlessly controversial position when he says that "the more recent developments of psychological and social theory indicate that it is possible to formulate explanatory principles for purposive action in purely nonintrospective terms." Whether Hempel is correct about "recent developments," we need not decide here. The important point is, it possible that there could be an explanatory theory without its being subjectively meaningful and, as Hempel maintained, Weber rules that out a priori. This is enough to condemn the classical doctrine.

Third, in the context of Hempel's other work it is clear that his acceptance of the Methodological Restraint Thesis (MRT) is based on his acceptance of the Nomological Model of Explanation (NME). Even in the quotations given above one sees that NME is implicitly assumed. For example, Hempel argues that the behavior of people belonging to other cultures may be "explainable and predictable in terms of general principles even though the scientist who establishes or applies these principles may not be able to understand his subjects empathetically." As Hempel's other writings testify, these "general principles" are scientific laws. Like Weber, Hempel believed that rational explanations in the social sciences are a special case of causal explanations. However, Hempel did not suppose that acceptable causal explanations in the social sciences were limited to rational explanations. Moreover, in contrast to Weber, he explicitly connected rational explanation with the existence of general laws. In his formulation of rational explanation, general laws in terms of statements of psychological tendencies play an essential role.[6]

However, Hempel's rejection of Verstehen theorists' restrictions on understanding is unnecessary and needlessly controversial. Despite the fact that advocates of nomological explanations in the social sciences can mount a strong defense for their thesis,[7] Hempel should not base the case on NME. NME is still a controversial thesis and MRT can be and should be defended on independent grounds. All that is required is that cases be adduced where there is social scientific understanding and yet Verstehen in the traditional sense is not present. I did this in chapter 1 where I held that one can understand a revolution when one sees it as part of a larger social movement. This understanding assumes neither nomological explanation nor Verstehen in any of the traditional senses. The existence of social laws applicable in this case is controversial and the need for Verstehen is questionable. What is neither controversial nor questionable is that knowledge that the revolution is part of a larger trend helps one understand it.

Finally, Hempel also implicitly assumes that having a social scientific explanation and having social scientific understanding are roughly the same. To be sure, he does not suppose that having a social scientific explanation is the same as having empathetic understanding since he does not deem this type of understanding scientific. But he does assume some version of the Equivalency Thesis (ET). Thus, in the following quotation he closely identifies scientific understanding and NME: "But the kind of '[empathetic] understanding' thus conveyed must be clearly separated from scientific understanding. In history as anywhere else in empirical science, the explanation of a phenomena consists in subsuming it under general empirical laws; and the criterion of its soundness is. . .whether it rests on empirically well supported assumptions concerning initial conditions and general laws."[8]

However, ET is not needed to advocate MRT. One can argue that social scientific understanding should not be restricted to Verstehen and maintain that having an explanation and having social scientific understanding are not the same. Thus, for example, a psychotic episode might be understood in terms of its manifold physiological, psychological, and social manifestations. However, it would be a mistake to suppose that these provide an *explanation* of it. This is clearly seen once it is realized that these manifestations come after the episode. However, as one normally understands an explanation, the explanans— what explains—cannot come after the explanandum—what is explained.

Interestingly enough, some of what Hempel says allows for the separation of understanding and explanation. Thus, at one point, he says, "A class of phenomena has been scientifically understood when it can be fitted into a testable and adequately confirmed theory or a system of laws. . . ."[9] However, a phenomenon can be so fitted without necessarily having an explanation of it. Suppose that testable and adequately confirmed general laws and initial conditions enable us now to infer that an earthquake occurred in Brazil in 1990. The quake can be fitted into a pattern of laws but it is not explained by these laws for the same reasons that a psychotic episode is not explained by its manifestations: the explanans cannot come after the explanandum.[10]

Hempel is not unique in rejecting the restriction of social scientific understanding to Verstehen. This position was also taken by the philosopher of science, Ernest Nagel, whose views were influenced by the naturalist and logical empiricist movements. Although Nagel did not use the term "Verstehen," what he says in "The Subjective Nature of Social Subject Matter," a section of *The Structure of Science*, his major work on the philosophy of science, is directly relevant to the methodological issues connected with Verstehen.[11] Nagel considered three interrelated questions: (1) Are the distinctions required for exploring the subject matter exclusively "subjective"? (2) Is a behavioristic account of social phenomena inadequate? and (3) Do imputations of "subjective" states to human agents fall outside the scope of logical canons employed in inquiries into "objective" properties? In answering the last question he advanced AVC and in answering the first two questions he offered MRT.

(1) While admitting that human behavior is frequently purposeful, Nagel said that "social sciences do not confine themselves to using only distinctions that refer to psychological states exclusively; nor is it clear, moreover, why these disciplines should place such restrictions upon themselves." In addition, explanations of social behavior may use assumptions that do not refer to the subjective states of the actors. For example, cotton planters in the United States before the Civil War mistakenly believed that the use of animal manure would preserve indefinitely the fertility of the soil. In order to explain why under this mistaken belief cotton production gradually deteriorated and why as a result "there was an increased need for virgin land to raise cotton if the normal cotton crop was not to decrease,"[12] social scientists had to go beyond the subjective categories of the actors and appeal to modern laws of soil chemistry. Obviously, Nagel's argument relates to Weber's emphasis on rational explanatory Verstehen and his claim that the aim of sociology is to provide subjectively meaningful causal explanations. Explanations that rely on modern laws of soil chemistry go beyond Weber's restrictions.

(2) Nagel argued that behaviorism "does not have a precise doctrinal connotation; and students of human conduct who designate themselves

as behaviorists do so chiefly because of their adherence to a methodology that places a premium on objective (or intersubjectively observable) data."[13] Behaviorists, Nagel argued, need not deny the existence of subjective mental states and might only assert that "the controlled study of overt behavior is . . . the only sound procedure for achieving reliable knowledge concerning individual and social action."[14]

Nothing precludes behaviorists from "postulating various mechanisms that are not open to direct public observation." Although behaviorists who eschew the explanatory value of mental states and opt for explanatory theories in terms of purely physical categories are following a research program that has not yet achieved success, "it cannot be ruled out on a priori grounds as illegitimate or as intrinsically absurd."[15] Nagel concluded that behaviorism has not been shown to be inherently inadequate despite repeated claims to the contrary. This argument is also relevant to Weber's views on rational explanatory Verstehen insofar as Weber's theory seems to entail the inadequacy of behaviorism. Nagel is suggesting that one can understand human behavior in behavioristic terms, which means that social scientific understanding is not restricted to subjectively meaningful explanations.

(3) Nagel argued that even if the distinctive aim of the social sciences was to understand social phenomena in terms of the subjectively meaningful categories, the question remains whether the logical canons used in the imputation of subjective states to social actors "are different from those employed in connection with the imputation of 'objective' traits to things in other areas of inquiry."[16]

Recall that Weber argued that a causal relation R between A and B is subjectively meaningful if and only if R is understood in terms of some intuitively plausible relation R^1 holding between A^1 (some subjective state of the actors associated with A) and B^1 (some subjective state of the actors associated with B). Nagel argues that neither the claim that a causal relation holds between A and B nor the claim that the social actors in states A^1 and B^1 are "self-certifying, and evidence is required for each of them if the explanation of which they are part is to be more than an exercise in uncontrolled imagination."[17] This evidence, Nagel argued, is not obtained by empathetic identification. To be sure, a person's ability "to enter into relations of empathy with human actors in some social process may indeed be heuristically important in his efforts to *invent* suitable hypotheses which explain the process. Nevertheless, his empathic identification with those individuals does not, by itself, constitute *knowledge*."[18] Nagel concluded that the imputations of "subjective" states to human agents do not fall outside the scope of the logical canons employed in inquiries into "objective" properties. Nagel was aware that his position on this question was similar, if not identical, to Weber's who realized that imputation of subjective states to social actors must be based on objective evidence and procedures. In short, Nagel answered the question by giving the AVC of Verstehen. However, unlike some other critics influenced by positivism, he did not suppose that classical Verstehen theorists such as Weber held this view.

In another section of *The Structure of Science*, "Methodological Individualism and Interpretative Social Science," Nagel also considered methodological issues connected with Verstehen. Here he showed the problems and limitations of interpretative social science, which he characterized as maintaining that the distinctive aim of social science, is to "'understand' social phenomena by explaining them in terms of 'motivationally meaningful' (or 'subjective') categories of human experience."[19] Arguing that such a view is often tied to a thesis about the reducibility of all statements about social phenomena to a special class of psychological statements about individual human conduct, Nagel showed the difficulties with such a reduction. In addition, he argued that although explanations in terms of cultural values and other "subjective" dispositions have "frequently illuminated social change," it would be absurd to claim that such explanations account for all social change or to deny that explanations in terms of other variables (such as physical environment, state of technology, population density, forms of economic organization) often have as much "predictive and systematizing power" as do explanations in terms of subjective categories.[20]

Like Hempel, Nagel was committed to the Nomological Model of Explanation (NME). In *The Structure of Science* he argued that "the distinctive aim of science" is to provide "systematic and responsibly supported explanations."[21] Nagel made it clear that explanations in science—including social science and history—are based on general or probabilistic laws.[22] Further, Nagel tacitly assumed a close connection between the scientific explanation of social phenomena and scientific understanding of social phenomena— the Equivalency Thesis (ET). In general, Nagel drew no clear distinction between the two, often using the terms "explanation" and "understanding" together. Indeed, he seems to have assumed that understanding presupposed having an explanation. Although he distinguished interpretative social scientific understanding from other types, he believed that it is simply having a special kind of explanation in terms of subjective categories. Presumably, understanding social phenomena noninterpretatively would be in terms of giving explanations not in terms of subjective categories. Further, although, as far as I am aware, he did not consider the issue explicitly, he assumed that social scientific understanding is always connected with social scientific explanation. Thus, it would not have occurred to Nagel to question whether one could have a scientific understanding of something without a scientific explanation of it.

Nagel's commitment to NME and ET, like Hempel's, is not needed to argue MRT, however. To return to his example of cotton planters in the United States before the Civil War, Nagel's claim that an adequate explanation of their behavior cannot be restricted to explanation in terms of subjectively meaningful categories is not contingent on the assumption that such explanation must be in terms of laws. Whether or not there are laws of soil chemistry that help explain the farmers' behavior, Nagel's point remains that the explanation cannot be restricted to subjectively meaningful categories. A similar point can be make with respect to Nagel's example of behaviorism. Even if there are no behavioristic laws, explanations of social behavior cannot be restricted a priori to those in terms of meaningful categories: Behavioristic explanations are possible without behavioristic laws.

With respect to Nagel's implicit commitment to ET a similar point can be made. The assumption of ET is not needed to maintain MRT. The behavior of the cotton farmers may be understood in terms of theoretical principles that link events occurring after their behavior—for example, depletion of virgin land—to their behavior. Since the explanans cannot be temporally posterior to the explanandum, such events could not provide an explanation of the behavior. However, we can understand their behavior in these terms. We usually explain and understand a later event as being a consequence of earlier events. But we can understand and do not explain an earlier event as being a causal factor of some later events without explaining it. However, such understanding without explanation is not limited to meaningful categories.

A Typical Response

Unfortunately, traditional defenders of Verstehen attacked the well-known but irrelevant Anti-Verification Criticism (AVC) and did not pay attention to the relevant but little-known Methodological Restraint Thesis (MRT). When methodologists accused the critics of Verstehen of misunderstanding it, their accusations were usually directed at the best known of these attackers, namely, Theodore Abel.

The sociologist Murray Wax's response was typical. Claiming that Abel attempted "to demolish and debunk" Verstehen, Wax tried to defend Verstehen against his criticism.[23] In order to do so he distinguished four levels or varieties of Verstehen: extracultural Verstehen, intracultural Verstehen, Verstehen as pattern recognition and interpretation, and Verstehen as interpersonal intuition. Arguing that the most important variety is intracultural and that Abel's criticism is directed only to the least important and most problematic variety, interpersonal intuition, Wax maintained that Abel's criticism was largely irrelevant.

According to Wax, intracultural Verstehen is neither a procedure for generating hypotheses nor for verifying them but a "precondition of research."[24] With respect to Abel's example of one's neighbor chopping wood to keep warm, Wax said, "the real Verstehen in this account has been completely overlooked, namely the recognition by the observer that the social objects involved were 'neighbor,' 'desk,' 'ax,' 'woodshed,' and so on, and that the actions were 'chopping with an ax,' 'lighting (kindling) a fire,' 'writing (seated) at a desk,' and so on." According to Wax, Abel failed to perceive "the vast background of shared meanings"[25] that the social scientists and social actors have in common—a background brought about by socialization—and without which sophisticated research techniques would be impossible to use. Indeed, the function of field work is precisely to give the social scientist an insider's view of a culture and thus to provide what Wax called secondary socialization.

Another important type of Verstehen is what Wax called pattern recognition and interpretation. In the recognition and interpretation of ethnological and linguistic patterns, the perspective of the actors is crucial since their categories and distinctions—many of which they are unaware of—play an essential role. As in intracultural Verstehen, socialization and participation often play a crucial role in developing the skill necessary to recognize and interpret patterns.

Identifying interpersonal intuition Verstehen with Weber's concept, Wax found it problematic. However, it is not clear whether Wax understood Weber's crucial distinction between explanatory Verstehen (the requirement of subjective meaningfulness for acceptable causal explanation) and empathetic Verstehen (a technique of hypotheses generation).

Abel attempted to answer Wax by arguing that when he used the term "Verstehen" he had in mind the technical meaning adopted by

German sociologists.[26] Although the term "Verstehen" is rich in meaning in the German language, Abel argued that German sociologists did not use the term in Wax's first three senses. According to Abel, these sociologists used the term "Verstehen" in the technical meaning developed by Weber. Thus, he considered Wax's criticism irrelevant to his purposes.

Maintaining that, despite what Wax might think, he did not intend to demolish and debunk Verstehen, Abel said he believed that Verstehen is the "chief source of hypotheses in sociology." Indeed, Verstehen can lead to knowledge such as "the disclosure of connections between social phenomena and other insights" and, consequently, Verstehen "is an important tool for the explanation of knowledge in the social sciences."[27]

Whether or not Abel was correct that the term "Verstehen" was not used by German sociologists in three of the four ways specified by Wax, he neglected one crucial sense of Verstehen used by Weber, namely, explanatory Verstehen. Moreover, it is not clear whether Wax's four varieties of Verstehen include Weber's explanatory Verstehen. How exactly Wax's interpersonal intuition Verstehen connects with Weber's explanatory Verstehen is uncertain. Wax's claim that intracultural Verstehen is a precondition of research is not relevant to Weber's explanatory Verstehen. If Weber's explanatory Verstehen is to be considered a precondition at all, it is not a precondition for doing research, but for having acceptable causal explanations.

We have seen that there is reason to doubt Weber's requirement for acceptable causal explanations. There is also reason to doubt Wax's precondition for doing social scientific research. Wax makes it sound as if a social scientist's understanding a society or culture in the same terms as the social actors is a precondition of understanding it in any way. Thus, the social scientist must be socialized in such a way that he or she acquires at least to some extent the same background of shared meaning as the social actors. But there are many ways to understand a culture. Some of these might make it necessary to comprehend it in the natives' terms before it can be understood at all. However, I see no reason to suppose that this is true for all ways of understanding. Understanding social actors in terms of the categories of an abstract sociological theory need not involve using the concepts of the actors or even relating these concepts to the actors' concepts. Wax's preconditions for research are only a precondition for doing research in a certain way.

In short, Wax not only fails to defend Verstehen from the MRT but assumes without argument that Verstehen puts restrictions on research. Although he correctly shows the irrelevance of the AVC of Abel, he is completely unaware of the type of criticism given by Hempel and Nagel. As far as Abel's retort to Wax is concerned, it also fails to come to grips with the MRT and continues to defend the irrelevant AVC despite the fact that the latter has little to do with the classical conception of Verstehen.

Notes

1. Carl G. Hempel, *Aspects of Scientific Explanation* (New York: The Free Press, 1965), p. 258.
2. Ibid.
3. Ibid. Hempel derives this example from Edgar Zilsel.
4. Ibid., p. 257-58.
5. Ibid., p. 163-64.
6. Ibid., pp. 470-77.
7. See Lee C. McIntyre, *Laws and Explanation in the Social Science* (Boulder, CO: Westview Press, 1995).
8. Hempel, *Aspects of Scientific Explanation*, p. 240.
9. Ibid., p. 329.
10. See Michael Martin, *Concepts of Science Education* (Lanham, MD: University Press of America, 1985), p. 60.
11. Ernest Nagel, *The Structure of Science* (New York: Harcourt, Brace and World, 1961), pp. 473-85.
12. Ibid., p. 476.
13. Ibid., pp. 477-78.
14. Ibid., p. 480.
15. Ibid.
16. Ibid., p. 481.
17. Ibid., p. 482.
18. Ibid., p. 484.
19. Ibid., p. 540.
20. Ibid., p. 546.
21. Ibid., p. 15.
22. See Ibid., chapters 14, 15.
23. Murray Wax, "On Misunderstanding Verstehen: A Reply to Abel," in Marcello Truzzi, ed., *Verstehen: Subjective Understanding in the Social Sciences* (Reading, MA: Addison-Wesley Publishing Co., 1974), p. 71.
24. Ibid., p. 74. A similar critique of Abel is mad by Thomas McCarthy, "On Misunderstanding 'Understanding'", *Theory and Decision* 3, 1973, pp. 351-70.
25. Ibid.
26. Theodore Abel, "A Reply to Professor Wax," in Truzzi, ed., *Verstehen: Subjective Understanding in the Social Sciences,* pp. 83-86. Abel uses a similar reply against McCarthy's criticism. See Theodore Abel, "Verstehen I and Verstehen II," *Theory and Decision* 6, 1975, pp. 99-102.
27. Wax, "On Misunderstanding Verstehen: A Reply to Abel," p. 86.

4

Verstehen and Ordinary Language Philosophy

The best known positivists' critique of Verstehen that Verstehen was not a method of verification (AVC) but was at best a methodological device useful for hypothesis generation was challenged in the late 1950s by Peter Winch and William Dray. Showing sympathy with the tradition of Dilthey, Weber, and Collingwood, Winch and Dray maintained that Verstehen was neither a method of verification nor a method of hypotheses generation but a necessary condition for social scientific and historical understanding. Dray was well aware of the positivists' account of Verstehen as only a methodological device for generating hypotheses and explicitly rejected this view. In his discussion of Popper's critique of Weber, Winch also shows awareness of this sort of criticism and rejects its application to Weber's view and indirectly to his own.

Whether Winch and Dray were aware of the less well known positivists' critique that Verstehen was not necessary for social scientific understanding is uncertain. Although this criticism is found in papers Hempel wrote in the 1940s, it is unclear whether Winch ever read them since he does not cite the papers in his work. Dray was very much aware of Hempel's early work on explanation, especially his 1942 paper "The Function of General Laws in History," and attacked Hempel's Nomological Model of Explanation (NME) as being inapplicable to history. But Dray does not seem to have considered Hempel's critique of the doctrine that Verstehen was not necessary for social scientific understanding and that this critique could be formulated independently of NME. This is not surprising since Hempel's criticism is deeply embedded in his defense of NME and the argument that the rejection of Verstehen could be based purely on the Methodological Restraint Thesis (MRT) is not well known.

In any case, Winch's and Dray's approaches to Verstehen set the stage for much of the discussion that followed. Although sympathetic to the traditional view, they showed that a defense of Verstehen did not have to be based on this view and could be argued for on independent grounds. Indeed, just when it might have appeared historically that the positivists had carried the day and showed that traditional Verstehen was defunct, Winch and Dray revived Verstehen, placing it in a new and exciting philosophical context of Wittgensteinianism and Ordinary Language Philosophy, which dominated Anglo-American philosophy during the 1950s and 1960s.

In the *Tractatus*, Wittgenstein argued that there was an ideal logical form which pictured the structure of the world that was hidden beneath the surface of ordinary discourse. However, in his later writings, in particular in *The Philosophical Investigations*, he rejected this conception of language in favor of an account of concrete "language games" as "forms of life."[1] According to Wittgenstein, there are manifold uses of language in ordinary life that are tied to actions and social practices. These various uses of language (language games) are governed by rules and comprise different "forms of life."[1] A philosophical problem is generated by the misuse of language and is dissolved by getting a clear view on the ordinary uses of language in the context of the problem.

Ordinary language, according to Wittgenstein, is acceptable as it stands and should not be thought of as incorporating a set of theories with deep conceptual problems. Although Wittgenstein was primarily concerned with Western ordinary language, he believed that all societies have ordinary languages that are also in order as they are. Thus, he claimed that Frazer was mistaken in the *Golden Bough* in the same way that a philosopher is typically mistaken concerning ordinary language. Frazer believed that the sentences used in native rituals were indicative sentences analogous to scientific theoretical claims. But, according to Wittgenstein, this was a serious misunderstanding. Wittgenstein argued that the native language used in ceremonies should be interpreted as religious utterances and that because these utterances have a purely expressive function, they are neither true nor false.[2]

Except for a few brief comments, such as his remarks about Frazer, Wittgenstein did not concern himself with understanding social scientific phenomena. However, some philosophers influenced by his views developed their implications for the social sciences. The best known of these is Peter Winch. In his book, *The Idea of a Social Science* (1958), and his paper, "Understanding a Primitive Society" (1964), Winch develops and applies what he takes to be Wittgenstein's insights to the social sciences.[3]

The Idea of a Social Science

The View Explained

Winch took over Wittgenstein's concept of forms of life and applied it to the understanding of social activities. Thus, he held that one understands the actions or utterances of actors in terms of the rules governing a form of life. For example, science is one form of life and religion another, and each has different "criteria of intelligibility peculiar to itself."[4] Consider the criteria of logic. According to Winch, it does not make sense to say that a form of life is either logical or illogical. It is non-logical.[5] Winch argued that actions within a certain form of life promote certain "considerations" or purposes that are characteristic of this form of life. "Magic, in a society in which magic occurs, plays a peculiar role of its own and is conducted according to considerations of its own."[6]

What is involved in understanding social behavior? Winch agrees with Max Weber that in understanding social behavior one is concerned with understanding it as meaningful behavior.[7] For him as for Weber understanding the meaning of the behavior could consist of knowing the reasons why an actor does what she does. Once one knows these reasons the action becomes meaningful. To use Winch's example, if one knows the reason N voted Labor, N's action becomes meaningful. Although he says that N's reasons may not be known to N but only to a psychoanalyst, in order to be meaningful N must be able to grasp such reasons and to eventually accept them.

According to Winch, however, meaningful behavior extends beyond actions based on a person's reasons. Thus, for example, traditional behavior such as voting for Labor because one's parent did can be considered meaningful. The behavior becomes meaningful because "the tradition is regarded as a standard which directs choice between alternative actions."[8] In other words, it is understandable in terms of a standard or rule; in short, it is rule-governed. Indeed, Winch argued that behavior which is meaningful (therefore all specifically human behavior) is ipso facto rule-governed. Both the action of a monk and that of an anarchist can be understood in terms of rules. The difference between them is not that one follow rules and the other does not but that they follow different rules. Thus, Winch rejected the view that Verstehen involves some private inner sense or intuition and that advocates of Verstehen confuse the familiar with the intelligible. Grasping this meaning, Winch argues, need not involve any intuition and the meaning grasped need not be familiar.

Although Winch does not acknowledge it, Winch's theory is somewhat closer to Dilthey's view than to Weber's if Dilthey's theory is given the reconstruction interpretation. Unlike Weber, neither Winch nor Dilthey connected Verstehen with causal explanations. One assumes that for Winch Verstehen is simply what he called understanding human action and this involves understanding human action, that is, meaningful behavior, in terms of the rules of social life. For Dilthey on the reconstruction account, Verstehen is understanding an action as a manifestation of an underlying idea, intention, or feeling of the actor. There is obvious overlap between these two notions of Verstehen since for Dilthey the underlying idea might be related to a social rule.

The View Evaluated

A. The Scope of Social Inquiry

It is difficult to determine just how important Winch believes understanding meaningful behavior in terms of the rules of social life is relative to the overall task of social science. Indeed, one may distinguish two different theses:

(1) The only task of social science is to understand the meaningful behavior of social actors in terms of the rules of social life.

(2) The main task of social science is to understand the meaningful behavior of social actors in terms of the rules of social life.

The stronger thesis, (1) above, is out of contact with the social sciences in the late 1950s.[9] (2) also seems too strong for it suggests that once one has discovered and specified the rules of social life and has understood social practices in terms of them, little work of any importance remains for social science. But, on the contrary, almost all important questions that social scientists actually are interested in and are working on remain. Perhaps one should say

(3) Understanding the meaningful behavior of social actors in terms of the rules of social life is a necessary condition for doing any other social scientific investigation.

But even (3) is liable to serious misunderstanding. It is surely mistaken to maintain that social scientists must understand the meaningful behavior of social actors in terms of the rules of social life *before* any other investigations can begin. Increased knowledge of the rules of social life and understanding in terms of them can go hand in hand with the study of their origin, their acquisition, their effects on personality, and so on. Perhaps all that can be said is this:

(4) The existence of meaningful behavior, that is, rule-governed behavior, is a necessary conditions of doing social science.

But (4) is hardly news. Indeed, as Robert Brown, a philosopher of the social sciences, has argued, "'To say that social scientists depend upon the notion of rule conforming behavior is to utter a platitude."[10] Without rules of social life there is no society and hence no social scientific investigation is possible.

Which of the above theses is closest to Winch's own view? Unfortunately, this is not clear. The only task he explicitly specified for the social sciences is to understand the meaningful behavior of social actors in terms of the rules of social life. This suggests that his view is closest either to (1) or (2) and, indeed, this is how most of his commentators have interpreted him.[11] So interpreted, however, his theory has serious problems.

First of all, insofar as Winch limited the tasks of the social sciences to (1) and (2) above, his view is restricted and arbitrary. There are many other jobs social scientists have undertaken, many other kinds of investigations they have conducted. Consider, for example, the work of Robert Merton on bureaucratic structure and personality. Merton's work is typical of the sociology practiced at the time Winch's book appeared and was and still is considered a contribution to the field. Winch's account of social science does not allow for, or at least does not show awareness of, the sort of problems Merton dealt with. To be sure, Merton was interested in the rules of social life, but he did not limit his investigation to the discovery and specification of what these rules are or to understanding social life in terms of these rules. Indeed, these tasks would have been only the beginning for Merton.

Consider some of the kinds of questions Merton raised and tried to answer in his study of bureaucracy.[12]

(a) What are the functions of the social rules in a bureaucratic institution?[13]

(b) Why do these rules have these functions?

(c) What are the dysfunctions of these rules in a bureaucratic institution?

(d) Why do these rules have these dysfunctions?

(e) What effects do conforming to these social rules have on the personality of people in a bureaucratic institution?

(f) Why do they have these effects?

(g) Does a bureaucratic institution attract a certain personality type?

(h) If so, why does it do this?

In one of his studies, Merton argued that part of the function of bureaucratic rules is to insure devoted and efficient performances and the elimination of personalized relationships and nonrational considerations. But such rules might also be dysfunctional since they result in "trained incapacitates," that is, blind spots and inflexibilities. Other questions have also been asked by social scientists that are beyond the purview of Winch's conception of a social science. For example,

(i) What are the origins of bureaucratic institutions?

(j) How did social rules develop in bureaucratic institutions?

B. Nature of Explanation

Winch's views on the nature of social science lead him to make certain inferences about the nature of explanation in the social sciences. In particular, he seems to maintain all of the following theses:

(a) Social scientific explanations must be in terms of rules of social life.

(b) Social scientific explanations are always of rule-governed behavior.

(c) Social scientific explanations of rule-governed behavior must be in terms of rules of social life.

(d) Social scientific explanations must be in terms of what the actor can understand.

My justification for attributing (a), (b), and (c) to Winch is not based on anything he says explicitly but on what follows from the most plausible reading of what he says.[14] Thus, he emphasizes throughout his book the need of explaining meaningful behavior in terms of following the rules of social life. He mentions no other types of explanations. Since he never mentions nonmeaningful behavior he seems to imply that meaningful behavior is the only thing social science should be concerned with. Winch explicitly makes claim (d). In his example of understanding N voting Labor he says that the concept used in an explanation of why N voted Labor must be grasped *"by N himself."*[15]

Theses (a)-(d), although closely connected, raise different issues.

(1) As already noted there is reason to doubt thesis (a). Social scientists explain the origin and development of rules in a social institution,[16] the learning of social rules, the attitudes people have towards rules, the effects of conforming to these rules on personality, the adoption of one set of rules rather than another, and so on. In general, such explanations are not in terms of rules of social life.[17] It is perhaps only because Winch takes such a narrow view of the task of the social sciences that he seems unaware of these obvious points.

(2) It should be clear from the above considerations that (b) is mistaken. Sometimes social scientific explanations are about rule-governed behavior, but sometimes they are about the rules themselves, e.g., their origin, how they are learned. Moreover, social scientists are also interested in explanations of why people profess to follow social rules but do not. This failure to follow rules may or may not itself be rule-governed. That behavior does not conform to social rules does not entail that it is meaningless. According to Winch an action governed by a social rule can be done in a right or wrong way.[18] However, it would seem that one can perform an action not covered by such standards of right and wrong. For example, Alasdair MacIntyre questions whether there is a right and wrong way of going for a walk.[19] There is no reason why social scientists could not explain actions that are not governed by social rules. Moreover, sometimes social scientists explain behavior that is not an action. Winch gave an example of a berserk lunatic.[20] Supposing the behavior of the lunatic consists of meaningless movements, there seems to be no reason why social science could not explain it. This, of course, is not to say that the lunatic's behavior could be *completely* explained in social scientific terms; after all, psychology and physiology may be relevant. But a *partial* explanation may come from social science, e.g., in terms of the social class or social origin of the lunatic.

(3) Thesis (c) is weaker than (a). One may grant that social scientists sometimes do explain the origin of social rules, the learning of social rules, and so on and that these explanations are not always in terms of

social rules and yet still insist that rules-governed behavior must be explained in terms of these rules. This weaker thesis is wrong, however. Indeed, Winch gave what seems to be a counterexample to his own view. He considered a man N who votes Labor and yet has no reason for doing so.[21] This man's behavior, according to Winch, is meaningful: It is governed by certain standards of appropriateness, i.e., the rules of voting behavior. However, although we understand *what* he has done when we see his behavior in the context of these voting rules, we do not understand *why* he voted Labor in terms of his reasons. Moreover, since he has no reason for voting Labor rather than, say, liberal or conservative, we do not know *why* he voted Labor in terms of his reasons. Hence, rules of social life (standards of appropriateness or reasons) do not explain why he voted the way he did. However, a social scientist might still attempt to explain this man's voting behavior in terms of, say, his social or economic class.

But even if N did vote Labor and could give reasons for his choice it is still dubious that his reasons would furnish a complete causal explanation for his behavior. Yet depending on one's purpose a complete causal explanation may be precisely what is wanted. Citing his reasons may, of course, completely *justify* his choice; there might be no more one could say in construing a rationale for N's voting Labor.[22] But giving a complete rationale for someone's choice is not necessarily to completely answer the question of why he did what he did, in the sense of what causal factors brought about his actions. If one is asking for the complete causal explanation of N's action, N's reason may be only one part of this account. That this is true is shown by the fact that N may sometimes not vote Labor although his reasons have not changed. His having certain reasons is not sufficient to explain his action.

Winch would, of course, object to the above suggestion. He does not believe that rule-governed behavior can be causally explained. Winch assumes the controversial thesis that reason explanations are not a subspecies of causal explanation and gives two reasons in its support.[23]

First, Winch maintained that reasons justify someone's action whereas causes do not.[24] However, reasons can justify an action *and* having reasons can be causal factors that bring about the action. There is nothing incompatible about these two claims. Second, Winch argued that part of learning the concept of cause is learning techniques of prediction. But, although one can sometimes predict what someone will do by means of knowing his reasons, learning techniques of prediction is not involved in learning the concept of reason. Hence, reasons cannot be causes.[25] Not enough is known about the details of language learning to know whether Winch's view is correct;[26] in relation to our present knowledge Winch's view is pure speculation. But even granted that we do learn language in the way Winch said, nothing of philosophical interest follows. It still might be true that reasons can be usefully assimilated to causes.

Consider an analogous case: The notion of number may not be learned as a notion that is set-theoretically defined, but it may still be useful to assimilate numbers to sets in a systematic account of mathematics. The same thing may be true of cause and reason: it may be useful to assimilate having reasons to causes in a systematic account of social science.

(4) Now thesis (d), social scientific explanations must be in terms of what the actor can understand, is parasitic on thesis (a), social scientific explanations must be in terms of rules of social life, and thesis (b), social scientific explanations are always of rule-governed behavior.

Explanations of the origins of rules of institutions, for example, may not be in terms the members of the institutions understand, for the members of the institutions may be ignorant of history or theoretical sociology. For obvious reasons the explanations of the behavior of a lunatic may not be in terms the lunatic can understand since his mental capacity may prevent him from understanding the theory that explains his behavior.

But even an explanation of a piece of meaningful behavior need not always be in terms that the actor can understand. Thus an explanation of N's choice to vote Labor when N has no reason might be in terms of a sociological theory which uses abstract theoretical notions beyond N's ken, for example, group cohesiveness. Moreover, even if N has reasons for voting Labor, the complete explanation—the total cause—may transcend N's understanding. The total cause may be specified in terms of an abstract sociological theory which N cannot grasp.

Winch argues sometimes for a much more moderate thesis than that social scientific explanations must be in terms of what the actor can understand. He maintains in places that although the concepts that a social scientist uses might transcend the understanding of the participants, the use of these concepts must "presuppose" the participants' understanding. For example, an economist might use a technical concept that is not understood by business people. For this concept to be explanatory, however, it must be "logically tied" to concepts, such as money, profit, cost, and risk, which are understandable to business people. Or a psychoanalyst

> may explain a patient's neurotic behavior in terms of factors unknown to the pa-
> tient and concepts which would be unintelligible to him. Let us suppose that the
> psychoanalyst's explanations refer to events in the patient's early childhood. Well,
> the description of those events will presuppose an understanding of the concepts
> in terms of which family life, for example, is carried on in our society; for those
> will have entered, however rudimentarily, into relations between the child and his
> family.[27]

The important question here is what is meant by "logically tied" and what is meant by "presuppose." Alan Ryan in defending Winch holds a similar position. Ryan believes that Winch is correct to maintain that, whatever explanations we end up with, "we must root our story in that which is told by the agents themselves."[28] He links this restriction explicitly to the doctrine of Verstehen and argues that to construe Verstehen as a heuristic device is "quite inadequate."[29] The crucial question is what Ryan means by "root." His meaning is clarified by the following quotation:

> For the point is that the identification of the events to be understood necessarily
> depends on understanding the rules which make them count as events of whatever
> kind it may be. Thus when we describe a set of actions as *praying*, the necessity is
> to employ religious criteria, when we describe an act as that of voting the neces-
> sity is to employ *political* criteria.[30]

From this one gathers that commonsense categories of the actors are used to identify the subject matter to be explained. Once it has been identified, then explanatory theory and categories can be introduced that go beyond the actor's point of view.

It is likely that Winch meant something similar: Although the concepts of actors do not dictate the explanations offered by social scientists, they do determine the subject matter under investigation. However, even this restriction on social science explanations is too much. Why must social scientists start by identifying their subject matter in terms of the categories of the actor? Suppose a social scientist wants to find out why a certain pattern of group behavior occurs in an alien society. Suppose further that the members of this society do not recognize this pattern and indeed do not even have a concept for it. It would seem that Ryan's and Winch's restrictions would prevent social scientists from explaining this pattern of social behavior. And this does not seem justified.

Now it might be argued that, as the examples from economics and psychoanalysis suggest, the concepts that determine the subject matter of social scientific investigation should generally be the ones the subjects use and understand. It might appear that if one departs, too, from the maxim that the subject matter of scientific investigations must be determined by the actors' concepts, one risks making the investigation irrelevant. However, this is not necessarily true. Economists and psychoanalysts may have good theoretical reasons why the subject matter of their fields of investigation should be defined by concepts that depart in significant ways from the concepts of business people or patients. Traditional concepts such as money, profit, cost, etc., might be much too crude and simple for a systematic definition of the field of economics as it matures; the commonsense categories of family life referred to in psychoanalytic explanations might have to give way to more theoretical ones as psychoanalysis develops as a science. Such departures from the concepts of the social actors might at first make it seem as if economics or psychoanalysis were irrelevant to business or family life. However, the new conceptualizations of these fields might indirectly help us understand business and family life better than the old conceptualization that used the actors. After all, physical sciences departed significantly from common sense in how they characterized their subject matter, yet few would deny the relevance of natural science not only to understanding the everyday physical world but to predicting and controlling it.

Winch on Weber

Winch's view is related to Weber's in that both Winch and Weber argue that social science should attempt to interpret social behavior in meaningful terms. However, Winch sees himself as correcting Weber's theory. According to Winch, Weber was mistaken in attempting to argue that plausible interpretations of human actions must be verified by statistical evidence. Winch attributed to Weber the assumption that Verstehen is something which is

> logically incomplete and needs supplementing by a different method altogether, namely, the collection of statistics. Against this, I want to insist that if a proffered interpretation is wrong, statistics, though they may suggest that it is so, are not the decisive and ultimate court of appeal for the validity of sociological interpretations in the way Weber suggests. What is needed is a better interpretation, not something different in kind. . . . Someone who interprets a tribe's magical rites as a form of misplaced scientific activity will not be corrected by statistics about what members of that tribe are likely to do on various kinds of occasions (though this might form *part* of the argument); what is ultimately required is a *philosophical* argument. . . .For a mistaken interpretation of a form of social activity is closely akin to the types of mistakes dealt with in philosophy.[31]

However, Winch's critique of Weber's notion of Verstehen can be questioned. According to Winch, Weber is mistaken to suppose that the verification of Verstehen needs statistics. But how is someone's explanatory account in terms of social rules to be verified? Unfortunately, Winch does not say. The only thing that he says is that statistical evidence is not decisive in this validation and that a philosophical argument is required to correct serious interpretive mistakes. Winch says, "What is needed is a better interpretation, not something different in kind." However, he does not tell us in any clear way what a better interpretation is.

Let us suppose he is correct about the two things he does say. Of course, similar points might well be made about understanding natural phenomena. Statistical data is not decisive in validating interpretation of many kinds of natural phenomena. For example, determining whether the Copernican theory was a valid interpretation of the heavens was hardly something that was decisively decided by statistics.[32] Moreover, even interpretations in the natural sciences on a much less grand scale are often not decided by statistics. For example, deciding whether Jones has disease D, given he has symptoms S, is not usually determined by statistical data. In addition, one might argue that incorrect views of nature, for example, the Aristotelian worldview, which have been overthrown, have not been accomplished by appealing to statistical data, but by the use of metaphysical arguments.[33]

My view is that an interpretation of social actions in terms of the rules of social life is validated in the same way as interpretations of phenomena in the natural sciences are, namely, by seeing if it accounts for the evidence in a more simple and comprehensive way than do rival interpretations. Weber may have been wrong to suppose that statistics were necessary to validate social interpretations, but he was certainly not wrong to insist that an interpretation should not be accepted simply because it is plausible; that is, because the social behavior to be explained would be meaningful if the interpretation were true. After all, there could be incompatible plausible interpretations that make the same social behavior equally meaningful. That is to say, there could be incompatible sets of social rules that explain some social behavior equally well. To determine which interpretation social scientists should accept might not involve statistics but it must involve an appeal to objective evidence.

This is not to say, of course, that this evidence itself will need no interpretation. In other words, this evidence will be theory-laden. However, this does not differ from the natural sciences where the evidence that is used to validate an interpretation is also theory-laden. In later chapters the problem of the "hermeneutic circle" will be confronted, that is, one interprets the whole in terms of the part and the part in terms of the whole. Although it is important to his defense of Verstehen, Winch, however, shows little awareness of such a problem in *The Idea of a Social Science.*

In fact, tending to avoid any problems about the validation of interpretations of social behavior, Winch posed a misleading contrast between Weber and himself by his ambiguous use of the term "interpretation." By "an interpretation" in the context of social inquiry Weber usually meant a hypothesis in terms of the subjective meaning of the actor. Statistical considerations aside, Weber's point is well taken: An interpretation in *this* sense is incomplete since it is not scientifically acceptable as it stands, but needs validation by objective evidence. In this sense of "interpretation," Verstehen does indeed need to be supplemented by a "different method altogether," namely, some objective method of validation.

By "an interpretation," Winch included what Weber meant to include and also what Weber intended to exclude. For I think it plausible to suppose Winch meant by interpretation a hypothesis in terms of subjective meaning of the actors *plus* some objective validating procedure and that the evidence for this hypothesis would be generated by this procedure. (This procedure and evidence remain unspecified.) Given *this* meaning of interpretation, Winch could well claim, "what is needed is a better interpretation, not something different in kind." Of course, in *this* sense of "interpretation" a better interpretation might simply involve better evidence or better validation procedures and consequently would not be something of a different kind.

On my reading of Winch, he makes it look as if he were in radical disagreement with Weber only by using "interpretation" in a different sense from Weber. His reliance on statistics aside, Weber might well agree that in Winch's sense of "interpretation," Verstehen needs no supplementation and stands on its own. On the other hand, if one sticks to Weber's original meaning, interpretation does need supplementation and does not stand on its own. In this sense, Winch's appeal to better interpretations, not something different in kind, will not do.

Understanding a Primitive Society

Several years after Winch's book appeared, he wrote a paper entitled "Understanding a Primitive Society," in which the theory put forth
in *The Idea of a Social Science* was clarified and extended.

The View Explained

In "Understanding a Primitive Society," Winch argued that the views
of primitive people such as the African Azande put a "strain" on Western anthropologists who study them[34] and that this strain poses problems for the Verstehen approach. He asked how one can understand the
Azande's action from their point of view and yet make sense of this
action. On the one hand, an anthropologist wants to make the action of
these people intelligible. "This means presenting an account of them
that will somehow satisfy the criteria of rationality demanded by the
culture to which he and his readers belong: a culture whose conception
of rationality is deeply affected by the achievements of the sciences,
and one which treats such things as a belief in magic or the practice of
consulting oracles as almost a paradigm of the irrational."[35] On the
other hand, Zande believe that "certain of their members are witches,
exercise a malignant occult influence on the lives of their fellows. They
engage in rites to counteract witchcraft; they consult oracles and use
magic medicines to protect themselves from harm."[36]

While rejecting the common view that one can simply say that
Zande's views about witches and magic are illusory and that the scientific picture of the world accepted by Western anthropologists is in
accord with objective reality, Winch did not accept what he called extreme Protagorean relativism, that is, the view that there is no independent reality against which to check our views. He insisted that "what is
real and what is unreal shows itself *in* the sense that language has.
Further, both the distinction between the real and the unreal and the
concept of agreement with reality belong to our language. . . . If then
we wish to understand the significance of these concepts, we must examine the use they actually have—*in* the language."[37]

The first question Winch considered is whether the Azande view of
the world "constitutes a coherent system of discourse like science, in
terms of which an intelligible conception of reality and clear ways of
deciding what beliefs are and are not in agreement with the reality."[38]
He argued that an affirmative answer to this question does not commit
him to accepting as rational all beliefs couched in terms of magical
concepts. After all, he said, not all beliefs that are in the name of sci-

ence are rational. In particular, Winch argues that he was not committed to the view that the magic beliefs held by people in Western society are rational, since magic beliefs in our culture are "parasitic on, and a perversion of other orthodox concepts."[39] Zande magic belief is quite different since it is not parasitic on other concepts but is basic and fundamental to their culture.

To come to grips with the question of whether Zande's picture of the world makes sense, Winch asked what criteria one has for saying that something makes sense. He said that a partial answer is that a set of beliefs and practices makes no sense insofar as it involves a contradiction. With respect to consulting an oracle, a contradiction can arise in two different ways: Two oracular pronouncements may contradict one another or an oracular pronouncement may conflict with future experience. However, according to Winch, Zande have a variety of ways of explaining away the seeming contradictions that are built into their network of beliefs. For example, they may say that an oracle is adversely influenced by witchcraft or that the operator of the oracle is ritually unclean.

Winch admitted that sometimes Zande seem to have no explanation for contradictions within their system of thought. In such cases it appears to us that they leave obvious contradictions "where they are, apparently unresolved."[40] For example, witches are supposedly detected in postmortem examinations by examination of the suspects' intestines for witchcraft-substance. The contradiction arises in the following way. If a man is proven a witch, then, according to Zande belief, all members of his clan are also. It follows that a few positive results from postmortem tests would show that all members of a clan were witches. But it would also follow that a few negative results among members of the same clan would show that none were witches. However, according to Evans-Pritchard, the Azande "do not perceive the contradiction as we perceive it because they have no theoretical interest in the subject, and those situations in which they express their belief in witchcraft do not force the problem on them."[41]

One may be inclined to say that the Azande's irrationality is shown by their not pressing their thought to its logical conclusion. Winch rejects this interpretation, however. He said that Evans-Pritchard's statement that "they have no theoretical interest in the subject" indicates that

the context from which the suggestion about contradiction is made, the context of our scientific culture, is not on the same level as the context in which the belief about witchcraft operates. Zande notions of witchcraft do not constitute a theoretical system in terms of which Azande try to gain a quasi-scientific understanding of the world. This in turn suggests that it is the European, obsessed with pressing Zande thought where it would not naturally go—to a contradiction—who is guilty of misunderstanding, not the Zande. The European is in fact committing a category-mistake.[42]

According to Winch, one should not try to understand Zande's witchcraft in quasi-scientific or quasi-technical terms. Witchcraft is used neither to understand the world nor to control things. Here one sees a clear application of what Henderson has called "the special principle of charity." The principle allows Winch to reject the interpretation that magic is an erroneous protoscientific theory.

The next question Winch attempted to answer is, what are we to make of the possibility of understanding primitive institutions, like Zande magic, if the situation is as he outlined it? According to one commentator, in order to bring about this understanding, Winch proposed "a sort of dialectical process in which, by somehow bringing the subject's conception of intelligible behavior into relation with our own, we create a new unity for the concept of intelligibility."[43] Winch put it this way:

We are not seeking a state in which things will appear to us just as they do to members of [society] S, and perhaps such a state is unattainable anyway. But we *are* seeking a way of looking at things which go beyond our previous way in that it has in some way taken account of and incorporated the other way that members of S have of looking at things. Seriously to study another way of life is to necessarily extend our own.[44]

Winch made some suggestions about "ways of thinking in our own society that will help us to see the Zande institutions in a clearer light."[45] There are, he said, certain analogies holding between primitive ways of life and ours. For example, there is an analogy between the Christian view of a human being's complete dependence on God and Azande's nontechnical view of magic. Christians do not consider prayers as ways of influencing God; in a somewhat similar way Zande do not consider magic as a technique for bringing about certain things they want done. Apparently following Wittgenstein's theory, Winch argued that both prayers and magic have similar expressive functions. Witchcraft, he said, is used to "*express an attitude* to contingencies; one, that is, which involves recognition that one's life is subject to contingencies, rather than an attempt to control these."[46] This can be interpreted as an application of the general principle of charity. Winch interprets Zande's attitude of apparently unacceptable irrationality in pressing a problem to its logical conclusion as expressing an acceptable and understandable attitude. No contradiction is involved or avoided.

There are other analogous notions that Winch calls limiting notions—the major ones having to do with birth, sex, and death—that help us understand primitive societies. "Their significance here is that they are inescapably involved in the life of all known human society in a way that gives us a clue where to look, if we are puzzled about the point of an alien system of institutions."[47] Presumably utilizing these limiting concepts in combination with the general principle of charity, an interpreter would attempt to understand what appears at first as unintelligible as serving some way of life connected with birth, sex or death.

The View Evaluated

Winch's position in "Understanding a Primitive Society," as applied to the social sciences has many of the same problems presented in his book. For example, he still seems to assume a very narrow view of the task of the social sciences. Rather than go over this ground again, in what follows I will concentrate on problems connected with his principle of charity—a principle that is used in translating alien language and action into terms that are understandable to us. This principle allowed Winch to make sense out of prima facie incomprehensible and irrational social actions and language. A general and special principle can be distinguished in Winch's work with specific significance in his analysis of the Azande.[48]

These two principles of charity are closely related to the doctrine of Verstehen. According to this doctrine, human behavior must be understood in terms of the subjective states of the actor. The principles of charity put restrictions on this, requiring that the imputation of subjective states to the actor must meet certain demands that eliminate uncharitable interpretations. In this book, Winch required understanding action in term of social rules. The two principles of charity used by Winch assure that interpretations in terms of social rules do not put the actors' way of life in an unfavorable life. Thus, Winch sometimes relies on what David Henderson has called a *special version* of the principle of charity: When a social scientist says that what is said or done in a society expresses a certain unsatisfactory protoscientific theory, he or she is probably mistaken.[49] For example, social scientists, Winch said, often wrongly assume that some alien way of life is an instance of a scientific or protoscientific form of light. However, Henderson argues that Winch also assumes a *general version* of the principle. Winch assumes that ways of life (instances of various forms of life) serve their end or aim well. A proper interpretation must conclude that they do and if an interpretation does not conclude this, it is incorrect.[50] In other words, according to the general version of the principle of charity one must identify the meaning of actions or the pieces of language "within a way of life in a manner that leads us to see them as *effective* means to the ends (or points) of that way of life."[51] There are difficulties with Winch's views.

First, the general principle of charity seems to conflict with the evidence. It is empirically false that all ways of life serve their point well. Henderson cites German Nazism as an example of a way of life that did not serve its point well: "Nazism was a disaster which failed to serve many considerations [points] on any plausible list of the considerations that it was directed to serving."[52] If Winch were to reject this example on the grounds that Nazism was not a way of life, then it is unclear what he meant by way of life.

Second, with respect to the special principle of charity, it goes too far in rejecting *all* intellectual accounts of magic. Just because Frazer and other Victorian anthropologists made primitive people's views seem silly and stupid, it does not mean that no intellectual account of magic is plausible. Henderson suggests that a modified principle of tolerance would be adequate to eliminate the excesses of Victorian anthropologists. For example, one might require that the primitive people's errors be explainable in light of contemporary psychology.

Third, Winch's claim that Zande magic has a wholly expressive function is denied by contemporary anthropologists working in this area. As Henderson puts it: "[S]urely the reasonable presumption here is that the philosopher has overstepped his area of competence and erred."[53] Of course, this conflict with orthodox anthropologists only creates a presumption that Winch is mistaken, whereas Winch might be correct and the anthropologists wrong. The question is whether Winch has good reason for his unorthodox interpretation. He does not. As Henderson argues: "[H]e offers us no more than the objection that unless we see things his way we will impute inconsistencies and other errors to the practitioners of ritual."[54] In particular, Winch does not offer detailed accounts of Zande practices and speech that would convince anthropologists working in this area.[55]

In conclusion, Winch's theory of the social sciences in both his book, *The Idea of a Social Science* and his article "Understanding a Primitive Culture," has serious problems. His book imposes unacceptable a priori limits on the social sciences while his article assumes inappropriate principles of charity.

William Dray

Winch was not the only linguistic philosopher in the 1950s and 1960s who tried to defend the Verstehen approach against positivistic criticisms. In his book, *Laws and Explanation in History,* and in several papers, William Dray defended his version of Verstehen in history against the positivist emphasis on causal explanation by general laws so forcefully that he dominated the field of philosophy of history for many years. Maintaining that Verstehen was not a methodological device but a necessary aspect of historical understanding, Dray challenged the positivists' critique of Verstehen given by Hempel and Nagel and at the same time rejected the positivistic interpretation of Verstehen given by Abel and Rudner. Although in this respect his views on Verstehen were similar to Winch's, they were not specifically influenced by Wittgenstein. Moreover, they were focused primarily on history and Dray's theory was closer to the reconstruction interpretation of Dilthey than to Weber's explanatory Verstehen since, like Dilthey and unlike Weber, he did not connect acceptable explanations with causal laws. Although he was influenced by Collingwood, he interpreted him in ways that were congenial to Oxford Ordinary Language Philosophy of the late 1950s. Dray maintained that explanation by laws does not help us understand human action in the sense proper to the subject matter. Although he believed that the idealists were mistaken and confused to suppose that historians must literally re-think or re-experience historical events, Dray argued that they had an important point to make. He gave the point a logical basis by means of his analysis of historical explanations that maintained one can only understand a human action by giving a rational explanation of it. According to Dray, a rational explanation is one that takes the actor's point of view and attempts either to reconstruct the agent's actual rationale or to construct a possible rationale for the action. As Dray saw it, such an explanation shows that the action was the appropriate one to take under the circumstances.

Dray on Collingwood

In a 1958 article entitled "Historical Understanding as Re-thinking,"[56] Dray interpreted Collingwood's theory, "clarifying it where that is possible and amending it where that seems necessary."[57] In providing a sensitive interpretation of Collingwood's theory, his paper offers a useful introduction to his own version of Verstehen.

According to Dray, the "core" of Collingwood's theory can be stated by means of three theses:

> First, that human action, which is the proper concern of history, cannot be described as "action" at all, without mentioning the thought which it expresses—it has in Collingwood's terms, a "thought-side"; second, that once the thought in question has been grasped by the historians, the action is understood in the sense appropriate to action, so it is unnecessary to go on to ask for the cause which produced it, or the law which it instaniates; that the understanding of action in terms of thought requires the re-thinking of the thought in question by the historian, so that, in essence, all history is "the reenactment of the past in the historian's own mind."[58]

Dray pointed out that, unless one understands Collingwood's view that history is concerned with action in a certain way, it is open to a serious objection. Collingwood's requirement of a thought-side of action might be interpreted as meaning that an agent's behavior is not an action unless it is preceded by conscious reflection of the agent about what he or she should do. However, on this reading there would be very few actions and, consequently, the domain of historical inquiry would be quite small.

Acknowledging that Collingwood might have encouraged this interpretation by some of the things that he said, Dray argued that this reading of Collingwood is mistaken given the larger context of his work. Actions, according to Dray's interpretation of Collingwood, can express thoughts; propositions do not need to be recited to oneself before the action. Thus Collingwood's view that there is a thought-side to action is compatible with historians discovering the thoughts of historical agents "which were unknown, not only to any contemporary eyewitness of the action concerned, but even to the agents themselves." Furthermore, Dray argued that, on this interpretation of Collingwood's theory, even thought*less* action may express a thought. This does not mean that such action is without purpose; it only means that the actor acted without taking into account certain considerations which should have been taken into account.

With respect to the second thesis, Dray rejected Collingwood's theory that once one knows what an action is, one knows why it has happened; and, consequently, in order to explain an action it is not necessary to go beyond the action to further thoughts which are not part of the action. According to Collingwood, the thought-side of action must be included in the specification of the action. However, Dray argued,

> The thought which is required to make it the action it is, therefore, cannot be considered as something logically distinct from it, by reference to which the ac-

tion itself can be explained. The thought-side of an action might, of course, be called upon to explain the mere movement which is its own other "side": We might say, for instance, that Caesar's wanting to get to the other shore explains his physical progress across the river. But it is clear enough that in history, the problem will almost always be the explanation of actions, not mere movement; and in order to explain an action in terms of thought it will be necessary to refer beyond the action to a thought which is not itself part of the action as specified.[59]

Although it would be possible to incorporate this further thought into the specification of the action, Dray maintained that to do so would cause problems. For example, suppose one wanted to explain Caesar's crossing the Rubicon, for example, in terms of his desire to remove Pompey from the capital. One might incorporate this into the specification of the action. But now one cannot say that this thought explains his crossing the Rubicon. The action now is crossing the Rubicon in order to remove Pompey.

Dray seemed to agree with Collingwood that no laws are necessary in historical explanations. Collingwood, he said, would agree that in order to explain a human action the action must be shown to be necessary, but this necessity is in terms not of natural laws but of being rationally required. Thus Collingwood maintained that if and only if rational necessity can be shown, then one can understand what the agent did. But this does not require that it be shown "by the methods of natural science, that what happened was a natural necessity as well."[60]

In relation to that understanding a historical action requires re-thinking the thoughts of the actor, Dray argued that "there is nothing in Collingwood's theory which requires the historian to go through the same overt actions, or undergo the same private experiences, as the subject of his inquiry. The fact that the original thought may not have been thought propositionally would therefore be no barrier to its being re-thought propositionally—the way we should naturally expect the historian to re-think it."[61]

But what does this historical re-thinking by the historian amount to, according to Dray? On Dray's interpretation Collingwood's requirement of re-thinking simply becomes the requirement that in order for an explanation to be successful it must reveal the rationality of the agent. What does the rationality of the agent involve? On some occasions Collingwood seems to have supposed that the agent must be rational in some absolute sense; that is, the agent must be rational relative to the *actual* situation. But at other times, Collingwood was quite clear that what is rational is hypothetical; that is, the rationality of the action must be construed in the following way: *If* the situation had been as the agent envisaged it, then what he or she did would have been the rational thing to do.

Dray maintained, however, that even a commitment to hypothetical rationality may "lead us astray."[62] Although Collingwood believed that when historical understanding fails this is due to a breakdown of historical analysis and that historians should be blamed for the failure, Dray argued that there are other possibilities. First, the agent's reasoning about his or her situation might itself be mistaken. For example, an agent might wrongly conclude that some action is required by the situation as he envisages it and act accordingly. Second, what an agent does might not be intended. For example, an unwise speech by a cabinet minister might subvert his own government. Third, there are capricious or arbitrary actions. For example, suppose that there are two equally rational actions and an agent arbitrarily chooses one of them. In all of these cases, historical understanding in Collingwood's sense fails, but it would be wrong to suppose that historians are to blame for the failure.

Laws and Explanation in History

How does Dray's critique and modification of Collingwood relate to his own views as presented in *Laws and Explanation in History*?[63]

The bulk of Dray's book is a sustained critique of the Nomological Model of Explanation (NME) as applied to history, according to which a historical event is explained by subsumimg it under some general or statistical law. However, indirectly Dray's book was much more: It was an attack on positivism which was associated with NME and a defense of the fundamental difference between history and the natural sciences. One argument against the covering-law view is that even if human actions do fall under laws, such laws would not help us understand human action in a sense proper to history. Philosophers as well as historians, Dray says, have maintained that to understand historical agents the historian "must *penetrate* behind appearances, achieve *insight* into the situation, *identify* himself sympathetically with the protagonists, *project* himself imaginatively into the situation. He must *revive*, *re-enact*, *re-think*, *re-experience*, the hopes, plans, desires, views, intentions, etc., of those he seeks to understand."[64]

Dray pointed out that critics of this empathic view of historical understanding such as Hempel argued that empathy functions only as a heuristic device that might be useful in suggesting psychological hypotheses. However, according to Dray, this sort of criticism does not cut as deeply as covering-law theorists assume. These theorists "fail to notice what makes idealists want to say what they do. . . . What is left out, I wish to maintain, should properly be taken into account in a *logical* analysis of explanation as it is given in history."[65] In presenting this logical analysis, Dray said that his discussion might be regarded in part as an attempt to make sense of "what Collingwood, in particular, has to say of historical understanding"[66] without offering any close textual discussion of his account.

What is this logical analysis? According to Dray, what historians want when they want an explanation of the historical agent's actions is a *"calculation* of means to be adopted towards his chosen end in the light of the circumstances in which he found himself."[67] This calculation, Dray hastened to add, need not be an actual series of thoughts in the agent's mind. It might be the "one the agent would have gone through if he had time, if he had not seen what to do in a flash, if he had been called upon to account for what he did after he did the event, etc."[68] Calling explanations of this sort "rational," Dray argued that there is an element of appraisal connected to them: When one judges an action as rational one deems the action *appropriate* from the agent's point of view.

Dray maintained that it is misleading to suppose that empathetic understanding is simply a heuristic device used to suggest hypotheses. He admitted that there is a methodological side to the doctrine which can be expressed by the statement: "Only by putting yourself in the agent's position can you *find out* why he did what he did." However, he said that there is another way of formulating the doctrine: "Only by putting yourself in the agent's position can you *understand* why he did what he did." He argued that the "point of the 'projection' metaphor is, in this case, more plausible as interpreted as a logical one. Its function is not to remind us of *how we come to know* certain facts, but to formulate, however tentatively, certain *conditions which must be satisfied* before a historian is prepared to say: 'Now I have the explanation.'"[69]

Dray stressed that rational explanations are not beyond empirical inquiry but are constructed from the evidence. Nevertheless, he argued, that "the *direction* of inquiry in the explanation of action is generally from what the inquirer presumes the relevant agent calculation to be—using his own or his society's concept of rational purposes and principles—to what he discovers to be the peculiar data of the historical agent. . . ."[70] I take it that by this Dray meant that historical inquirers initially assume that historical agents are rational in terms of sharing our beliefs, goals, and principles. However, this presupposition can be defeated in light of the evidence and we may end up saying that the agent is rational in light of his or her beliefs, goals, and principles, which are very different from ours.

Rejecting the view that rational explanations assume general laws, Dray argued that they assumed "principles of action's." Principles of actions have the form: When in a situation of type C the thing to do is x. Unlike general laws, such principles are not falsified by negative instances in which some agent is in a situation of type C and does not do x. Of course, Dray admitted that if there was a large number of negative instances, this would "create a presumption against the claim of a given principle having universal validity"[71] but this would not compel us to abandon the principle. Furthermore, if a particular person "often acted at variance with a principle which he was said to hold, the statement that he held that principle would come into question."[72] However, even then, Dray said, the statement would not necessarily be falsified.

Evaluation

Dray's interpretation and revision of Collingwood does not meet some of the problems connected with Collingwood's theory. Moreover, since Dray adopted most of Collingwood's ideas after interpreting and revising them, these problems affect Dray's theory as well. First, Dray argued that Collingwood's view that action which is the proper concern of history must contain a thought-side should not be interpreted as referring to conscious thought. He admitted that very often there is no conscious thought in a historical action. Such actions, said Dray, can express propositions, even when the actor entertains no propositions. The crucial problem is, of course, how a historian can know what these propositions are that are expressed but not consciously entertained.

Collingwood's answer, according to Dray, is that a historian discovers what propositions are expressed by an action by re-thinking the thoughts of the historical actor. Dray, however, believed that this should not be interpreted literally. He seemed to adopt the dispositional interpretation of rationality discussed in chapter 1 as the correct interpretation of Collingwood and incorporated this idea into his own theory. One determines what proposition is expressed by an action by calculating what would be the rational thing for the historical agent to do given the circumstances. This involves assessing the truth of a contrafactual conditional: For example, if the agent had been asked to justify his or her action, he or she would have given such and such reason. But, as noted in chapter 1, this has two obvious problems that Dray did not address: A historical actor might not have performed a particular action if he or she had thought about it and, in any case, historians are often interested in the actual basis of the action (habit, convention, reflex) rather than the rationale a historical actor *would* have given *if* he or she had reflected.

As previously noted, it is difficult to understand how Collingwood could maintain that complex social behavior and group actions can be understood only by re-thinking the thoughts of individual social actors, especially when he rejected laws linking individual action with social wholes. Does Dray have the same problem? His dispositional interpretation of re-thinking by itself does not help to solve this problem. Even if one grants the premise that a social actor's thoughts can be interpreted dispositionally and construed as rational in the circumstances, this does not explain the group action of which this action is a part. Dray, as well as Collingwood, must assume methodological individualism: the view that social wholes can be explained by individual actions. Thus, while admitting that the analysis would "present difficulties," Dray argued that statements such as "Germany attacked Russia in 1941" are explained by the calculations of "those individuals who were authorized to act 'for Germany.'"[73] This controversial thesis is not argued for. Unlike Collingwood, he did not completely reject the use of laws in history, maintaining that "we give reasons if we can, and turn to empirical laws if we must."[74] However, it is unclear from what Dray said whether the explanation of the behavior of social entities and group actions is one of those occasions in which the use of empirical laws—for example, laws linking individual actions to group behavior—is necessary.

Dray gets into difficulty also with his thesis that rational explanation is based on principles of actions and not general laws. One does not have to maintain that general laws are necessary for historical explanations to see that principles of actions are not explanatory. A principle of action is normative; it tells us what is appropriate or rational to do in a certain circumstance. But it tells us nothing about what historical actors actually do or even are inclined to do.[75] Dray confused this issue by suggesting that empirical evidence is indirectly relevant to evaluating principles of action. He maintained that if there was a large number of negative instances this would create a presumption against the principle. But why should it? It would show that many people do what is not appropriate, but it would show nothing about whether the principle was incorrect; that is, whether the action was inappropriate.

In order to have an explanation, one needs knowledge about the agent's actual motives; that is, whether the actor is motivated by the principle of action. For this one needs to show not just that the historical actor held this principle but that the principle was the actual cause of the action. Suppose that Jones believes principle P that asserts that action A is appropriate in circumstances C. Jones might believe that C is present and do A but not because of P.

Furthermore, even if Jones believes that P caused her to do A, this would not be sufficient for an explanation in terms of P. Jones believes that P must bring about A in the *right* way.[76] Suppose that Jones believes that in the circumstances it is appropriate to alert Smith to some danger. She writes Smith a letter alerting him and walks to a mailbox to mail the letter. By chance, Smith see Jones posting the letter and is alerted by the worried expression on her face. Clearly in this case although Smith is alerted by Jones operating on P, he is not alerted in the right way.[77]

However, the most serious problem with Dray's theory has yet to be mentioned. In "Another Look at the Doctrine of Verstehen,"[78] Jane Roland Martin evaluated it as a theory of understanding and argues that Dray is mistaken to maintain: "Only by putting yourself in the agent's position can you *understand* why he did what he did." Martin first interpreted Dray's theory as a general theory of understanding and then as a specific theory of historical understanding and evaluates each separately. Furthermore, she argued that although Dray seems to identify putting yourself in the agent's place with giving a rational explanation, these two ideas must be separated since one can put oneself in the place of the agent without giving a rational explanation. Thus, there are four distinct theses to be evaluated:

> (2.1) Only by putting yourself in the agent's position can you understand his action.

> (2.2) Only by giving (or by being given) a rational explanation can you understand his action.

> (3.1) Only by putting yourself in the agent's position can you historically understand his action.

> (3.2) Only by giving (or by being given) a rational explanation can you historically understand his action.

Utilizing the distinction between internal and external understanding that was introduced in the evaluation of Dilthey in chapter 1, Martin argued that one can understand something in many different ways. Both external and internal understanding, Martin argued, can take many different forms depending on how the thing understood is described, e.g., as a war, as a civil war, as a revolution. Dray has arbitrarily restricted understanding, she maintained, to one type of internal understanding, that is, internal understanding based on descriptive terms used by the agent. Moreover, even if one construed his claim to apply only to historical contexts, she continued, there are many ways to understand historical events.[79]

She argued that the Verstehen doctrine formulated in (2.2) in effect claims that external understanding is inapplicable to human action. Understanding an action in terms of rational explanation is a form of internal understanding, that is, the action is considered a unity and the relation of its parts—the agent's goals, beliefs about goals, beliefs about means, etc.—are investigated. These elements or parts would be related to one another as the parts of a plan or calculation would be related. But this is not the only way to understand an action. "As a matter of fact, we do find it illuminating to be shown the connection between an action and some antecedent event, e.g., a childhood experience, or some standing condition, e.g., a state of society or of an individual, and we consider it illuminating on occasion to be shown that an action fits into a larger context, e.g., a historical trend, or falls under some interesting and surprising category."[80]

The Verstehen doctrine formulated in (2.1), she argued, is also unduly restrictive in that it rules out external understanding as well as various forms of internal understanding. Martin maintained that we do not understand a thing *per se* but under a particular description. The trouble with the Verstehen doctrine represented both as (2.1) and as (2.2) is that it requires "not only that actions be understood internally but that they be understood under a particular description, namely the one the agent himself would give." However, various other descriptions are possible. For example, one can understand an action described in terms of unconscious motives or in technical terms that are beyond the agent's ken.

Martin held that the doctrine of Verstehen as represented in (3.1) and (3.2) might also be too restrictive. She argued that one would test them by carefully examining the conditions under which historians are willing to say "I understand." However, she maintained that this testing raises certain problems. Consider historians who understand events but do not use action descriptions in their accounts. Would this count as negative evidence to (3.1) and (3.2)? Martin suggested that it would *if* action descriptions were also available. Often they are. For example, a historian who describes a nonaction as "serfdom changed or disappeared" could use action terms, e.g., "the landlords abolished or modified serfdom." Since historians understand the historical event in nonaction terms but could use action terms, (3.1) and (3.2) would be falsified.

Of course, Martin pointed out that it would be possible to reject this interpretation of (3.1) and (3.2) and refuse to look behind the historian's initial description to see if action descriptions were possible. This reading would block many counterexamples, Martin argued, but at a great price. On this account the Verstehen doctrine would be purely hypothetical. It would say that *if* one describes events as actions, *then* in order to have historical understanding, one must do so and so. However, she maintained that this interpretation does not capture the intent of Verstehen theorists such as Dray. It would allow historians to use technical and theoretical vocabularies and would prevent drawing a sharp line between history and science, and is at odds with the Verstehen doctrine.

In concluding her argument against Dray, Martin said that although her suggestion that theories of understanding should be tested against historical practice should please Dray, who "prides himself on sticking fairly close to what the historian actually does," the result of this test might not be what he apparently expects. "As everyone knows, but as those philosophers and historians who write about history tend to forget, history is immensely various. I would expect (3.1) and (3.2) gaining confirmation from some historical practice but not from all historical practice."[81] However, she warned that this test must range over the whole of historical practice and not stack the deck for (3.1) and (3.2) by ruling out historical practice that would refute them "as bad perhaps, as parasitic, or nonprimary, or as nonstandard."[82] To be sure, (3.1) and (3.2) could be revised to claim:

(4.1) Putting yourself in the agent's position is one way to understand action historically.

(4.2) Giving (or by being given) a rational explanation is one way to understand action historically.

Martin pointed out that the doctrine of Verstehen so construed would have "an easier time of it when confronted by the facts of practice. But then, of course, the doctrine of Verstehen would lose much of its interest; for surely it is the very lack of modesty of its various claims that on the one hand endangers its truth but on the other hand makes it worthy of discussion and extended investigation."[83]

Conclusion

In conclusion, I have shown that Winch's views on the social sciences and Dray's theory of historical understanding have serious problems. The Wittgensteinian approach expressed in Winch's *The Idea of a Social Science* limited the goals of the social sciences in an a priori manner, and failed to provide an adequate account of the validation of social scientific interpretations. Winch's views expounded in his more recent paper, "Understanding a Primitive Society," do nothing to overcome these problems. Indeed, given his principle of charity and his interpretation of Azande witchcraft, this paper expresses in a more acute form the problems inherent in his theory.

Influenced more by Collingwood than Wittgenstein, Dray's versions of the doctrine of Verstehen have different problems from Winch's. In his account of rational explanation of historical actions, Dray, like Collingwood, adopted a hypothetical account of rational calculation and ran into similar problems. Dray's reliance on principles of action in historical explanations also raises a serious problem. Their purely normative status precludes them from explaining actual action. In addition, his theory when interpreted as a theory of understandings is too restrictive. It excludes external understanding and internal understanding based on descriptions that are not given by the actor.

Notes

1.   Fred R. Dallmayr and Thomas A. McCarthy, eds., "Introduction to Part Three," *Understanding and Social Inquiry* (Notre Dame, In: University of Notre Dame Press, 1977), p. 138.
2.   See David K. Henderson, "Winch and the Contraints of Interpretation: Versions of the Principle of Charity," *The Southern Journal of Philosophy* 25, 1987, pp. 164-65. See Ludwig Wittgenstein, *Remarks on Frazer's "Golden Bough,"* ed. Rush Rees (Atlantic Highlands, NJ: Brynmill, Notts, and Humanities Press, 1979).
3.   This chapter is based on a revised version of my paper, "Winch on Philosophy, Social Science, and Explanation," *Philosophical Forum* 23, 1966, pp. 23-41.

4. Peter Winch, *The Idea of a Social Science and Its Relation to Philosophy* (New York: Humanities Press, 1958), p. 100.

5. Ibid., pp. 100-101.

6. Ibid., p. 99.

7. Ibid., p. 45.

8. Ibid., p. 49.

9. Cf. Leo Goldstein, review of Winch, *The Idea of a Social Science and Its Relation to Philosophy* in *Philosophical Review* 69, 1960, pp. 411-14.

10. Robert Brown, *Explanation in Social Science* (Chicago: Aldine Publishing Co. 1963), p. 98.

11. For example, see reviews by L. Goldstein (*Philosophical Review* 69, 1960, pp. 411-14) and I. C. Jarvie (*British Journal for the Philosophy of Science* 12, 1961, pp. 73-77); papers on Winch (E. Geller, "The New Idealism—Cause and Meaning in the Social Science," pp. 377-406; P. Cohen, "The Very Idea of a Social Science," pp. 406-22; J. W. N. Watkins, "Anthropomorhism in Social Science," pp. 423-26, E. Geller, "Reply," pp. 426-32) in *Proceedings of the International Colloquium in the Philosophy of Science*, London, 1965, vol. 3, published in Imre Lakatos and Alan Musgrave, eds., *Problems in the Philosophy of Science* (Amsterdam: North-Holland Publishing Co, 1968); the exchange between Louch and Winch (A. R. Louch, "The Very Idea of a Social Science, " *Inquiry* 6, 1963, pp. 273-87, Peter Winch, "Mr. Louch's Idea of a Social Science," *Inquiry* 7 1964, pp. 202-208; A. R. Louch, "On Misunderstanding Mr. Winch," *Inquiry* 8, 1965, pp. 212-16); Richard Berstein's discussions of Winch in *Beyond Objectivism, and Relativism: Science, Hermeneutics, and Praxis* (Philadelphia: University of Pennsylvania Press, 1983), pp. 25-29, and *The Restructuring of Social and Political Theory* (New York: Harcourt, Brace, and Jovanovich, 1976), pp. 63-74; Richard Rudner's criticism in *Philosophy of Social Science* (Englewood Cliffs, NJ: Prentice-Hall, Inc., 1966), pp. 81-82; Alasdair MacIntyre's paper, "The Idea of a Social Science," in Alan Ryan, ed., *The Philosophy of Social Explanation* (London: Oxford University Press, 1973), pp. 15-32, and Alan Ryan, *The Philosophy of Social Science* (London: Macmillan and Co. 1971), chapter 7; and Mark B. Okrent, "Hermeneutics, Transcendental Philosophy and Social Science," *Inquiry* 27, 1984, pp. 23-49.

12. Robert K. Merton, *Social Theory and Social Function* (Glencoe, IL: The Free Press, 1957), chapter 6 and 7.

13. Winch, *The Idea of a Social Science*, p. 116, says that function is a "quasi-causal notion, which is perilous to apply to social institutions." Winch gives no justification for this judgment.

14. Ibid., pp. 46-65.

15. Ibid., p. 46.

16. Cf. Goldstein, review of winch (note 9).

17. Cf. Brown, Explanation in Social Change, chapter 7, 8.

18. Winch, *The Idea of a Social Science*, p. 58.

19. Cf. MacIntyre, "The Idea of a Social Science," p. 21.

20. Winch, *The Idea of A Social Science*, p. 53.

21. Ibid., p. 49.

22. Cf. Morton White, *Foundations of Historical Knowledge* (New York: Harper and Row, 1965), chapter 5.

23. This thesis has been subjected to extensive criticism since his book appeared. See, for example, White, ibid.; Donald Davidson, "Action, Reasons, and Causes," *Journal of Philosophy*, 1963, pp. 685-700; Fred Dretsky, *Explaining Behavior*

(Cambridge, MA: MIT Press, 1988); Kathleen Lennon, *Explaining Human Action* (LaSalle, IL: Open Court, 1990).

24. Winch, *The Idea of a Social Science*, p. 81.
25. Ibid., pp. 82-83.
26. Cf. Paul Ziff, *Semantic Analysis* (New York: Cornell University Press, 1960), pp. 35-36n.
27. Ibid., pp. 89-90. Winch's position here is similar to Alfred Schutz who argues that a social scientist can erect a second-order concept on the first-order concept of social actors. See Alfred Schutz, "Concept and Theory Formation in the Social Sciences," in Dorthy Emmet and Alasdair MacIntyre, eds., *Sociological Theory and Philosophical Analysis* (London: Macmillan and Co., 1970), p. 15.
28. Alan Ryan, *The Philosophy of Social Science* (London: Macmillan and Co., 1971), p. 193.
29. Ibid.
30. Ibid.
31. Winch, *The Idea of a Social Science*, pp. 113-14.
32. Thomas S. Kuhn, *The Copernican Revolutions* (New York: Random House, 1959).
33. See E. A. Burtt, *The Metaphysical Foundations of Modern Science* (Garden City, NY: Doubleday Anchor Books, 1954).
34. Peter Winch, "Understanding a Primitive Society," in Fred R. Dallmayr and Thomas A. McCarthy, eds., *Understanding and Social Inquiry* (Notre Dame, IN: University of Notre Dame Press, 1977), pp. 159-88. Originally published in *American Philosophical Quarterly* 1, 1964, pp. 307-24.
35. Ibid., pp. 159-60.
36. Ibid., p. 159.
37. Ibid., p. 162.
38. Ibid., p. 163.
39. Ibid., p. 164.
40. Ibid., p. 170.
41. E. E. Evans-Pritchard, *Witchcraft, Oracles and Magic among the Azande*, p. 25, quoted by Winch, "Understanding a Primitive Society," p. 171.
42. Ibid., p. 172.
43. Thomas McCarthy, "On Misunderstanding 'Understanding'," *Decision and Theory* 3, 1973, p. 360.
44. Winch, "Understanding a Primitive Society," p. 176.
45. Ibid., p. 180.
46. Ibid., p. 181.
47. Ibid., p. 183.
48. I am indebted in what follows to Henderson, "Winch and the Constraints of Interpretation: Versions of the Principle of Charity," pp. 153-73.
49. Ibid., p. 157.
50. Ibid.
51. Ibid., p. 158.
52. Ibid., p.168.
53. Ibid., p. 170.
54. Ibid., p. 171.
55. Brian Fay gives a more charitable reading of Winch. He may be suggesting that the value of Winch's expressive interpretation of magic is to show that the principle of charity "must be augmented by an explicit sense of cultural diversity that varies from culture to culture." See Brian Fay, *Contemporary Philosophy of Social Science* (Cambridge, MA: Blackwell, 1996), p. 109.

56. W. H. Dray "Historical Understanding as Re-thinking," *University of Toronto Quarterly*, 1958, pp. 200-13, reprinted in *Readings in the Philosophy of Science*, ed. E. D. Klemke, Robert Hollinger, and A. David Kline (Buffalo, NY: Prometheus Books, 1980), pp. 124-26.
57. Ibid., p. 125.
58. Ibid.
59. Ibid., p. 130.
60. Ibid., p. 132.
61. Ibid., p. 133.
62. Ibid., p. 135.
63. William Dray, *Laws and Explanation in History* (Oxford: Oxford University Press, 1957).
64. Ibid., p. 119.
65. Ibid., p. 121.
66. Ibid., p. 122.
67. Ibid.
68. Ibid., p. 123.
69. Ibid., p. 128.
70. Ibid., p. 130.
71. Ibid., p. 132.
72. Ibid.
73. Ibid., p. 141.
74. Ibid., p. 138.
75. See Carl G. Hempel, *Aspects of Scientific Explanations* (New York: The Free Press, 1963), pp. 470–71.
76. On this point, see Jon Elster, "The Nature and Scope of Rational Choice Explanations," in M. Martin and Lee C. McIntyre, eds., *Readings in the Philosophy of Social Science* (Cambridge, MA: The MIT Press, 1994), p. 314.
77. In addition to these problems Dray's principle of action wrongly assumes that there is one appropriate or rational thing to do in the circumstances. However, there might be several alternatives that are equally appropriate. Further, there are different criteria of what is appropriate or rational that lead to different accounts of what is appropriate. Dray seems to suppose that there is one. See Ibid. and Carl G. Hempel, *Aspects of Scientific Explanations,* pp. 463-69.
78. Jane Roland Martin, "Another Look at the Doctrine of Verstehen," in M. Martin and Lee C. McIntyre, ed., *Readings in the Philosophy of Social Science*, pp. 247-58. First published in *The British Journal for the Philosophy of Science* 20, 1969, pp. 53-67.
79. Whether the position defended may be compatible with Brian Fay's views in *Contemporary Philosophy of Social Science* (Cambridge, MA: Blackwell, 1996), chapter 5, is unclear. On the one hand, Fay argues that in general we must assume agents are rational. On the other hand, I am arguing that depending on our purposes and the context, rational explanations are unnecessary. I would be more inclined to agree with Fay if he is interpreted in this way: certain kinds of internal explanation presuppose that humans are in general rational. But even this claim is dubious in light of Henderson's critique of the principle of charity. See David Henderson, *Interpretation and Explanation in the Human Sciences* (Albany, NY: SUNY Press, 1993).
80. Martin, "Another Look at the Doctrine of Verstehen," p. 251.
81. Ibid., p. 257.
82. Ibid.
83. Ibid.

5

Verstehen and Situational Logic

In chapter 4, we saw that a Verstehen approach was developed within the analytic tradition of Wittgenstein and Oxford Ordinary Language Philosophy. Thus, despite Verstehen's continental origins, it was able to thrive in quite another kind of intellectual environment. It is remarkable that Verstehen could flourish in still a different type of intellectual environment, one influenced by the philosophy of Karl Popper, a thinker with no sympathy with either continental metaphysical thought, Ordinary Language Philosophy, or logical positivism.[1]

Popper's theory of science is based in large part on a critique of induction, that is, nondemonstrative inference.[2] His critique is derived primarily from the objections against induction raised by David Hume. Hume argued that no inference that goes beyond the evidence is rationally justified. To be sure, such inferences are made by everyone. But, according to Hume, they are irrational; they are without logical foundation. Hume argued that one cannot make a deductive inference to any conclusion that goes beyond the evidence and one cannot make probabilistic inferences to any conclusion that goes beyond the evidence *unless* one assumes (without justification) that the world beyond the evidence is similar to the world revealed by the evidence.

In brief, this is Hume's argument and philosophers ever since have been trying to show Hume to be mistaken and nondemonstrative inferences are warranted. Popper, however, accepted Hume's argument; indeed, he maintained that no one has ever answered it. Many philosophers of science have thought that if Hume were correct, it would be the end of science. Popper argued, however, that this is not so. The irrationality of nondemonstrative inference is perfectly compatible with rational scientific inquiry. Popper proposed a radical new way of looking at science as a rational enterprise—a way that is free from Hume's problem. According to Popper, science proceeds not by the proposal of hypotheses and their verification. Science proceeds rather by the proposal of hypotheses and their falsification—by "conjecture and refutation." Hypotheses are proposed and then vigorous attempts are made to refute them. False hypotheses are thus eliminated and truth approximated by the elimination of error.

Since the refutation of a hypothesis is a deductive procedure no inference is made that goes beyond the evidence. In eliminating a hypothesis we deduce consequences from the hypothesis that turn out to be false. We can then be deductively assured that the hypothesis is in error. But Hume had no objection to deduction. Thus, science proceeds simply by the elimination of error which is accomplished purely by deduction, that is, by deduction of the consequences of conjectured hypotheses that prove to be false.

According to Popper, falsification not only provides a way of doing science that is rational despite Hume's problem, it also provides a way of distinguishing science from nonscience. Scientific statements are falsifiable, that is, if they are false, it is possible that empirical evidence can refute them. Nonscientific statements are not falsifiable; they can be maintained in the face of any empirical evidence. Popper believed that this criterion provides an adequate explication of the difference between the scientific status of Einstein's theory of relativity and Freud's theory of psychoanalysis. According to Popper, Einstein's theory is a scientific theory but Freud's theory is not. The reason is that Einstein's theory is falsifiable and Freud's theory is not.

Popper was opposed to the logical positivists' approach to science. First Popper rejected induction; the logical positivists based their theory on induction. Indeed, Rudolf Carnap and Hans Reichenbach developed comprehensive inductive approaches to science. Second, Popper distinguished science from nonscience by his criterion of falsifiability. The positivists distinguished science from nonscience by the verifiability theory of meaning. According to Popper and the positivists nonscience is metaphysics. But there was a crucial difference. For the positivists metaphysical discourse was noncognitive; that is, it was neither true nor false and was cognitively meaningless and should be eliminated from science. 'This was not Popper's view.' Metaphysics was not cognitively meaningless, according to Popper, and was often useful to science. In other words, unlike the positivists, Popper drew the line between science and nonscience *within* the realm of cognitive discourse. Third, although Popper agreed with the positivists that

Verstehen could not be a method of testing hypotheses, I will argue that he accepted the view that Verstehen is essential to social scientific explanations. However, Popper and the logical positivists agreed on at least one point: They both embraced the Nomological Model of Explanation (NME). NME entailed that a causal explanation must be in terms of laws that specify causally sufficient conditions for the event to be explained.[3]

To be sure, since Popper advocates the unity of scientific method[4] and Verstehen advocates do not, Popperian philosophy of science is not usually associated with Verstehen in the social sciences. Indeed, what Popper calls "intuitive understanding" is apparently one of the doctrines of the historicism that he rejects.[5] However, Popper[6] and his followers, especially I. C. Jarvie,[7] have argued that the primary method of the social sciences should be "situational logic." However, situational logic explanations are explanations set in institutional contexts in terms of beliefs, aims, and rationality of the actors, and the unintended consequences of their action. This sort of explanation is, in fact, one type of Verstehen explanation.

How does Popper's situational logic contrast with the intuitive understanding that he seems to reject? Does it have problems of its own? In this chapter I will answer these questions.

Popper's Critique of Intuitive Understanding

In 1957 in *The Poverty of Historicism*, Popper characterized what he called "intuitive understanding" as one aspect of the antinaturalistic doctrines of historicism that he rejected. He distinguished three different variants of intuitive understanding:

> The first asserts that a social event is understood when analyzed in terms of the forces that brought it about, i.e., when the individuals and groups involved, their purposes and interests, and the power they can dispose of, are known. The actions of individuals or groups are here understood as being in accordance with their aims—promoting their real advantage. Or, at least, their imagined advantage. The method of sociology is here thought of as an imaginative reconstruction of either rational or irrational activities, directed towards certain ends.[8]

The second variant of intuitive understanding includes everything the first does and adds that we must understand the meaning or significance of the social event, by which he meant the event's "situational value." He believed that this latter involves understanding the role that the event plays in the whole situation. In this way, Popper argued, this variant goes beyond causal explanations. This suggests that Popper believes that the first variant of intuitive understanding does not go beyond causal explanations. The third variant of intuitive understanding includes everything the first and second variants do but in this variant it is also necessary to understand the underlying historical trends and tendencies. According to Popper this involves comparing similarities between historical periods and the use of inference by analogy. This variant, he sees, tends to rely on the analogy between an organism and a group and to operate with ideas such as the mind or spirit of the age.

Popper objected to intuitive understanding for two reasons, both of which seem irrelevant. Arguing in a way similar to that of the positivists he maintained that, although intuitive understanding can be a means of generating hypotheses, it is not a method of testing them. He admitted that we have more intuitive understanding of ourselves than we do of physical objects such as atoms. We can use this knowledge, he said,

> [T]o frame *hypotheses* about some other people, or about all people. But these hypotheses must be tested, they must be submitted to the method of selection by elimination. . . . The physicist, it is true, is not helped, by direct observation when he frames hypotheses about atoms; nevertheless, he quite often uses some kind of sympathetic imagination or intuition which may easily make him feel that he is intimately acquainted with even the "inside of the atoms"—with even their whims and prejudices. But this intuition is his private affair. Science is interested only in the hypotheses which these intuitions inspired, and then only if these are rich in consequences, and if they can be properly tested.[9]

However, there is nothing in his characterization of intuitive understanding to indicate that he considered it is either a way of testing or generating hypotheses.

Popper also seemed to object to intuitive understanding because of its alleged connection with holism; that is, the grasping of social wholes (in the sense of totalities) by intuition.[10] Since he argued that the scientific study of such totalities is impossible, he rejected intuitive understanding. However, there is nothing in his first variant to suggest any connection with holism.

The upshot of Popper's criticisms is that they seem to leave untouched the first variant of intuitive understanding. This is significant for, as we shall see shortly, although he did not refer to situational logic explanations as a type of intuitive understanding this type of explanation bears close similarities to the first variant of intuitive understanding.

Popper on Situational Logic

In *The Poverty of Historicism*, Popper made passing reference to what he called "the logic of situations."[11] After rejecting many aspects of historicism, he admitted that it had some sound elements. In particular, he argued that the rejection of the spirit of an age, of a nation, and so on "leaves a vacuum, of a place which it is the task of sociology to fill with something sensible such as the problems arising within a tradition. There is room for a more detailed analysis of the *logic of situations*. The best historians have often made use, more or less unconsciously, of this conception. . . ."[12] He did not explicitly relate the logic of the situation to any variant of intuitive understanding, however.

In a 1969 paper entitled "The Logic of the Social Sciences," Popper returned to situational logic and provided more details, saying "the logical investigation of economics culminates in a result which can be applied to all social sciences. The result shows that there exists a *purely objective method* in the social sciences which may well be called the method of *objective* understanding, or situational logic."[13] The method of situational logic, he said,

> consists in realizing that the action was objectively *appropriate to the situation*. In other words, the situation is analyzed far enough for the elements which initially appeared to be psychological (such as wishes, motives, memories, and associations) to be transformed into elements of the situation. The man with certain wishes therefore becomes a man whose situation may be characterized by the fact that he pursues certain objective *aims*; and the man with certain memories or associations becomes a man whose situation can be characterized by the fact that he is equipped objectively with certain theories or with certain information.[14]

Popper argued that situational logic enables us to understand actions in an objective sense so that one can say, "Admittedly I have different aims and I hold different theories (from, say, Charlemagne): but had I been placed in his situation, thus analyzed—where the situation includes goals and knowledge—then I, and presumably you too, would have acted in a similar way to him."[15]

Popper went on to say that explanations in terms of situational logic are "rational theoretical reconstructions. They are oversimplified and overschematized and consequently, in general, *false*. Nevertheless, they possess a considerable truth content and they can, in the strictly logical sense, be good approximations to the truth, and better than certain other testable explanations. . . .Above all, however, situational analysis is rational, empirically testable and capable of improvement."[16] Situational logic, he argued, assumes a physical world with physical resources and barriers and a social world with other people and social institutions. He suggested that the fundamental problem of a theoretical sociology is "the general logic of the situation and the theory of institutions and traditions." This would include the problem of developing a theory of the "quasi-actions of institutions" since institutions do not act—only individuals act in, or for, or through institutions. It would also include a theory of the intended or unintended institutional consequences of purposive actions.[17]

In "Models, Instruments, and Truth: The Status of the Rationality Principle in Social Science," the full text of which was not made available until 1994, Popper connected situational logic to a generalized model of the simplifying explanatory scheme found in theoretical economics.[18] According to this model the actor is animated by the desire to act in accordance with the logic of the situation which is based on four basic factors: physical objects, social institutions, the aim of the actor, and the knowledge the actor has of the situation. Thus, a pedestrian who desires to cross the road will take into account the cars. the social institutions such as crosswalks, traffic signals, and so on. Given the pedestrian's knowledge of the situation and his desire to cross the road, his action is predictable.[19]

Situational logic explanations have important similarities to what Popper calls the first variant of intuitive understanding in *The Poverty of Historicism*. In both the first variant of intuitive understanding and situational logic, human action is explained in terms of the agent's purposes and beliefs: both types are "reconstructions"; both seem to be causal explanations; both eschew any appeal to wholes, the spirit of the age, and so on. However, there are some differences. In situational logic, the rationality of the agent is assumed, whereas in the first variant of intuitive understanding Popper spoke of the reconstruction of either rational or irrational action. Situational logic explanations apparently include explaining the unintended consequences of an action in terms of the beliefs and purposes of the agents and it is not clear if this is included in the first variant of intuitive understanding.

Whatever the precise connection between situational logic and the first variant of intuitive understanding and despite Popper's failure to categorize situational logic in this way, there is good reason to suppose that situational logic is a form of Verstehen. From the work of Max Weber we know that one form of Verstehen is understanding social action in terms of the beliefs, goals, and rationality of the actors.

To be sure, Popper rejected the idea that in order to understand an action we have to relive or imagine in our own minds the experience of the actor. However, this was also rejected by Weber. Further, just as Weber argued that causal explanations in the social sciences should be in terms of rational explanatory Verstehen, so Popper maintained that situational logic explanations are causal.

Although Popper's situational logic approach has remarkable similarities to Weber's rational Verstehen, it is notably different from Dilthey's, Collingwood's, Winch's, and Dray's views. Dilthey, Winch, and Dray all developed their views of Verstehen without recourse to causal considerations. Causal considerations play virtually no role in Dilthey's theory. For Winch, understanding social behavior was to interpret such behavior in terms of social rules and not as explaining such behavior in terms of causal laws couched in terms of the logic of the situation; for Dray, historical explanations were not in terms of causal laws but in terms of principles of actions. Although Collingwood did not rule out causes in historical explanations, these causes were internal events and were not formulated in terms of general causal laws. For Popper, on the other hand, situational logic explanations were so formulated and relevant causal factors specified in these laws were not just in terms of internal events.[20]

Jarvie's Situational Logic

Following Popper, Jarvie has argued that the correct explanatory approach to anthropological phenomena and presumably to all social scientific phenomena is in terms of "situational logic."[21] By this he means roughly that in the social institution in which the social actors operate their underlying aims and beliefs and some other factors should serve as the explanation of both their actions and the consequences of their actions. Thus, Jarvie maintains that although people's actions may superficially seem irrational, deeper analysis would usually reveal that, given their aims and beliefs about the world, their actions are perfectly reasonable.[22] Like Popper, Jarvie does not relate situational logic to any traditional notion of Verstehen, although his approach is close to Weber's rational explanatory Verstehen.

According to Jarvie, people's aims, beliefs, social context, and their rationality in light of these explain what they do. Consequently, he has urged anthropologists to return to Frazer's notion that primitive myth and magic are rational in light of the natives' beliefs and goals and social context. On this view, situational logic explains myth and magic while the accounts in terms of functions that they serve do not. Explanation in terms of the logic of the situational can work in two ways: First, knowing what people value and believe we may explain the *intended* results of their action. For example, obtaining food would normally be an intended action of hunting and would be explained by situational logic. On the other hand, it can also explain *unintended* consequences of action, for example, a low standard of living that results from crude agricultural practice in a primitive society.

Evaluation

There are a number of questions that must be raised about situational logic as presented by Popper and Jarvie: (1) What is the relation between situational logic and the method of conjecture and refutation? (2) What is the meaning of rationality? (3) Are situational logic explanations uniquely adequate in the social sciences? (4) What is the causal importance of beliefs, aims, and rationality in causal explanations?

(1) The Relational between Situational Logic and the Method of Conjecture and Refutation

A hasty reader might be led to suppose from Popper's and Jarvie's writings that situational logic explanations in the social sciences are somehow implied by the method of conjecture and refutation. Thus, one might suppose that once we have seen the errors of inductivism and the virtues of the method of conjecture and refutation, the acceptance of situational logic as the fundamental method of social science follows as a matter of course. However, that this is not so can easily be seen. The method of conjecture and refutation does not prescribe any particular content for the conjecture. A hypothesis in terms of people's beliefs, aims, and rationality would simply be one possible hypothesis among many. One might accept the method of conjecture and refutation as the method of science and with no inconsistency be opposed to situational logic as the method of explanation in social science.[23] Conversely, one can accept situational logic and yet not accept the method of conjecture and refutation. Indeed, situational logic is perfectly compatible with, e.g., the use of hypothetical inference. Hypotheses about peoples' expectations, aims, and rationality might be construed as verified by verbal and nonverbal behavior. Thus there is no inconsistency in using situational logic and one form of inductive inference, a mode of inference that Popper opposes.[24] So unless independent arguments are produced, the advantages of situational logic in social science are by no means confirmed by establishing the method of conjecture and refutation as the fundamental method of social science.

Actually, unless independent arguments were given, the method of situational logic would seem to be inconsistent with the method of conjecture and refutation.[25] To see this we must recall that Popperians emphasize that the method of conjecture and refutation would justify bold and speculative theories in social science. Presumably an essential part of bold and speculative theorizing might involve the introduction of new and unfamiliar notions, the postulations of unheard of processes and entities. However, far from justifying such freewheeling speculation, the method of situational logic as a fundamental method in social science would put some restrictions on it. Jarvie himself has said that in social science explanations are to be in terms of the familiar, i.e., in terms of the actor's goals and beliefs and the rationality of acting in terms of these values and beliefs. But, surely, restricting anthropological explanations to explanations in terms of familiar notions of aims and beliefs and rational actions prevents the formulation of bold explanatory hypotheses, for example, those not couched in such familiar terms. Many explanations in the social sciences are formulated in these unfamiliar terms. How do Popperians justify this restriction? In order to answer this question we must first clarify the notion of rationality which plays a crucial role in situational logic.

(2) The Meaning of Rationality

Although Jarvie uses the notion of rational action throughout his work it is surprising how he does little to clarify it. At times he seems to identify goal-directed activity and rational action,[26] but surely this cannot be his view for not all goal-directed activity is rational. For example, a native might want to produce rain and believe that doing a rain dance is the only way to do this and yet do a war dance instead. Although his action is goal directed it would not be rational in the light of his beliefs (unless we found out, e.g., that he thought he was doing a rain dance). Goal-directedness may be a necessary condition of rational action, but it is surely not a sufficient condition. It does not uniquely separate rational from nonrational action.

A closer reading of Jarvie suggests that he may think that what is a rational action is a goal-directed action in which the goal is in keeping with the beliefs of the native in the situation in which he finds himself, in keeping with the native's "horizon of expectations."[27] The native's action would be rational in our rain dance case if he did the rain dance believing that the rain dance was necessary to achieve rain and he wanted rain.

However, much more than this needs to be included in any plausible account of means-end rationality. For example, any viable means-end rationality would exclude inconsistent beliefs and incoherent preferences. Thus, the transitivity of preferences—if A prefers X to Y, and Y to Z, then X prefers X to Z—would have to be part of the standards of a viable means-end rationality. Moreover, Jarvie's simple model of rational action can give no plausible account of complex rational action. Consider a native with various goals G_1, G_2,.....G_n and beliefs B_1, B_2,.....B_n about the likelihood of reaching these goals. One may suppose that these goals have different utilities for the native. What is the rational thing to do in this situation?

The mathematical theory of decision—so-called decision under risk— is useful in cases of this sort. The usual procedure is to define rational action as that which maximizes expected utility. Expected utility is computed by multiplying, say, the believed likelihood of obtaining each goal G with the utility of achieving the goal. It should be noted that two or more courses may have equal expected utility; hence these courses of action are equally rational. Clearly, in this case there is no one course of rational action relative to the person's expectations and goals.

This problem of defining rationality is even more pronounced when we come to other situations where probabilities are not known (so-called decisions under uncertainty). Suppose that on one's beliefs B_1, B_2,..... B_n a set of mutually exclusive courses of action A_1, A_2,....A_n are possible with mutually exclusive outcomes C_1, C_2,....C_n for each course of action; suppose further that each outcome has an associated utility. For example, suppose a native in a nonliterate society believes the following two courses of action are open to him: he can pray to the Sun God or he can pray to the Moon God (he believes he cannot do both). Suppose that he believes that if he prays to the Moon God there will either be rain (1) for a week or (2) for five minutes; if he prays to the Sun God there will either be rain (3) for a day or (4) for an hour. Now suppose the native values each outcome in the following way: (1) 1000: (3) 100: (4) 10: (2) 1, that is, suppose these are subjective utilities of the native for each outcome.

What the rational thing to do is depends on the rule in terms of which his action is viewed. The *maximin rule* would direct him to choose that action in which the worst possible outcome is at least as good as the worst possible outcome of any alternative. In this case he would be directed to pray to the Sun God. On the other hand, the *maximax rule* would direct him to pray to the Moon God. This rule directs us to choose a course of action whose best possible outcome is at least as good as any alternative. Moreover, various alternative rules have been proposed.[28]

To say that Jarvie is not alive to these complexities is perhaps to understate the case: he speaks glibly of *the* rational principle[29] as if there were one criterion of rationality. Moreover, even if a criterion of rationality is chosen, it does not always uniquely determine one course of action as rational. Although Jarvie allows that action can be rational, he argues that beliefs cannot be.[30] This is because a belief can be rational only if it is justified. However, according to Popperians, beliefs can be justified only if induction is valid and they argue that it is not. Jarvie does allow that attitudes can be more or less rational: A person's attitude is rational in proportion to his or her willingness to take account of criticisms. This account of a rational attitude completely coheres with the Popperian characterization of scientific rationality in terms of conjecture and refutation: Science should put forth easily criticizable theories and subject these to rigorous criticisms.

(3) The Unique Adequacy of Situational Logic Explanation

Given the Popperian claim for the unique adequacy of situational logic explanations in social science, Popperians must somehow show that other types of explanations, i.e., nonsituational logic explanations, are not worth considering; they must show that one ought not to conjecture in terms of these other hypotheses. But how *could* this be shown?

Presumably it could not be shown by refuting existing alternative explanatory theories on factual grounds. Thus even if it is shown that existing functional theories (Malinowski's and Radcliffe-Brown's) have false premises, this would not show that other new types of functional theories will have false premises, let alone that new nonfunctional, nonsituational logic explanations will have such premises.[31] Jarvie's argument would have to proceed on methodological grounds; he would have to show that all possible nonsituational logic explanations are methodologically inadequate. Has Popper or Jarvie done this?

Jarvie, as well as other Popperians, advocates one type of institutional methodological individualism—the view that individuals operating in the context of social institutions explain social phenomena. They are opposed to both methodological holism, i.e., the view that the explanation of social phenomena should be in terms of the social whole, and any type of methodological individualism where social institutions play no explanatory role. The issue is an extremely complicated one, but at least this can be said here. It is quite possible that the issues between these opposing positions are not methodological ones at all but can be resolved into purely factual questions about the existence of certain laws.[32] In any case, even if considerations of social institutions are an essential part of the explanations of social phenomena, and methodological holism is eliminated, it does not follow that situational logic is shown to be uniquely adequate. Situational logic explanation is merely one kind of institutional methodological individualistic explanation; psychological explanation set in the context of social institutions, for instance, is another type. Situational logic explanation uses the commonsense categories of the actor such as beliefs, aims, and rationality. But there are other psychological theories that use technical concepts such as psychic energy and valance. Such psychological theories need not be purely individualistic since the psychological factors appealed to could be placed in an institutional setting.

It is curious that although all of these possibilities must be eliminated as live options to establish the Popperian thesis, Popperians like Jarvie do little to eliminate them. Jarvie excluded explanations in terms of the irrationality of the actor as beyond the purview of social science on the grounds that to "appeal to irrationality [is to] give up the possibility of any explanation at all."[33] No argument is given for the contention that the irrationality of the actor could not explain—at least partially—what he did. Surely, the only thing that is necessary to explain a person's action (if Popper's view of explanation is correct)[34] is to deduce a description of the action from general laws and initial conditions. There is no a priori reason why the predicate "is irrational" could not appear in the antecedent of a general law and in the statement of initial conditions. Naturally other factors besides the irrationality of the actor would have to be taken into account to provide a complete explanation. But the same thing is true in situational logic explanation; more factors than the rationality of the actor must be taken into account.

It is possible that Jarvie supposes that an irrational action cannot be subsumed under some general law. But this is surely not the case. One might speculate that he has confused two senses of "irrational." In the one sense, "irrational" means "not lawful, spontaneous or random." In another sense, "irrational" means "not guided by reason or rational principles." Irrational action in the second sense—presumably the sense Jarvie is talking about—does not entail irrational action in the first sense.

Although Jarvie explicitly rejects physiological explanations his arguments are far from persuasive. He argues that S. F. Nadel, a theoretical anthropologist, is wrong to suppose that there are levels of explanation and that social phenomena, e.g., joking relations, can be explained at the level of neurophysiology. His argument seems to be that since neurophysiological processes are influenced by environmental factors (including social environment), and conversely, social phenomena could not therefore be explained in terms of neurophysiology.[35] Situational logic alone seems able to take into account the mutual influence between environment and people in his view.

Whatever the validity of Nadel's position, Jarvie is guilty of a nonsequitur. One need not suggest that only neurological factors alone are sufficient to explain the joking relations. But one might argue that neurophysiological and environmental variables together might be sufficient to explain social phenomena, e.g., joking relations. One might suggest that beliefs, goals, etc. are not needed. Thus the refutation of completely physiological explanations of social phenomena does not leave situational logic as the only alternative.

Jarvie does not explicitly consider behavior theory, despite the fact that this theory has been used in anthropological studies.[36] When he does consider psychological theories which are not in terms of beliefs, aims, and so on, his argument is the same as the one he used in regard to neurophysiology: since psychological variables are influenced by social variables, and conversely, purely psychological explanations are inadequate.

But advocates of psychological theories in social science need not argue that psychological factors (for instance, action potentials, mental energy) alone provide a sufficient condition for social phenomena any more than Jarvie needs to maintain that beliefs, aims, and rationality provide a sufficient condition. Psychological theorists might argue that psychological factors are a necessary but insufficient part of a sufficient but unnecessary condition of some social phenomena.[37]

Jarvie hints at times that other types of explanations—nonsituational logic explanations—are or at least tend to be untestable (unfalsifiable).[38] No argument is given for this remarkable contention. Surely this thesis cannot be decided on a priori grounds. Even if all existing alternative theories are shown to be untestable (something Jarvie does not begin to show), this would not show that all alternative theories are untestable.

Indeed, not only has Jarvie failed to justify the unique adequacy of situational logic explanation but there are cases where their use seems particularly problematic. How, for example, can situational logic explanations explain beliefs? In his book *The Revolution in Anthropology*, Jarvie tried to give an explanatory account of cargo cults in Melanesia. However, part of his account is the explanation of the beliefs connected with these cults. For example, he attempted to explain the idea behind the cult doctrine and the failure of the cults, including various cognitive reactions.[39] Can this be done in terms of situational logic?

David Henderson has pointed out a serious problem in Jarvie's account.[40] The problem is that Jarvie wanted to explain cult doctrines in terms of aims, beliefs, and rationality of the cult followers and yet he maintained that religious belief is not rational. This seemed initially paradoxical. Henderson argued that Jarvie dealt with this problem by considering beliefs as actions, not states. On this interpretation of Jarvie, phrases such as "religious belief" should be understood as referring to "acts of believing" of some religious doctrine. So understood, Jarvie can apply means-ends rationality appropriate to the actions. When a social actor learns scientific rationality, that is, the attitude of being open to criticism, this can be considered as part of the actor's situation—part of the actor's aims and beliefs—and factored into the means-end rationality. But in a closed society where the standards of scientific rationality are not used, for example, in Melanesia, the natives use the only standards that they know. Given these standards, Jarvie suggests, the native belief in cargo cults is a rational action.

The trouble with this reply is that magico-religious beliefs obtain in societies where scientific rationality is known and appreciated. Jarvie cited prayer services in the Bible Belt in order to bring about rain as an example of something that could be explained by situational logic.[41] However, given his view that beliefs can be explained by situational logic, he presumably would maintain that the relevant beliefs of inhabitants of the Bible Belt could be so explained. Henderson has pointed out a serious problem with Jarvie's thesis.

However, having spent a number of years in that region, I have this to report. The situation there is not at all like the situation in Malaysia (as described by Jarvie). Christian beliefs are not held only by those who have no familiarity with the theoretical explanations of modern science and who have a theoretically barren technology. Rather, such beliefs are held by many lawyers, engineers, chemists, and so on. To attempt a logic of the situation explanation of such beliefs would require either ad hoc adjustments in the standards of rationality appealed to, or dubious claims that threaten to elevate the purported rationality into an a priori truth. (For example, it might be held that although the relevant believers have been exposed to alternative theoretical models and to standards of critical reasoning, they failed to appreciate these things. However, it looks as though the evidence for this is just that, had they appreciated such things, they would not have acted as they did.)[42]

Henderson has pointed out another problem as well.[43] According to Jarvie, mysticism is one reaction to the failure of cargo cults. He attempts to explain this mystical reaction in terms of situational logic. Mysticism beliefs, Henderson has argued, seem to be not only contradictory but mystical doctrine sanctions a violation of logical standards. However, any plausible means-ends rationality excludes violations of elementary logic principles. Thus, it seems difficult to understand how situational logic can explain mystical beliefs.

In sum, we must conclude that Jarvie has done nothing to establish the unique adequacy of situational logic explanations[44] and, indeed, there is good reason to question whether these explanations can be used always in the circumstances where Jarvie tries to apply them.

(4) The Causal Importance of Beliefs, Aims, and Rationality

Jarvie admits that beliefs, aims, and rationality of the members of a society operating in an institutional setting taken alone cannot provide the causally sufficient condition explanation of their behavior that is essential for Popperian explanations. But what else he wants to include is uncertain.[45] Perhaps Jarvie's thesis is only that some unspecified factors must be included. If so, it is certainly true that sometimes situational logic so interpreted can provide a causally sufficient explanation of human behavior. But this is surely of little importance and may well be unfair to Jarvie's intentions. For he above all wants to emphasize the importance of beliefs, aims, and rationality in causal explanations whatever other factors may be causally relevant.

Thus, one may perhaps interpret Jarvie as claiming that beliefs, aims, and rationality in their institutional setting are the most important causal factors[46] in the total cause of a piece of behavior, e.g., cargo cult activity, whatever else the total cause may include. The truth of Jarvie's thesis so interpreted will depend on what is meant by "the most important causal factor or factors." On some analyses Jarvie's thesis may not be true.

Let us consider a contextual analysis of causal importance. On this account whether the beliefs, aims, and rationality are the most causally important will be dependent on the purposes of the inquiry and how the problem is described. As already noted, understanding is a contextual notion that depends on the purpose of the investigation and description of the thing understood. A similar contextual approach can be taken with respect to causal importance. Given that there are many causal factors in a total cause that can be described in many ways, what is the most important cause and how it will be described will vary with context and the purpose of the inquiry. For example, a macroeconomic anthropologist might describe cargo cults in terms of macroeconomic theory and cite macroeconomic factors as the most important cause in explaining them, while an anthropologist interested in psychoanalysis might describe cargo cults in psychoanalytic terms and cite psychoanalytic factors as the most important causal factor in explaining them. In both of these analyses, beliefs, aims, and rationality play an unimportant role in anthropologists' explanations, despite the fact that these factors are part of the total cause.

Another analysis is this:[47] Suppose factors A and B when taken together are causally sufficient for C although neither A nor B taken alone is sufficient. Thus, all A's and B's are C but it is not the case that all A's are C and it is not the case that all B's are C. Now if most A's are C and it is not the case that most B's are C, then let us say that A is a more important causal factor than B. However, if most B's are C and it is not the case that most A's are C, let us say that B is more important than A. Finally, if most A's are C and most B's are C, let us say that A and B are equally causally important.

The application of this to situational logic should be obvious. Let A be the complex factor of beliefs, aims, and rationality and let B be all other causal relevant factors, e.g., physiological and environmental factors. Now it is an empirical question whether the factors Jarvie emphasizes in situational logic explanation are the more important causal factors in any given situation; it is not something that can be decided by a priori reasoning.

Let us illustrate this more fully. Suppose we are interested in knowing the most important causal factors in a native's hunting for game. Let us suppose we know that the native is rational, and in relation to his desires and beliefs the rational thing to do would be to hunt game.

However, the native will not hunt if, for example, he becomes ill or if certain environmental factors prevent him. Now it is an empirical question whether (1) "Most natives for whom hunting game is the rational thing to do and who are rational hunt game" is true and whether (2) "Most natives who are not ill and when certain environmental factors obtain hunt game" is false or vice versa or whether (1) and (2) are both true.

Thus, in general, the sentences resulting from interpreting the schemata,

(1)[1] Most people, for whom doing x is the rational thing to do given their aims y and beliefs w who are rational, do x.

(2)[1] Most people who are in physiological condition c and environmental condition e do x,

will be true or false depending on the particular values of x, y, w, c, and e which are substituted even if the sentence is true, which results from substituting in the following schema:

(3) All people, for whom doing x is the rational thing to do given their aims y and beliefs w, who are rational and who are in physiological condition c and environmental condition e, do x.

Thus, on this analysis of causal importance, the causal importance of beliefs, aims, and rationality may vary from context to context. Jarvie's thesis interpreted as stressing the importance of beliefs, aims, and rationality in all or most contexts will require the support of evidence not found in his work. But even if this is not Jarvie's thesis, the above considerations throw light on an important aspect of social scientific explanation. If it were true that beliefs, aims, and rationality were not in general important causal factors in the explanation of human behavior, social scientists might well choose to ignore them.

To be sure, it might be true that slightly more precise predictions could be had by taking into account beliefs, aims, and rationality than if only physiological and environmental factors were taken into account. But such precision may not be needed and indeed may be had only at a high price. For example, it is often difficult to find out what a person's beliefs and aims are. This difficulty may be too high a price to pay for a slight increase in predictive accuracy.

On the other hand, if beliefs, aims, and rationality are causally important and environmental and other factors are not, Jarvie's apparent stress on the former may indeed be vindicated. Social scientists may well be advised to concentrate on beliefs, aims, and rationality rather than on environmental and other factors despite the problems involved in discovering what an actor's beliefs and aims are. For if one takes beliefs, aims, and rationality into account, a large increase in predictive accuracy will result. Environmental factors, in this case, may be relatively ignored.

However, if Jarvie is not stressing the causal importance of aims, beliefs, and rationality above other factors and in fact is urging social scientists to concentrate equally on both sorts of factors, this view may prove ill-advised as social science progresses. Either sort of factor might warrant special concentration in the light of new evidence and theories. It is difficult to discern exactly what Jarvie's thesis is on this issue. But that he does not discuss these crucial issues is obvious.

Conclusion

I have argued that Popperian situational logic is a form of Verstehen and has serious problems. Unless nonsituational logic explanations are excluded from social science on a priori grounds, the advocacy of situational logic is inconsistent with Popper's stress on bold speculation in social science. Popperians do not provide such grounds. Although Jarvie's account of situational logic is the most systematic account offered by Popperians, it has serious problems. His views on rationality—an essential notion in situational logic explanations—are too simple; a precise characterization of situational logic is never given; his stress on aims and beliefs is never justified; there is good reason to suppose that situational logic explanations cannot be applied to some of the very cases that Jarvie uses as examples of its application.

Notes

1.   This chapter is based in part on my article "Popperian Anthropology," *Methodology and Science* 4, 1971, pp. 41-79.
2.   Karl Popper, *The Logic of Scientific Discovery* (New York: Basic Books, 1959), and *Conjectures and Refutations* (New York: Basic Books, 1962).
3.   Whether Popper's acceptance of NME in *The Logic of Scientific Discovery* is compatible with his thesis that social scientific laws are impossible, expounded in his later work, cannot be explored here. For a critique of his argument, see Lee C. McIntyre, *Laws and Explanation in the Social Sciences* (Boulder, CO: Westview Press, 1996).

4. Karl Popper, *The Poverty of Historicism* (Boston: The Beacon Press, 1957), pp. 130-43.
5. Ibid., pp. 19-24.
6. Ibid., pp. 147-52; Karl Popper, "The Logic of the Social Sciences," in *The Positivist Dispute in German Sociology*, T. Adorno et al. (New York: Harper Torch Books, 1969), pp. 102-103.
7. See I. C. Jarvie. "Nadel on the Aims and Methods of Social Anthropology," *The British Journal for the Philosophy of Science*, 1961, pp. 1-24; I. C. Jarvie, *The Revolution in Anthropology* (New York: The Humanities Press, 1964).
8. Popper, *The Poverty of Historicism,* pp. 20–21.
9. Ibid., p. 138.
10. Ibid., pp. 78-79.
11. Ibid., p. 149. For a different and more detailed account of the evolution of Popper's situational logic, see Peter Hedström et al., "Popper's Situational Analysis and Contemporary Sociology," *Philosophy of Social Sciences*, vol. 28, 1998, pp. 39-64.
12. Ibid.
13. Karl R. Popper, "The Logic of the Social Sciences," p. 102.
14. Ibid., pp. 102-103.
15. Ibid., p. 103.
16. Ibid.
17. Ibid., p. 104.
18. Karl Popper, "Models, Instruments, and Truth: The Status of the Rationality Principle in Social Science," in Karl Popper, *The Myth of the Framework*, M. A. Notturno (London: Routledge, 1994).
19. See Egon Matzner and Ian C. Jarvie, "Introduction to the Special Issue on Situational Analysis," *Philosophy of Social Sciences*, vol. 28, 1998, pp. 333-38.
20. Although commentators have failed to relate Popper's situational logic to Verstehen, they have noted the connection between Popper's views and the movement called "economic imperialism" that started in the 1930s and began to gain prominence in the 1950s: the movement to apply a model of rational behavior used in theoretical economics to other social sciences. See ibid., p. 335.
21. Jarvie, *The Revolution in Anthropology,* pp. 34-42, 113-30, 163-69, 223-34; Jarvie, "Nadel on the Aims and Methods of Social Anthropology," pp. 11-24; see also I. C. Jarvie, Review of Robert Brown, *Explanation in Social Science, in The British Journal for the Philosophy of Science*, 1964, pp. 143-50.
22. Jarvie's position following Popper is based on what he calls the trivial general law that sane people as a rule act more or less rationally given their interests, aims, and beliefs. See Ian Jarvie, "Situational Logic and Its Reception," *Philosophy of Social Sciences*, vol. 28, 1998, p. 370.
23. For example, if it could be shown that situational logic explanations are difficult to refute. The tension between Popper's falsification principle and the simplifying—and thus false—assumptions of situational logic has been noted by Hedström et al., "Popper's Situational Analysis and Contemporary Sociology," pp. 351-53. However, they do not note the related problem discussed here.
24. See, for example, the use of such explanations by Hempel. See C. G. Hempel, *Aspects of Scientific Explanation* (New York: The Free Press, 1965), pp. 463-89.
25. Jarvie argues that, according to Popper, social science methodology should be disciplined by practical considerations, for example, the elimination of suffering. However, he believes that this does not affect the unity of scientific method in the social and natural sciences. See Jarvie, "Situational Logic and Its Reception," p. 366.

26. Jarvie, *The Revolution in Anthropology,* pp. 132, 137.
27. Ibid., p. 134.
28. Hempel, op. cit.
29. Jarvie, *The Revolution in Anthropology,* p. 218. For a similar critique of Popper, see Hedström et al., "Popper's Situational Analysis and Contemporary Sociology," pp. 356-57.
30. Jarvie, *The Revolution in Anthropology,* p. 132.
31. Ibid., pp. 176-98; see also Jarvie, "The Nature and Value of Functionalism in Anthropology," *Functionalism in the Social Sciences,* ed. Don Martindale (Philadelphia: The American Academy of Political Science, 1965), pp. 19 -35. See also Brown's critique of Jarvie's critique of functionalism. Robert Brown, Review of I. C. Jarvie, *The Revolution in Anthropology, The British Journal for the Philosophy of Science,* 1964, pp. 143–50.
32. For this view, see Arthur Danto, *Analytic Philosophy of History* (Cambridge: Cambridge University Press, 1965), chapter 12; Michael Martin, "Methodological Individualism and the Reduction of Cultural Anthropology to Psychology," *Scientia* 9-10, 1969, pp. 482-502.
33. Jarvie, *The Revolution in Anthropology,* p. 92.
34. Popper, *The Logic of Scientific Discovery,* pp. 59-64.
35. Jarvie, " Nadel on the Aims and Methods of Social Anthropology," pp. 16-17.
36. John W. M. Whiting and Arvin L. Child, *Child Training and Personality* (New Haven: Yale University Press, 1953).
37. See David Braybrooke, *Philosophy of Social Science* (Englewood Cliffs, NJ: Prentice-Hall, Inc., 1987), p. 24.
38. Jarvie, *The Revolution in Anthropology,* p. 73.
39. Ibid., pp. 71-72.
40. David K. Henderson, "The Role and Limitation of Rationalizing Explanations in the Social Sciences," *Canadian Journal of Philosophy* 19, 1989, pp. 267-88.
41. Jarvie, *The Revolution in Anthropology,* pp. 35–36.
42. Henderson, "The Role and Limitation of Rationalizing Explanations in the Social Sciences," pp. 274-75 .
43. Ibid., p. 277.
44. Jarvie fails to face this problem even in his recent publications. For example, in "Situational Logic and Its Reception," pp. 374-78, he distinguishes his type of methodological individualism from others but does not show that these others are in error.
45. See Michael Martin, "Popperian Anthropology," *Methodology and Science* 4, 1971, pp. 413-16. See also Hedström et al., "Popper's Situational Analysis and Contemporary Sociology," p. 339, who also complain of the vagueness of Popper's view on this point.
46. I cannot find any specific passages in Jarvie to justify this interpretation; however, this interpretation does make sense out of his apparent emphasis on these factors in explanations in the social sciences.
47. Cf. Morton White, *Foundations of Historical Knowledge* (New York: Harper and Row, 1965), chapter 4.

6

Verstehen and Phenomenology

Background

Although a Verstehen approach has been developed from within a Popperian approach to science, Verstehen is usually associated with continental philosophy. It has, for example, been associated with phenomenology and will be considered from this perspective here.

Understood literally, phenomenology is the study of appearances. Thus, "any description of how things appear, especially if sustained and penetrating, can be called phenomenology."[1] More specifically the term "phenomenology" has come to designate the philosophical movement started by Franz Brentano (1838-1917) and developed by Edmund Husserl (1859-1938). Initially emphasizing the description of human experience as directed onto objects real or imaginary, it then shifted and stressed a description of those objects of experience which were considered to be essences or structures intuited by the mind. Calling this study of essences "eidetic analysis," Husserl believed that in pursuing this study it was necessary to bracket all preconceptions based on the scientific worldview and the natural attitude; in other words, to put aside the unquestioning stance of common sense.[2] On this view, bracketing reveals the "transcendental ego" for which everything that exists is an object.[3]

This phenomenological approach generated two major problems when applied to the social sciences. One is that Husserl's stress on essences and structures tended to ignore the uniqueness and changeability of social phenomena. In addition, his emphasis on the transcendental ego gave phenomenological investigation a solipsistic orientation which threatened to exclude intersubjective meanings and experiences.[4] Although he struggled to overcome these problems, he had only limited success. As Fred Dallmayr and Thomas McCarthy have argued,

> To alleviate the first quandary, Husserl juxtaposed to eidetic analysis a more "mundane" type of inquiry—labeled "descriptive psychology"—designed to explore individual motivations and intentions operative on the level of the "natural attitude." With respect to the second issue, the focus on the "life-world" (Lebenswelt) evident in his later work reflected the desire to bridge the gulf between ego consciousness and social context. Despite strenuous efforts, however, the goal of integration remained elusive. Husserl's opus left unresolved both the relationship between eidetic and mundane approaches and their pertinence to the investigation of the life-world.[5]

In any case, Husserl's study of life-world provided a point of departure for many of the phenomenologically oriented social scientists who came after him.[6] Arguing in his last book that a study of culture since Galileo shows that the world of our common, lived experience has been replaced by an objectively true world of science, Husserl maintained that this objective world is derived from the life-world. Indeed, the world of science is a construction based on this latter. As a sympathetic commentator put it,

> It becomes clear that the scientific universe is but a network of interlocking ideal constructs. These constructs are but the theoretico-logical "substructure" of immediately given things and relationships . . . . The whole of theoretical truth, including the logical and mathematical truth of the positive sciences, finds its ultimate justification and validity in the type of evidence that concerns events and occurrences in the life-world . . . . This means that the theoretical scientific world must find its foundation in the life-world rather than the life-world finding its ultimate justification in scientific theory.[7]

Schutz's Phenomenological Social Sciences

The work of Alfred Schutz, who had been described as "the principal pioneer and architect of phenomenological sociology,"[8] is the ideal place to examine Verstehen in the context of phenomenology. In *The Phenomenology of the Social World* (1932), he utilized Husserl's method of bracketing and argued for the importance of reflections of the transcendental ego. In his later writing Schutz moved progressively away from transcendental-egological concerns in the direction of a sociology of the life-world—but without relinquishing the accent on "subjective intentionality and motivation."[9] His concern with the sociology of the life-world is evident in two representative papers, "Concept and Theory Formation in the Social Sciences"[10] and "Common Sense and Scientific Interpretations of Human Action,"[11] both of which offer some of the clearest presentations available of a phenomenologically based view of the social sciences.[12] The first paper is especially relevant to our purposes here for Schutz criticizes Nagel's evaluation of Max Weber's claim that social science seeks to "understand" social phenomena in terms of "meaningful" categories of human experience and explicitly links his own analysis to Verstehen.[13] The second paper, although covering some of the same ground, presents a more detailed comparison between Schutz's phenomenological approach to social science and a naturalistic and positivistic approach. Thus, an examination of these papers gives us an opportunity not only to evaluate Schutz's own theory of Verstehen, his interpretations of Weber and Nagel, but to appraise the methodological differences he posits between his theory of the social sciences and the standard naturalistic alternative.

Interpretation of Verstehen

Schutz linked understanding of the life-world with Verstehen as follows:

Verstehen is, thus, primarily not a method used by social sciences but the particular experiential form in which common sense thinking takes cognizance of the social cultural world. It has nothing to do with introspection; it is a result of processes of learning or acculturation in the same way as the common sense experience of the so-called natural world. Verstehen is, moreover, by no means a private affair of the observer which cannot be controlled by the experience of other observers. It is controllable at least to the same extent to which the private sensory perceptions of an individual are controllable by any individual under certain conditions.[14]

Schutz cited as an example of this controllability the prediction based on Verstehen that a duly stamped and addressed letter will reach its destination.

According to Schutz, the confusion plaguing discussions of Verstehen is partially the result of a failure to distinguish between Verstehen "(1) as the experiential form of commonsense knowledge of human affairs, (2) as an epistemological problem, and (3) as a method peculiar to the social sciences."[15] The epistemological problem is, "How is Verstehen possible?" that is, how is it possible that we have knowledge of other minds and intersubjective experience of the natural and cultural world? Arguing that a satisfactory solution to this problem has not yet been found, he maintained that a solution has been "taken for granted in our commonsense thinking and practically solved without any difficulty in each of our everyday actions."[16] Emphasizing our experience of the life-world is "the unquestioned but always questionable background within which inquiry starts and within which alone it can be carried out," Schutz argued, that this "insight sheds light on certain methodological problems peculiar to the social sciences."[17]

According to Schutz, "the assumption that the strict adoption of principle of concept and theory formation prevailing in the natural sciences will lead to reliable knowledge of social reality is inconsistent itself."[18] Even an ideally refined behaviorism "will not tell us anything about the social reality as experienced by men in everyday life."[19] If social science wants to explain social reality, it has "to develop particular devices foreign to the natural sciences in order to agree with commonsense experience of the social world."[20] This is because there is an essential difference in structure between the constructs used in the natural and the social sciences. Unlike the facts, events, and observation fields studied in the natural sciences, the facts, events, and observation fields in the social sciences are "pre-interpreted." Arguing that the world of nature does not mean anything to the objects studied by the natural sciences, Schutz held that the social world means something to the social actors studied by the social sciences:

> The thought objects constructed by the social scientists, in order to grasp this social reality, have to be founded upon the thought objects constructed by the commonsense thinking of men, living their daily lives within the social world. Thus, the constructs of the social sciences are, so to speak, constructs of the second degree, that is, constructs of the constructs made by the actors on the social scene, whose behavior the social scientist had to observe and to explain in accordance with procedural rules of science. [21]

Schutz went on to say,

> Consequently, if the social sciences aim indeed at explaining social reality, then the scientific constructs on the second level must include a reference to the subjective meaning an action has for the actor. This is, I think, what Max Weber understood by his famous postulate of subjective interpretation, which has, indeed, been observed so far in the theory formation of all social sciences. The postulate of subjective interpretation has to be understood in the sense that all scientific explanations of the social world *can*, and for certain purposes, *must* refer to the subjective meaning of the actions of human beings from which social reality originates.[22]

For Schutz, then, the first task of the methodology of the social sciences is "the exploration of the general principles according to which man in daily life organizes his experiences, and especially those of the social world."[23] What are some of these principles? Phenomenological analysis of the natural attitude shows that the unique objects of our experience in the life-world are unique only "within a horizon of typical familiarity and pre-acquaintance."[24] Whether I consider a unique object as unique or as a typical example and which traits of an object I single out as unique and which as typical depends on my interests and system of relevances; that is, it depends on the practical or theoretical problem at hand. An actor bestows subjective meaning upon his or her actions in the same way, viz., in terms of the actor's interests and system of relevance. "This implies that, strictly speaking, the actor and he alone knows what he does, why he does it, and when and where his action ends."[25]

Arguing that everyday life is from the outset also a social-cultural world, Schutz said that one learns in particular situations and only in a fragmentary way to experience the subjective meaning that other actors ("the Others") place on their actions. One can experience them more easily in their typicality, leading one to construct typical patterns of action, motivation, and personalities. Another principle of organization of the social aspect of the life-world is an idealization which Schutz calls the reciprocity of perspectives: If I were to exchange places with my fellow human being I would experience things as he or she would.[26] Still another organizing principle is that knowledge is socially distributed, that is, each individual knows "merely a sector of the world and common knowledge of the same sector varies individually as to its degree of distinction, clarity, acquaintanceship, or mere belief."[27]

Schutz's view of Verstehen has important similarities to and differences from other Verstehen theories considered in earlier chapters. Like Dilthey on the reconstruction interpretation, Weber, Collingwood, Winch, Dray, and Jarvie, he rejected Verstehen as involving empathetic identification with the social actors. Moreover, unlike Scriven, Schutz's Verstehen is not a method of verification and, unlike the positivists such as Abel, it is not a method of hypotheses generation. Schutz, like Weber, Collingwood, Winch, Dray, and Jarvie, argued that Verstehen was a necessary condition for social scientific understanding. However, unlike Weber and Jarvie, Schutz did not believe this understanding was connected with causal explanations. In this respect, his view was closer to Winch and Dray. On the other hand, his emphasis on ideal types and idealizations shows the influence of Weber. However, the fundamental difference of Schutz's theory from the others considered is his phenomenological orientation in that only Schutz attempts to ground his insights in the phenomenology of the life-world.

The Methodology of the Social Sciences

How then should social scientists proceed according to Schutz? They should observe facts and events within social reality and construct the typical behavior or course-of-action patterns of an ideal actor. Social scientists should ascribe to this ideal actor a fictitious consciousness and typical purposes and goals:

> This homunculus or puppet is supposed to be interrelated with interaction patterns to other homunculi or puppets constructed in a similar way. Among these homunculi with which the social scientist populated his model of the social world of everyday life, sets of motives, goals, roles—in general, systems of relevances— are distributed in such a way as the scientific problem under scrutiny requires. Yet . . . these constructs are by no means arbitrary. They are subject to the postulate of logical consistency and to the postulate of adequacy.[28]

By the postulate of logical consistency Schutz meant that the conceptual framework must be "fully compatible with the principles of formal logic."[29] But what is the principle of adequacy? It means that "each term in such a scientific model of human action must be constructed in such a way that a human act performed within the real world by an individual actor as indicated by the typical individual would be understandable to the actor himself as well as to his fellow-men in terms of the commonsense categories of everyday life."[30] In "Common Sense and Scientific Interpretations of Human Action," Schutz suggested another requirement that he called the postulate of subjective interpretation:

> In order to explain human action the scientist has to ask what model of an individual mind can be constructed and what typical contents must be attributed to it in order to explain the observed facts as the result of the activity of such a mind in an understandable relation. The compliance with this postulate warrants the possibility of referring all kinds of human action or their result to the subjective meaning such action or result of action has for the actor.[31]

It seems clear from what Schutz said in a third paper, "The Problem of Rationality in the Social World," that the models constructed by social scientists assume that the typical idealized actors that made up the models—the homunculi or puppets—are rational in the sense assumed by classical economics.

> The ideal type of social action must be constructed in such a way that the actor in the living world would perform the typical act if he had a clear and distinct scien-

tific knowledge of all elements relevant to his choice and the constant tendency to choose the most appropriate means for the realization of the appropriate end . . . The postulate of rationality implies, furthermore, that all other behavior has to be interpreted as derivative from the basic scheme of rational acting.[32]

This model can be verified by empirical observation at each step in its construction. However, Schutz stressed that this observation must not be limited to sensory observation, but must also include "the experimental form, by which commonsense thinking in everyday life understands human actions and their outcome in terms of their underlying motives and goals."[33]

Although according to the principles of adequacy and the subjective interpretation, social scientific theories must ultimately be based on subjective meaning and be understandable to the social actors, according to Schutz there are crucial differences between social science and commonsense constructs. Commonsense constructs are formed from "Here" within the world of lived experience. "They take a stock of socially derived and socially approved knowledge for granted."[34] But the social scientist has no "Here" within the social world, or more precisely "he considers his position within it and the system of relevances attached to it as irrelevant for his scientific understanding."[35] Rather "the scientific problem . . . determines alone the structure of relevance."[36] Despite this independence from common sense, Schutz insists that a social scientist "has to interpret [social action patterns] in terms of their subjective meaning lest he abandon any hope of grasping 'social reality.'"[37] Thus, in order to comply with the postulate of subjective meaning, "the scientific observer proceeds in a way similar to that of the observer of a social interaction pattern in the world of everyday life, although guided by an entirely different system of relevances."[38]

Schutz's Analysis of Nagel

According to Schutz, Nagel interpreted Weber as maintaining that the social sciences "seek to 'understand' social phenomena in terms of 'meaningful' categories of human experience and that, therefore, the 'causal functional' approach of the natural sciences is not appropriate in social inquiry."[39] On Nagel's interpretation of Weber, said Schutz, Weber maintained "all socially significant human behavior is an expression of motivated psychic states . . . ." Because of this "the social scientist cannot be satisfied with viewing social processes simply as concatentations of 'externally related' events, and that the establishment of correlations or even universal relations cannot be his ultimate goal. On the contrary, he must construct 'ideal types' or 'models of motivation' in terms of which he seeks to 'understand' overt social behavior by imputing springs of action to the actors involved in it."[40]

Schutz summed up Nagel's criticisms of Weber's theory of Verstehen as follows. First, Nagel rejected the view often associated with Verstehen that in order to know the springs of human action one must undergo the actor's psychic experience. Second, Nagel argued that the imputation of a psychic state to the actor by means of empathetic identification may be mistaken. Third, Nagel maintained that an objective or behavioristic social science in principle can provide as much understanding of social phenomena as an approach using subjectively meaningful categories.

Schutz and Nagel agree that all knowledge is discovered through processes of controlled inquiry and that it is statable in propositional and intersubjectively verifiable form. They also agree that in the empirical sciences that theory means "the explicit formulation of determinate relations between a set of variables in terms of which a fairly extensive class of empirically ascertainable regularities can be explained,"[41] and maintain that the fact that regularities in the social sciences are of limited scope and permit only a narrow range of predictions does not show a fundamental difference between the natural and social sciences. They are also in accord in maintaining that it is not necessary for the observer to identify with the social agent in order to understand the agent's motives. However, Schutz argued that he knew no social scientist who held the subjective position and "[m]ost certainly this was not the position of Max Weber"[42] and that in attributing this view to Weber, Nagel has seriously misunderstood him.

Critique of Sensationalistic Empiricism

Schutz saw Nagel's alleged misunderstanding of Weber as symptomatic of a deeper problem: his sensationalistic empiricism which "identifies experience with sensory observation and which assumes that the only alternative to controlled and, therefore, objective sensory observation is that of subjective and, therefore, uncontrolled and unverifiable introspection."[43] Rather than expose the hidden presupposition of this sort of empiricism, Schutz attempted to defend "a few rather simple propositions."[44]

Obviously influenced by Husserl's notion of the life-world, Schutz argued first that the primary goal of the social sciences is to obtain organized knowledge of social reality:

By the term "social reality" I wish to understand the sum total of objects and occurrences within which the social cultural world as experienced by the common sense thinking of men living their daily lives among their fellow-men, connected with them in manifold relations of interaction. It is the world of cultural objects and social institutions into which we all are born, within which we have to find our bearings, and with which we have to come to terms. From the outset, we, the actors on the social scene, experience the world we live in as a world both of nature and culture, not a private but intersubjective one, that is, as a world common to all of us, either given or potentially accessible to everyone; and this involves intercommunication and language.[45]

Schutz argued next that all forms of naturalism and logical empiricism assume this life-world: "Intersubjectivity, interaction, intercommunication, and language are simply presupposed as the unclarified foundations of these theories. They assume, as it were, that the social scientist has already solved his fundamental problem before scientific inquiry starts."[46] Controllable sensory observation—the method of logical empiricism—presupposes the life-world in which scientist A understands what scientist B observed, what A's goals of inquiry are, why A thought the observed fact worthy of being observed, and so on. This understanding, according to Schutz, is not achieved by introspection, behavioral explanations, or identification with social actors.

Finally, Schutz maintained that the empiricist restriction of experience to sensory observation excludes several dimensions of social reality from possible inquiry. For example, the meaning of overt behavior to the social actors, the behavior of the observer, negative actions (intentional refrainings), delusory beliefs that seem true to the participants, social relations that are not experienced in face-to-face contacts. He held that although knowledge of these aspects of experience is fragmentary, often inconsistent, and comes in various degrees of clarity, it is as much a part of the life-world as the sensory experience of the empiricists.

Evaluation of Schutz's Position

What can one say about Schutz's phenomenological-based social science? Fortunately for our purposes here we need not evaluate the foundations of Husserl's phenomenology in order to come to grips with the basic problems of Schutz's position. In what follows, I will consider: (1) the a priori limitations placed on social scientific theorizing by the postulates of subjective interpretation and adequacy, (2) the particular limitations placed on social science by Schutz's restricted view of social scientific theories, (3) the epistemological status of Schutz's characterization of the life-world, (4) Schutz's critique of sensationalistic empiricism and of Nagel's interpretation of Verstehen, (5) Schutz's interpretation of Weber's views on Verstehen.

(1) The a Priori Limitations Created by the Postulates

Schutz's methodology imposes a priori limitations on the social sciences. Why must social scientific theories be formulated so that it is possible for the actors to understand them in terms of their commonsense categories? Why should it make any difference to social scientists if their theories allow the actors to understand their own behavior in terms of social scientists' theories? The crucial question surely is whether the social scientists can understand the actors' behaviors in terms of their own theories. Schutz realizes that social scientists are guided by "a different system of relevances" and that the scientific problem "determines alone" the structure of relevance. Yet he inexplicably insists that a social scientific theory be formulated in such a way that it is not dictated entirely by the system of relevances of social scientists.

On general methodological grounds restrictions like Schutz's are surely harmful. Since the commonsense categories of the actor may be imprecise and muddled, a reformulation, an explication, or even a replacement of the commonsense categories would certainly seem to be in order as it is in other scientific fields. Furthermore, scientific practice seems to belie such a restriction. Thus, for example, Tom Burns has shown that in several sociological studies the scientific explanation given of people's behavior is in sharp contrast to those given by the actors themselves.[47] As a case in point, "Vilhelm Aubert's study of the judiciary in Norway, when it was first published, evoked violent reaction among the legal profession precisely because it pointed to the fact that, in giving sentences, judges appeared to be following a tacit code which contravened the explicit code of equality before the law."[48] Indeed, Burns has argued that sociology has a crucial function, namely, that of exposing the falsehoods and deceptions of the commonsense ideas of the actors about their own actions. In turn, Victor Turner in his study of Ndembu ritual[49] has introduced theories and concepts based upon psychoanalytic and sociological theory that clearly transcend the primitive thinking of the natives concerning the use of symbols. And Lévi-Strauss has introduced explanatory notions that go well beyond those of the natives whose behavior he was attempting to understand. This, of course, is not to say that all of these social scientists' explanations are successful. Far from it. Lévi-Strauss' theory, for example, has been severely criticized.[50] But the problems with his work do not stem from the fact that, departing from the commonsense thinking of the natives, it does not provide an interpretation of meaning for the social actors. On the contrary, the assumption has been that social scientists are perfectly justified in introducing explanatory categories and theories that are quite foreign to the people whose behavior they are trying to explain.

It is difficult to believe that Schutz would really be opposed to these sorts of social scientific theories. Perhaps a weaker interpretation of his position is possible. So far I have considered the postulate of adequacy as a restriction on social scientific explanations. However, at one point he said that the categories of the actors' needs in social situations are "first order constructs" of the social sciences and the second level constructs must be "erected" on these.[51] This suggests that explanatory concepts which are different from commonsense categories can be introduced so long as they are based in some unspecified way on the commonsense categories of the actors. The crucial question is exactly how these second order constructs must be related to the first order constructs for there is a clear danger here of making the relation either too restrictive or too empty.

On the one hand, this restriction is empty unless it clearly excludes some second order concepts. On the other hand, if some second order concepts are excluded, what a priori grounds could be given to justify their exclusion? A similar problem was noted when we discussed Winch. It will be recalled that he at one point spoke vaguely of scientific concepts "presupposing" the understanding of the social actor, and what he meant was not clear. Alan Ryan has interpreted Winch to mean that categories of the actors are used to identify the subject matter to be explained, but once this has been identified, explanatory theory and categories can be introduced that go beyond the actors' point of view. Perhaps this is close to what Schutz has in mind by saying that the second order concepts of social scientists must be erected on the first order concepts of the social actors. If so, this restriction on social science explanations is too much. However, as in the case of Winch, there is no good reason why social scientists should start by identifying their subject matter in terms of the categories of the actors.

A similar objection can be made to the postulate of subjective interpretation. This seems to require that the basic explanatory model of all the social sciences must be formulated in terms that are subjectively meaningful to the actor. This requirement is urged "lest [the social scientist] abandon any hope of grasping 'social reality.'" But the social scientist can grasp social reality in many ways, not all of which are in terms that are meaningful to the social actor.

Now Schutz at times seemed to identify explanations in terms of everyday common sense categories with ones in terms of subjective meaning of the actor and to identify subjective meanings of explanations with ones in terms of motives, beliefs, emotions, and the like. Now although such an identification may be the correct one to make in our society and culture, it is not obvious that it is the correct one to make in all cases. For it is not implausible to suppose that in the case of some nonliterate cultures commonsense categories will not be in terms of motives, beliefs, emotions, etc. A native might believe that a person has been possessed by an evil spirit and that this is why he is acting the way he is. He might not believe, what is in fact the truth, that this person thinks that he has been possessed by evil spirits and because of this he is acting in certain ways. An explanation that is understandable in terms of common sense in this case would be one in terms of evil spirit possession, and not in terms of belief in evil spirit possession. Thus to require explanations to be understandable in what are to the natives commonsense terms is unacceptable.

(2) A Priori Limitations on the Type of Theories

Schutz also placed unnecessary limitations on social science by his narrow construal of what can constitute a social scientific explanation when he maintained that the only legitimate type of explanation is in terms of the typical behavior of ideal actors. However, the typical behavior of idealized actors is surely only one type of explanation used in the social sciences and is not even appropriate in answering certain types of questions. For example, functional explanations account for the persistence of a societal practice because of the benefits (social cohesion, stability, economic efficiency, outlet to antisocial behavior, etc.) that they confer on the society. Thus, Marvin Harris explained the practice of prolonged lactation found in hunter-gatherer societies as a means of depressing fertility.[52] It is far from clear, however, that this and other functional explanations can be fitted into Schutz's model. The same can be said for structural explanations. Here the attempt is to explain some important feature of a society as a causal sequence of some social structure, for example, state forms, economic systems, or transportation networks. For example, Samuel R. Williamson, Jr., has argued that the prewar European alliance structure was an important causal factor of the outbreak of World War I.[53] Here again Schutz's model does not seem to fit very well.

In addition, Leon Goldstein has persuasively argued that social scientists try to account for the development of some particular social world and explanations of this sort seem difficult to account for in terms of Schutz's model. According to Goldstein, metaphorically speaking, this sort of inquiry is outside the subjective standpoint of actors:

> Consequently, it is clearly not social science of the sort that the phenomenological philosophers insist is the only proper way to achieve the most desirable type of social knowledge. Any historical account which is not an attempt to reconstitute a social world which once was but is no more, but is, rather, an attempt to trace the development of institutions, must, perforce, fail to satisfy the requirements of the phenomenological approach.[54]

Indeed, Schutz's model seems to come closest to what Daniel Little has called rational aggregate explanations. As Little has described this type of explanation, individuals are assumed to have a set of interests against which they rationally evaluate alternative courses of action. Social actions are explained as the aggregate result of a large number of individuals acting on the basis of rational choice.[55] But this model of explanation does not exhaust all the varieties of explanations discussed by Little, let alone all types of rational explanation. Rational aggregate explanation relies on a "thin" theory of explanation since it depends on abstract descriptions of the goals in terms of interests and utilities and also postulates a simple mode of reasoning. In contrast to thin theory, "thick" theories of rationality rely on detailed accounts of norms, values, cultural assumptions, metaphors, religious beliefs and practices.[56] However, whether the thin theory is adequate in all cases where rational explanation is appropriate is uncertain.

(3) The Epistemological Status of Schutz's Characterization of the Life-World

One important question that should be asked is how one is to tell that Schutz's characterization of the life-world is correct. He gives many descriptions of commonsense knowledge in his work which are usually of a general nature, in at least two senses of "general." First, these statements do not seem to be simply descriptions of Schutz's own commonsense knowledge but purport to have a much wider scope, presumably at least as wide as our culture and perhaps much wider. Second, they are general in that they do not purport to be descriptions of particular contents of commonsense thinking but rather of the descriptions of the structure of commonsense thinking. Yet they are not obviously empirical generalizations that can be subjected to empirical test. How then can they be objectively checked? For example, how does one reconcile a disagreement between different phenomenologists over a description of some structure of commonsense thinking?

To make matters worse, Schutz's characterization is typically couched in the specialized language of phenomenology. For example, he speaks of "the horizon of familiarity," "pre-acquaintance," "system of relevances," "biographical determined situations, " "We-relationship," and "course-of-action types," and so on in describing the life-world. But then, in order to evaluate his characterization of commonsense thinking, it will often be necessary either to translate his descriptions into other terms or to learn his specialized vocabulary.[57] Yet it is not clear what language would be an appropriate translation medium or exactly how learning the language of phenomenology would help in testing it.

The difficulties of validating Schutz's statements about commonsense thinking can be illustrated by his discussion of the Reciprocity of Perspectives. According to Schutz, in commonsense thinking the same object means something different to different people because of their different perspectives and biographies. But commonsense thinking "overcomes the differences in individual perspectives" by two basic idealizations. First, there is the idealization of the interchangeability of standpoints: "I take it for granted—and assume my fellow-man does the same—that if I change places with him so that his 'here' becomes mine, I shall be at the same distance from things and see them with the same typicality as he actually does."[58] Second, there is the idealization of the congruency of the system of relevances: "Until counterevidence, I take it for granted—and assume my fellow-man does the same—that the differences in perspectives originating in our unique biographical situations are irrelevant for the purposes at hand and that he and I, that 'We' assume that both of us have selected and interpreted the actual or potential common objects and their features in an identical manner or at least an 'empirically identical' manner, i.e., one sufficient for all practical purposes."[59]

What is the status of these so-called idealizations? Are they hypotheses postulated by Schutz in order to account for certain behavior? If so, have these hypotheses been tested and how? Are there alternative explanations of this behavior? If so, why are they to be preferred to these alternatives? If these idealizations are not hypotheses, what are they? If they are not, why should we believe them to be true? The difficulty of understanding the epistemological status of Schutz's characterizations of the structure of commonsense thinking seems to be a special case of the difficulty of understanding the epistemological status of phenomenological statements in general.[60]

The problematic epistemic status of Schutz's characterization of the life-world raises doubts about his claim concerning its importance to the foundations of the social sciences. Even if the life-world is basic to social understanding, do we have any reliable knowledge about what its characteristics are? The world of common sense may indeed be presupposed by naturalism and logical empiricism, as Schutz contended, but given the problem of verifying his descriptions of it, we have no reason to suppose that its makeup matches his descriptions.

(4) Critique of Sensationalistic Empiricism and Nagel

Although Schutz was critical of what he called "sensationalistic empiricism" he made no attempt to define clearly what he meant. I will take him to mean the view that all immediate experience is of private sense data, for example, of color patches, shapes, smells, tastes, and the like. Empiricists of this kind deny that I can see directly that a brown table is front of me, let alone that I can see that the table is hard and made from oak. What I can see directly is that there is a brown rectangular patch in my visual field and everything I believe concerning the table is based on inference from my sense data.

Now it is true that some empiricists have advocated this view. For example, Ernst Mach advocated sensationalism.[61] But not all empiricists or even all logical empiricists have done so. Indeed, there was a controversy among logical positivists about the methodological status of private experience, that is, about whether sense data language should be the basic language of science.[62] Although Ernest Nagel was never completely identified with logical empiricism he was influenced by this movement. The question remains, however, of what view Nagel held on sense data. Although this is impossible to tell from the 1952 article criticized by Schutz in his 1954 paper, his view is clearly stated in his major work, *The Structure of Science* (1961). There Nagel said,

As a matter of psychological fact, elementary sense data are not the primitive material of experience out of which all our ideas are built like houses of initially isolated bricks. On the contrary, sense experience normally is a response to complex though unanalyzed patterns of qualities and relations, and the response usually involves exercise of habits of interpretation and recognition based on tacit beliefs and inferences which cannot be warranted by any single momentary experience. Accordingly, the language we normally use to describe even our immediate experience is the common language of social communication and collective experience, and not a language whose meaning is supposedly fixed by references to conceptually uninterpreted atoms of sensations. [63]

So whatever Nagel's position at the time Schutz criticized him, his later views are far removed from sensationalistic empiricism.

Now, according to Schutz, sensationalistic empiricists exclude several dimensions of social reality from possible inquiry, among which are the meaning of overt behavior to the social actors, the behavior of the observer, negative actions (intentional refrainings), delusory beliefs that seem true to the participants, social relations that are not experienced in face-to-face contacts. However, even if experience is given a rather narrow interpretation such that we cannot have, for example, *direct* experience of the meaning of overt behavior to the social actors, negative actions (intentional refrainings), and so on, there is no reason on empiricist principles why these things cannot be investigated indirectly.

For example, the meaning of some piece of overt behavior to an actor can be investigated by proposing a hypothesis about what the behavior means to the actor and by testing this indirectly, for instance, by investigating what the actor would say in response to certain relevant questions about the behavior. Very much the same thing can be said for other items on Schutz's list of alleged exclusions. Negative actions (intentional refrainings), delusory beliefs that seem true to the participants, social relations that are not experienced in face-to-face contacts, can all be investigated by the method of hypothesis; that is, by hypothesizing unobservable mechanisms and processes and deducing test consequences. Obviously social scientists influenced by logical empiricism can and have investigated the observers of social actors. For example, they have investigated the behavior of social scientists who are such observers. Of course, social scientists who investigate observers do not observe their own behavior in doing so: In order to preserve objectivity the subject and object of the research are kept separate. Whether this is preserved on Schutz's account is unclear.

Aside from his alleged commitment to sensationalistic empiricism, Schutz's main complaint about Nagel is his misunderstanding of Weber. Schutz implied that Nagel wrongly interpreted Weber as maintaining that understanding a social agent involves identifying with the agent. It is true that Nagel criticized this view in his 1952 paper, "Problems of

Concept and Theory Formation in the Social Sciences." However, it is doubtful that he was attributing it to Weber. Although Weber was footnoted once in this paper, the footnote related to a different point.[64] In *The Structure of Science*, Nagel made it clear that his position on a related issue was similar, if not identical, to Weber's. "Competent evidence for assumptions about the attributes and actions of other men is often difficult to obtain, but it is certainly not obtained merely by introspection of one's own or examining one's own belief, as to how such sentiments are likely to be manifested in overt action—as responsible advocates of 'interpretative' explanations have themselves often emphasized (e.g., with vigor and illumination by Max Weber.)"[65] Although a few sentences later he criticized the view that identification with a social actor is necessary for understanding, he certainly did not attribute this position to Weber. Indeed the close juxtaposition of his criticism and his favorable mention of Weber suggest that he did not think Weber held this view.

(5) Schutz's Interpretation of Weber

Schutz interpreted Weber as advocating that human action be understood according to the postulate of subjective meaning and, since he said that he held the same postulate, he argued that his theory was in accord with Weber. Indeed, he argued that this postulate is what was involved in Weber's notion of Verstehen. "The social scientist, such as Max Weber, however, called Verstehen subjective because its goal is to find out what the actor means in his action, in contrast to the meaning which the action has for the actor's partner or neutral observer."[66] Further, he argued that Weber did not maintain that identification with a social actor was necessary for understanding the actor's action.[67]

However, Schutz neglected two aspects of Weber's position. He ignored the causal aspect of Weber's methodology although when looked at in one way, what Schutz called the postulate of subjective meaning was for Weber a requirement that causal explanations must meet. For Weber, as for the positivists, the object of social sciences was to achieve causal explanation. He differs from the positivists in maintaining that social science is restricted to explanations of a certain kind. The function of rational explanatory Verstehen was to meet this additional requirement.

Second, Weber did not maintain that identification with the social actor is necessary for Verstehen when he restricted Verstehen to the rational explanatory kind, although Weber *did* suppose that identification was necessary for emotional empathetic Verstehen. To be sure, Weber emphasized rational explanatory Verstehen in his writings and said little about emotional empathetic Verstehen. However, as previously noted, he did suggest that it is a great help to be able to put oneself imaginatively in the place of the social actor and thus empathetically participate in his or her experience. This aspect of Weber's concept of Verstehen is also neglected by Schutz.

In short, Schutz eliminated all aspects of Weber's theory that did not fit his interpretation of social science. The causal aspect of Weber's view was exorcised and the obscure function of emotional empathetic Verstehen in Weber's methodology was not discussed.

Conclusion

The problems of Schutz's position indicate that he not only has misunderstood Nagel and the empiricist tradition represented by him but that his own account of Verstehen introduced a priori unjustified restrictions on social scientific inquiry. He wrongly maintained that Nagel embraced sensationalism and misconstrued Nagel's account of Weber. Schutz's general restrictions on social scientific theorizing, namely, that they must be formulated so that it is possible for the actors to understand them in terms of their commonsense categories, was unjustified. Moreover, the restrictions he placed on the type of social scientific explanation, namely, those in terms of typical behavior of ideal actors, is also unacceptable. In addition, the unclear and dubious epistemological status of his claims concerning the life-world suggest that the life-world cannot have the important role in the foundation of the social sciences that he claimed for it.

There is no a priori reason that a phenomenological approach to the social sciences must have some of the problems that are found in Schutz's theory. Such an approach could be considered useful for certain purposes and in certain contexts. A sensitive description of the life-world in terms of the commonsense categories of the actors and explanations in terms of the typical behavior of ideal actors might well be fruitful and important under certain conditions. Where this approach and Schutz go wrong is in supposing that it defines the limits of social inquiry.

Notes

1. A. R. Lacey, *Dictionary of Philosophy* (New York: Charles Scribner's Sons, 1976), p. 158.
2. Ibid. See also Joseph J. Kockelman, "Some Fundamental Themes of Husserl's Phenomenology," *Phenomenology*, ed. Joseph J. Kockelman (Garden City, NY: Doubleday and Company, Inc., 1967), pp. 24-36.
3. Richard Schmitt, "Edmund Husserl," *Encyclopedia of Philosophy*, vol. 4, ed. Paul Edwards (New York: Macmillan Publishing Co, Inc., 1967), p. 98.
4. Fred R. Dallmayr and Thomas A. McCarthy, eds., *Understanding and Social Inquiry* (Notre Dame, IN: University of Notre Dame Press, 1977), pp. 219-20.
5. Ibid., p. 220.
6. See Fred R. Dallmayr, "Phenomenology and Social Science: An Overview and Appraisal," *Explorations in Phenomenology*, ed. David Carr and Edward S. Casely (The Hague: Martinus Nifhoff, 1973), pp. 133-66. On the other hand, H. P. Neisser in "The Phenomenological Approach in Social Science," *Philosophy and Phenomenological Research* 20,1959, p. 209f, and Maurice Natanson in "A Study in Philosophy and the Social Sciences," *Philosophy of Social Science,* ed. Maurice Natanson (New York: Random House, 1963), p. 273, seem to deny the relevance of Husserlian phenomenological to what has come to be called phenomenology social science. But also see Natanson, ibid., p. 283, where he maintains that Husserlian phenomenology in the broad sense is relevant. See Leon Goldstein, "The Phenomenological and Naturalistic Approaches to the Social," *Philosophy of Social Science*, ed. Natanson, p. 287, for a fuller discussion.
7. Joseph J. Kockelman, "Life-World and World-Experience Life," *Phenomenology*, ed. Joseph J. Kockelman, p. 196.
8. Dallmayr and McCarthy, eds. *Understanding and Social Inquiry,* p. 220.
9. Ibid.
10. Alfred Schutz, "Concept and Theory Formation in the Social Sciences," *The Journal of Philosophy*, vol. 51, 1954, pp. 257-73: reprinted in Maurice Natanson, ed., *Philosophy of Social Science* (New York: Random House, 1963), pp. 231-49.
11. Alfred Schutz, "Common Sense and Scientific Interpretations of Human Action," *Philosophy and Phenomenological Research* 14, 1953, pp. 1-37; reprinted in Natanson ed., *Philosophy of Social Science*, pp. 302-46.
12. For an overview of Schutz's position, see Helmut R. Wagner, "Introduction," in Helmut R. Wagner ed., *Alfred Schutz on Phenomenological and Social Relations* (Chicago: The University of Chicago Press, 1970), pp. 1–50.
13. Schutz bases his evaluation of Nagel on Nagel's "Problems of Concept and Theory Formation in the Social Sciences," in *Science, Language, and Human Rights* (American Philosophical Association, Eastern Division, Philadelphia, University of Pennsylvania Press, 1952), vol.1, pp. 43-64; reprinted in Natanson, *Philosophy of Social Science*, pp. 189-209.
14. Schutz, "Concept and Theory Formation in the Social Sciences," p. 239.
15. Ibid., p. 240.
16. Ibid.
17. Ibid., p. 241.
18. Ibid.
19. Ibid.
20. Ibid.

21. Ibid., p. 242. The same point is made by Schutz, "Common Sense and Scientific Interpretations of Human Action," in Natanson ed., *Philosophy of Social Science*, p. 303.
22. Schutz, "Concept and Theory Formation in the Social Sciences," p. 245.
23. Ibid., p. 242.
24. Ibid., p. 243. See also Schutz, "Common Sense and Scientific Interpretations of Human Action," pp. 306-309.
25. Schutz, "Concept and Theory Formation in the Social Sciences," p. 243.
26. Schutz, "Common Sense and Scientific Interpretations of Human Action," pp. 310-12.
27. Schutz, "Concept and Theory Formation in the Social Sciences," p. 245. See Schutz, "Common Sense and Scientific Interpretations of Human Action," pp. 313-14.
28. Schutz, "Concept and Theory Formation in the Social Sciences," p. 247.
29. Schutz, "Common Sense and Scientific Interpretations of Human Action," p. 342.
30. Schutz, "Concept and Theory Formation in the Social Sciences," p. 247. See also Schutz, "Common Sense and Scientific Interpretations of Human Action," p. 343.
31. Schutz, "Common Sense and Scientific Interpretations of Human Action," pp. 342-43.
32. Alfred Schutz, "The Problem of Rationality in the Social World," Dorothy Emmet and Alasdair MacIntyre, eds. *Sociological Theory and Philosophical Analysis* (London:Macmillan and Co., 1970), p. 112.
33. Schutz, "Concept and Theory Formation in the Social Sciences," p. 248.
34. Schutz, "Common Sense and Scientific Interpretations of Human Action," p. 337.
35. Ibid., p. 338.
36. Ibid., p. 339.
37. Ibid.
38. Ibid.
39. Schutz, "Concept and Theory Formation in the Social Sciences," p. 233.
40. Ibid., pp. 233-34.
41. Ibid., p. 235.
42. Ibid.
43. Ibid., pp. 235-36.
44. Ibid., p. 236.
45. Ibid.
46. Ibid.
47. Tom Burns, "Sociological Explanations" in Emmet and MacIntyre, eds. *Sociological Theory and Philosophical Analysis*, pp. 55-76.
48. Ibid., p. 64.
49. Victor Turner, "Symbols in Ndembu Ritual," *Sociological Theory and Philosophical Analysis,* pp. 150-82.
50. For criticisms of Lévi-Strauss, see Edmund Leach, "Telstar and the Aborigines or la Pensée Sauvage," *Sociological Theory and Philosophical Analysis*, pp. 183-203, and Peter Worsley, "Groote Eylandt Totemism and Le Totémisme Aujour d'hui," ibid., pp. 204–23.
51. Schutz, "Concept and Theory Formation in the Social Sciences," p. 245.
52. See Douglas Little, *Varieties of Social Explanation* (Boulder, CO: Westview Press, 1990), pp. 94–97.

53. Ibid., pp. 102-106.
54. Goldstein, "The Phenomenological and Naturalistic Approaches to the Social," Natanson ed., *Philosophy of Social Science*, pp. 296-97.
55. Little, *Varieties of Social Explanation*, pp. 40–42.
56. Ibid., p. 41.
57. Wagner, for example, provides his readers with a glossary of terms. See Wagner, ed. *Alfred Schutz on Phenomenological and Social Relations,* pp. 316-23.
58. Schutz, "Common Sense and Scientific Interpretations of Human Action," p. 311.
59. Ibid.
60. See Richard Schmitt, "Phenomenology," *Encyclopedia of Philosophy*, vol. 6, ed. Paul Edwards (New York: Macmillan Publishing Co., Inc., 1967), pp. 135–51.
61. Peter Alexander, "Ernst Mach," *Encyclopedia of Philosophy*, vol. 5, ed. Paul Edwards, p. 116.
62. John Passmore, "Logical Positivism," *Encyclopedia of Philosophy*, vol. 5, ed. Paul Edwards, pp. 55–56.
63. Ernest Nagel, *The Structure of Science* (New York: Harcourt, Brace and World, 1961), pp. 121-22.
64. Nagel, "Problems of Concept and Theory Formation in the Social Sciences," p. 200.
65. Nagel, *The Structure of Science*, pp. 482–83.
66. Schutz, "Concept and Theory Formation in the Social Sciences," p. 240.
67. Ibid., p. 235.

7

Verstehen and the Sciences of Man

In previous chapters we saw that a Verstehen approach can prosper in various philosophical environments—from Ordinary Language Philosophy to Popperianism to phenomenology. Perhaps it should not come as a surprise, then, that a Verstehen approach can be developed without a well-developed philosophical ancestry as a foundation. In this chapter its use by the philosopher Charles Taylor will be considered.[1] Although Taylor mentions Dilthey, Gadamer, Ricoeur, and Habermas in the first paragraph of his well-known paper, "Interpretation and the Sciences of Man,"[2] he does not cite them again, and in contrast to Winch, Jarvie, and Schutz he does not tie his position to any particular thinker. Like Popper who did not use the term "Verstehen" but who spoke instead of the logic of the situation, Taylor typically forsakes the term "Verstehen," preferring the more fashionable "interpretation." However, despite Taylor's failure to use the term "Verstehen" in this paper his views are a variant to the Verstehen theory: Social practices are to be interpreted in terms of the social meaning of the actors.

Taylor's paper is one of the most frequently cited[3] and reprinted[4] English-language essays advocating an interpretive approach to the social sciences. There are several reasons for its popularity. First of all, his paper does not explicitly rely on European traditions of Verstehen and hermeneutics that English-speaking students often have difficulty understanding. Second, although Taylor's arguments are abstract and general, he cites social science literature, primarily from the field of political science, to illustrate his main points. Third, his position is an extreme one that can be sharply contrasted with the naturalistic, positivistic position that is usually associated with mainstream social science. Thus, he makes no attempt to argue, as David Braybrooke[5] does, that the naturalistic and the interpretive approaches have complementary insights.

Taylor presents a view that has appeal for many students of the social sciences. Drawing on the analogy of the interpretation of a literary text, he argues that the aim of the social sciences is to provide an interpretation of the social meanings connected with the social practices and institutions of particular societies, rather than to furnish causal explanations and predictions. The interpretation of social meanings involves, in his view, clarifying the field of concepts—the interconnections of a system of notions—that constitutes a social practice (intersubjective meaning) and provides for shared values and a sense of community (common meanings). The meanings to be clarified are those of the social actors who engage in the practice or are members of the institution in question.

According to Taylor there is no objective way of validating such interpretations. Rather, the validation of an interpretation is a circular procedure (the hermeneutic circle) and disagreements about interpretations ultimately rest on conflicting intuitions. In particular, objective validation by appeal to brute data—that is, data that one cannot question by further interpretations—is not available in the social sciences, although it is in the natural sciences. Nevertheless, he holds that the social meanings revealed by interpretive procedures are nonsubjective and that one can contrast these with the subjective meanings appealed to, for example, by mainstream political scientists. Although one can infer these subjective meanings from brute data, they fail to capture the social meanings expressed in interpretations. However, social meanings do not seem to be based on causal considerations.

Despite the popularity of Taylor's paper I know of only one extended critique of it.[6] This is unfortunate for the paper has many problems. In particular, Taylor's view of the scope of social science is too limited, his thesis that the interpretation of social phenomena does not involve causal considerations is mistaken, interpretations need not be circular, his reliance on nonsubjective meaning sits uneasily with his subjective methodology of interpretation, and nonsubjective meaning need not be for the actor.

Although Taylor's paper, "Interpretation and the Sciences of Man," will be the main critical focus of this chapter, towards the end I will consider how in some of his later papers on the philosophy of social science he has modified his position and will ask if his modifications are able to meet my criticisms of his crucial thesis.

The Scope of Interpretive Social Science

Taylor maintains that the aim of the interpretation of a text or a social practice is "to bring to light an underlying coherence or sense"[7] of the text or practice. According to him this aim presumes three things. First, there must be "an object or a field of objects, about which we can speak in terms of coherence or its absence, of making sense or non-sense."[8] What would this object or field of objects be in the social sciences? I take it that it would be a society, or else the institutions within a society, or perhaps the social practices of actors within the society or institutions. Second, there must be a distinction between the meaning embodied in a text or a social practice and the expression of that meaning. Third, the meaning of a text or social practice is for or by a subject. Taylor believes that it is this last requirement, when applied to a social practice, that distinguishes the human from the natural sciences. One can speak of the meaning or coherence of a certain object studied in the natural sciences, for example, a rock formation. But a rock formation neither has meaning for the rocks nor is an expression of meaning. In the social sciences, however, the meaning of a social practice has meaning for the social actors and the social actors in turn might give expression to this meaning.

Is it a misuse of language to speak of the meaning of a social practice? Do only linguistic expressions have meaning? Not according to Taylor. He admits that the meaning of a social practice is different from the meaning of a linguistic expression but maintains that it would be "hard to argue that it is an illegitimate use of the term."[9] We speak of the meaning of certain social actions or situations and we do so correctly, as for example when we say: "What is the meaning of this ritual?"

According to Taylor in order to understand the meaning of a social practice one must keep in mind three things. First, one must distinguish between the meaning of the practice and the practice itself. Second, one must understand the meaning that a practice has for a subject or a group of subjects. Third, one must remember that the meaning of a practice is always in a field; that is, it is connected with the meaning of other things. To use one of his examples, we might interpret some social practice in terms of the concept of shame. However, situations are shameful only for subjects. Further, there is a distinction between shame and the situation or action toward which a subject feels shame. Finally, the meaning of the term "shame" can only be "explained by reference to other concepts which, in turn, cannot be understood without reference to shame."[10]

Taylor is maintaining that the understanding of a social practice or a social institution or a society must be in terms of the meaning it has for the social actors. This interpretation consists in connecting some elements of the practice or institutions to other elements in a coherent pattern. It is not completely clear this could ever involve connecting the elements of a practice or institution with the elements outside the practice or institution, for example, to historical factors, geographical variables, or psychological dimensions. The general impression Taylor conveys is that, for him, understanding is necessarily internal understanding in the sense introduced in chapter 1: One understands a social practice or institution by considering the practice as whole and connecting its parts or aspects to one another rather than by connecting the practice or institution to things outside itself. In any case, it seems clear that Taylor assumes, as Dray did, that one must understand a social practice under a description that the social actor would give or at least find intelligible.

Now no one would deny that interpreting the meaning of social practices in this way is something that social scientists should be doing. The crucial critical question is how important is it? Perhaps the most plausible reading of "Interpretation and the Sciences of Man," is that Taylor holds either that the only task or the main task of social science is to interpret the meaning of social institutions, practices, and so on. There are two reasons for this. First, one would suppose that if he held a generous view of the scope of social science he would have said so. To be sure, he never explicitly denies that the social sciences have other jobs besides the interpretation of meaning. But none except the interpretation of the meaning of social institutions and practices is mentioned. Second, he argues against the standard empiricist approach to the social sciences which certainly attributed to the social sciences a larger scope than does Taylor. Taylor does *not* seem to maintain that the standard view is wrong only up to a point, e.g., that causal explanations are appropriate in certain areas of the social sciences or that they are appropriate relative to certain questions or goals, or that a hermeneutic approach should replace an empiricist approach only in certain areas of inquiry or only given some questions and goals. Indeed, he seems to be saying that the standard approach is wrong in all areas of the social sciences and with respect to all questions and goals.

Has Taylor exaggerated the importance of interpretation in the social sciences? There are good reasons to suppose so.[11] To be sure, many social scientists are interested in interpreting the meaning of social institutions and practices, but they do not limit themselves to this task. Indeed, there are many important questions that social scientists need to ask once an interpretation of a social practice in Taylor's sense has been given.

Consider some of the questions social scientists might ask about, for example, menstruation taboos that have been interpreted in terms of a field of concepts. In the anthropological literature menstrual blood and menstruating women are often interpreted as being considered polluting and dangerous, things that must be avoided by men in order to prevent contamination.[12] However, Marla N. Powers has recently argued that the standard negative picture of menstruation practices is the result of Western anthropologists reading their biases onto non-Western tribal cultures and has given a different interpretation of menstruation in the American Indian society of the Oglala.[13] One can understand Powers' work as giving an alternative and presumably more adequate interpretation of the meaning of menstrual taboos than the standard account, but it does more than this. Taking the concept of life stages from the work of Arnold Van Gennep[14] and deriving the concept of *communitas* or antistructure from that of Victor Turner,[15] Powers goes on to maintain that the function of the menstrual taboo "is to give structure to what otherwise is a period of antistructure."[16]

This type of functional investigation has played a large role both in sociology and anthropology. However, it is difficult to see that it would have any role at all to play if social science investigations were limited to the interpretation of meaning. It is one thing to consider what the meaning of the menstrual taboo in the Oglala society is and quite another to determine the function of this taboo. Powers does both, yet Taylor's concept of the social sciences seems to include only the former. One major obstacle to Taylor's incorporating a functional analysis into his scheme is that functional concepts need not be ones that members of the culture understand, and hence might have no meaning for the social actors. Thus, there is no reason to suppose that the function of menstrual taboos that Powers attributes to American Indian tribal societies had meaning for the members of these societies.

Given the limited scope of her paper, Powers does not ask other important questions about the menstrual taboos, but there is no a priori reason why she could not. She seems to assume that the defilement interpretation of menstruation is correct for Western societies. If she is right, then one naturally wonders what the basis of the difference between Western and non-Western societies is. Why does menstruation have a negative meaning in the one case and not in the other? Furthermore, if menstrual taboos have a function in non-Western societies, do they have a dysfunction in Western societies? If so, what is it? Another obvious line of inquiry has to do with the psychological effects of menstrual taboos on women. Social scientists have investigated similar questions in other contexts[17] and there seems to be no a priori reason to suppose that they could not investigate them in the present case. However, these questions seem to be excluded a priori from Taylor's scheme. A third line of inquiry would be to pursue questions about the origins of the menstrual taboos.[18] Why have they taken the form they do? Why have they developed so differently in Western and non-Western societies? Social science should be able to pursue these questions but it is not clear that Taylor's interpretive social science would allow them to.

The menstruation taboo example should make it clear that most plausible interpretations of Taylor suggested above, namely, that either the only task or the main task of social science is to interpret the meaning of social institutions, practices, and so on, exclude a variety of questions that social scientists could profitably consider. Unless Taylor gives good reasons why they should not be included in the purview of social science, his position does not seem reasonable. Does he provide such arguments? At one point in his paper he raises criticisms against what he calls "the influential 'developmental approach'" which relies on the concept of function.[19] However, he does not show that functional questions do not belong in the social sciences.[20] His opposition to a functional approach seems to be that this approach is ethnocentric and uses functions such as "interest articulation" and "interest aggregation" whose "definition is strongly influenced by the bargaining culture of our civilization, but which is far from being guaranteed appropriateness elsewhere."[21] However, there is no a priori reason why the functional approach must be ethnocentric in this sense. Social scientists obviously should attribute functions to social institutions that are appropriate to the cultural contexts they study. Power's use of function concepts did precisely this.

Can Taylor's position be interpreted in a more modest way so that it is not obviously wrong? One possibility is that he should be maintaining that interpreting the meaning of social institutions, practices, and so on is important to social inquiry and that many positivistic social scientists have neglected this. On this reading, although Taylor has exaggerated the importance of interpretation in social scientific inquiry, his views nevertheless bring to light aspects of social inquiry that have been neglected. Taylor's approach would then be seen as redressing the balance and providing a complementary approach to the standard view. Unfortunately, this more modest interpretation is not supported by what Taylor says.

Causality and Interpreting Meaning

As we have seen in previous chapters, Verstehen theorists either forsake causality or put limitations on the role of causality in the social sciences. Whereas Dray, Winch, and Schutz say very little about causality, Weber and Popper place restrictions on it. Taylor is in Dray, Winch, and Schutz's camp. Although the relevance of causality to Taylor's approach to the social sciences is difficult to determine, because he hardly uses the term "cause" in his paper, the most plausible reading is that he thinks that causality is not important. I say this for the following reasons. First, he seems to believe not only that interpretation is the main task or even the only task of the social sciences but that interpretation has nothing to do with causality. Thus, he never mentions "cause" or "causality" in connection with interpreting social phenomena or even with explanations. He seems to think that interpretation is all there is to explanation in the social sciences. Second, he associates causal analysis with empirical social science, precisely the position that he opposes.

Is Taylor correct to suppose that causality is not important? If one conceives of the task of social science as more than merely interpreting the meaning of social practices, as one should, then causality inevitably plays an important role. For example, understanding which social or cultural conditions bring about a menstruation taboo or what effects such a taboo has on women's personalities involves a consideration of causes. But what about the narrower social science task of interpreting social practice? Does this not involve considerations of causality also?

There are four reasons to suppose that it does. First, if one looks at the natural sciences, one sees that questions about the meaning of many concepts are closely connected with considerations of causality. By analogy one would expect the same thing to be true in the social sciences. Second, Taylor provides no explicit argument to suppose that the social sciences would be different from the natural sciences in this respect. Third, the most plausible argument that one can construct on his behalf is unsound. Fourth, some of Taylor's own descriptions of the meaning of concepts in the social sciences implicitly assume causality.

Since the meaning of a field of concepts in the natural sciences presupposes causal considerations, unless there are relevant differences, one would expect the same thing would be true in the social sciences. For example, in medicine an understanding of the field of concepts of cardiology presupposes understanding complex causal connections having to do with heart disease, its etiology, its symptoms, and its treatment. Thus, the meaning of coronary heart disease is closely connected with the formation of atheroma in the arteries that results in a lack of oxygen to the heart and angina. It is difficult to see how one could understand the conceptual connection between the disease, the formation of atheroma, and angina unless one understood the causal connections that are involved. By analogy, one might suppose that one could not understand the conceptual connections between a humiliating situation, the feeling of shame and a behavioral disposition unless one were to understand the causal connections that are involved.

Although Taylor gives no argument based on a relevant difference, could one construct an argument in his behalf? The best argument that I can think is this: Although in cardiology there is a field of objects, e.g., heart patients, and there is a distinction between the meaning of, e.g., angina and its expression in a medical interpretation of a heart patient, there is still a crucial difference from the social sciences. The meaning of a social practice is for or by a subject and this distinguishes the human from the natural sciences.

However, it is hard to see what relevance this has to the issue of causality. The argument from the premise that X has meaning for social actor A to the conclusion that X is not a cause of A's action or that X is not causally related to factors Y and Z that are closely connected with the meaning of X is invalid. Let us suppose that the meaning of angina is not for or by a heart patient whereas the meaning of shame is for or by people who engage in certain social practices involving shame. It does not follow that the feeling of shame is not causally related to other items that are part of the field of meaning of shame or that in order to understand shame one would not have to understand these causal relations.

When one sees how Taylor, in fact, talks about the field of concepts of shame, it is clear that he implicitly assumes causal notions:

> An emotion term like "shame," for instance, essentially refers us to a certain kind of situation, the "shameful," or "humiliating," and a certain mode of response, that of hiding oneself, of covering up, or else "wiping out" the blot. That is, it is essential to this feeling's identification as shame that it be related to this situation and give rise to this type of disposition. But this situation in its turn can only be identified in relation to the feelings it provokes; and the disposition is to a goal that can similarly not be understood without reference to the feeling experienced . . . . [22]

This passage fairly bristles with causal concepts. Taylor assumes that the feeling of shame is brought about because of some humiliating situation, that is, it is caused by this situation; and this feeling brings about, that is, causes, a certain disposition to hide oneself; and so on. Thus, the field of concepts of shame involves causal considerations. This is hardly surprising since the concept of shame is found in theories of commonsense psychology which are implicitly causal. When psychologists like Freud expand and explain the insights of commonsense psychology, the causal connections implicit in our concept of shame become explicit. Thus, for Freud, shame is causally connected to sexual inhibitions and to certain forms of sexual perversion. [23]

We can conclude that Taylor has failed to provide good reasons for excluding causality from the social sciences.

Objective Validation and the Hermeneutic Circle

According to Taylor, just as one should base one's understanding of texts on interpretations, so one should base one's understanding of societies and cultures on interpretations. But how can one validate these interpretations? Taylor says that the process of validation

> cannot but move in a hermeneutical circle. A given reading of the intersubjective meaning of a society, or of a given institution or practice, may seem well founded, because it makes sense of these practices or the development of that society. But the conviction that it does make sense of this history itself is founded on further related readings. [24]

This circularity of interpreting a text can be construed either in terms of passages or whole-part relations. In interpreting a text we try to establish a certain reading of one passage by appealing to our reading of other passages. But to accept this reading of the other passages we have to accept our reading of the first. Again we try to establish an

interpretation of a whole text by appealing to some part. But our interpretation of this part is dependent on our interpretation of the whole.
Our understanding of a society is circular in the analogous way. An
interpretation of one aspect A_1 of, for example, the political process of
a society at a particular time is dependent on our understanding of
another aspect A_2 at that time. But our understanding of aspect A_2 is
dependent on our understanding of A_1. Similarly, to understand some
part of a political culture, we must have some understanding of the
whole. However, in order to understand the whole one must understand the part.

Given this construal of the interpretive process, it is small wonder
that Taylor rejects appeals to rational argument to decide conflicts in
interpretation and instead relies on intuition. He argues,

> For it means that this is not a study in which anyone can engage, regardless of their
> level of insight; that some claims of the form "If you don't understand, then your
> intuitions are at fault, are blind or inadequate," some claims of this form will be
> justified; that some differences will be nonarbitrable by further evidence, but that
> each side can only make appeal to deeper insights on the part of the other.[25]

But since different people's intuitions are based on different ways of
life and value options, Taylor argues,

> in the sciences of man insofar as they are hermeneutical there can be a valid re-
> sponse to "I don't understand," which takes the form of, not only "develop your
> intuitions," but more radically "change yourself." This puts an end to any aspira-
> tion to a value-free or "ideology-free" science of man. [26]

The clear implication of this approach—one that Taylor does not seem
to shrink from—is that there is no objective way of validating interpretations of social phenomena and hence interpretations are ultimately
based on rationally unsupported intuitions and value decisions.

Is Taylor correct? In what follows I will first show that there is a
problem analogous to the hermeneutic circle in the natural sciences
but that this has not prevented natural scientists from objectively testing their theories. Next I will maintain that the same constraints and
checks that natural scientists use to test their theories objectively can
be applied to the interpretation of texts, social institutions, and practices.[27] Finally, I will maintain that some methodologists of hermeneutics have argued for an objective approach to interpretation and that
Taylor makes no attempt to refute their position.

It is important to note that Taylor does *not* suppose that circularity
exists in the verification process of the natural sciences. Indeed, he

makes a distinction between the social sciences and the natural sciences precisely on this ground: Natural science can appeal to some neutral observational basis—what he calls "brute data"—but interpretive social science cannot. Taylor neglects to mention that a circularity similar to the one he attributed to the social sciences has been alleged to exist in the natural sciences. Writing well before Taylor's paper appeared, Thomas Kuhn and other philosophers of science argued that observation in the natural sciences is theory-laden. According to them, theory-laden observation can only provide specious support for the theory it supposedly tests. This problem has led some philosophers of science to claim that theory acceptance in the natural sciences is based on irrational factors.

Once one takes the theory-laden nature of observation in the natural sciences into account, the difference that Taylor alleges between the validation of interpretations in hermeneutics and the testing of hypotheses in the natural sciences disappears. Moreover, since the theory-laden nature of observation in the natural sciences does not in fact make objective testing impossible,[28] there is reason to suppose that objective validation might not be impossible in textual interpretations either.

In the case of the natural sciences one must distinguish between the categories in which observations are couched and the observational reports themselves. Thus, for example, the observation report, "An electron passed through the cloud chamber," is couched in the theoretic categories of "electron" and "cloud chamber." Let us grant, then, that since observational reports must be made in the categories of some theory or other, they are theory-laden in this sense. But the existence of what one might call *theoretical category influence* does not mean that a theory predetermines the *particular* observational report that is made. Thus, for example, the theories of physics may predetermine that observational reports made in the context of physical experiments will be couched in the terms of physical theories. But this does not mean that someone who views an experiment in terms of the categories of a physical theory will observe that an electron is passing through a cloud chamber at some particular time even if this is what the theory predicts. An observational report, although stated in terms of the categories of a particular theory, can conflict with the premises of that theory. But then the existence of theoretical category influence does not necessarily undermine scientific objectivity. It does not mean that the support for a theory which an observational report provides is circular.

The theoretical dependency of observational reports would seem to be a more serious matter for scientific objectivity than the categories they are couched in. For if what is accepted as a true observational report is dependent on the observer's theoretical commitment to the premises of the theory, how can observation be an independent standard that can be appealed to in testing a theory? Theoretical commitment would in this case determine not only the categories of an observation report but the report itself.

It is necessary, however, to distinguish several different theses about what I will call *theoretical premise influence*:

(1) Theoretical premise influence is strong in some cases of observation.

(2) Theoretical premise influence is strong in all cases of observations.

(3) Strong theoretical premise influence, when it is present, can be detected and overcome.

(4) Strong theoretical premise influence, when it is present, cannot be detected and overcome.

Both the history of science and psychological experiments show that thesis (1) is true. The history of science shows that negative evidence in relation to some theory is often not recognized as such by scientists because of their prior theoretical commitments. An analog to this has been demonstrated in the well-known experiment of Bruner and Postman[29] in which subjects were asked to identify a series of playing cards in a short exposure. Subjects found it easy to identify the normal cards but difficult to identify abnormal cards as abnormal, for example, a black four of hearts. The tendency was to identify these as normal, for example, the black four of hearts as a black four of spades. Only after a long exposure were the abnormal cards correctly identified as abnormal by the majority of subjects and some of the subjects were unable to make correct identifications even after repeated exposures.

There is no reason at all, however, to suppose that (2) is true, for if it were, advocates of a theory would never make observational reports that were in conflict with it; a scientist's observational report would never be a shock to his or her expectations. But they sometimes are. Furthermore, even if (2) were true, this by itself would not undermine the objectivity of scientific theory testing via observation. For supposing that all observational reports were strongly influenced by the theoretical commitments of the observer, such theoretical influence might be detected and overcome. There is good reason to suppose that (4) is false, hence that (3) is true for there do seem to be means of detecting and correcting premise influence. Certainly, for most subjects in the Bruner and Postman experiment, repeated exposure to an incongruity was enough to bring it to light.

In addition to there being evidence that natural scientists are sometimes capable of recognizing observations that conflict with their theoretical beliefs, there are specific ways in which empirical observation can function as a constraint and a check on theory.[30] Suppose a doctor claims to observe that a patient has disease D, for example, measles, and that the observation is based on an alleged connection C between property D and symptom S. The extent to which this observation can function as a constraint on theory will depend on how justified we are in relying on C. This, in turn, might depend on whether our belief in C can be regarded as free from doubt given the context of inquiry in which C was tested.[31] Or it might be a function of the directness of the connection between D and S. Other things being equal, a connection that one establishes by long and complex causal chains gives us less security than one that is short and simple.[32] Or it might turn on the type of connection. The ideal case would be one in which our background knowledge warrants our believing that C has a biconditional form linking the bases for the observation to what one supposedly observes; in the present case, $(x)(Dx \longleftrightarrow Sx)$. Then, given that a patient has S, one could deduce that it has D. Weaker logical relations would, of course, give less security.

There are at least two other factors that affect the ways in which theory-laden observation can constrain and check theory.[33] One is the independence of observation from the theory under test. Suppose that a geologist claims to observe that a rock was formed by a glacier and she uses this observation to test some theory. If the geologist bases her observation entirely on theories that are not under test in the present context, her observation, although based on a theory, is independent of the theory under test and thus functions as a constraint on it.

Another factor is the convergence of independent and diverse sources of evidence that establish different but connected properties of an entity.[34] Suppose a doctor claims to observe that patient X has disease D that consists of interconnected properties P_1, P_2,....P_n and that her observations are based on heterogeneous and independent sources of theory-laden evidence E_1, E_2,....E_n. One supposes that it would be improbable in the extreme—indeed, it would be a virtual miracle—that these independent sources would converge in this way if this patient did not have D. In such cases, too, the observation would be a constraint and check on theory.

Might the approaches just outlined be relevant to the validation of interpretations?[35] Certainly there is a distinction to be drawn between the categories in which the interpretation of a text is couched and the statements of the interpretation itself. For example, on a Freudian interpretation, one would describe Hamlet's actions in terms of, say, an Oedipus complex.[36] But, unless psychoanalysis is an irrefutable theory, this does not mean that someone who accepts Freudian theory will necessarily interpret a given passage as being in accord with the premises of the theory. For example, a person might say: "In this scene with his mother Hamlet does *not* manifest any Oedipal reaction," although this sentence might be in conflict with the premises of Freudian theory. A Freudian interpretation of Hamlet would entail that in this sort of situation Hamlet would manifest an oedipal reaction.

The theoretical dependency of interpretive statements would seem to raise more serious matters for the objectivity of interpretations than the theoretical dependency of the categories they are couched in. Suppose one accepts as a particular interpretive statement, "Hamlet is manifesting an Oedipal reaction in this scene," and that this is dependent on the interpreter's theoretical commitment to the premises of the theory. How can such a particular interpretation serve as independent grounds for accepting the Freudian interpretation of the whole play? Theoretical commitment would in this case determine not only the categories used in an interpreter's particular judgment but the judgment itself.

Just as experience shows that in the context of science premise influence is sometimes very strong, it shows that premise influence is sometimes very strong in hermeneutic contexts. People committed to a given theory do not always recognize the negative textual evidence relative to an interpretation. But equally, experience shows that it is not strong in all cases, for if it were, a person committed to an interpretation of a whole text would never make particular judgments that were not in accord with it; the interpretation of a particular passage would never be a shock to the interpreter's expectations.

Further, even if premise influence were strong in all cases, it would not undermine the objectivity of interpretations. Sometimes one can detect premise influence and overcome it. Literary critics who are strongly committed to some particular interpretation sometimes change their minds when their interpretation is exposed to criticism and/or they flounder in their attempts to justify it; they acknowledge that their interpretation was biased or one-sided or that a key passage can be looked at in a different and more adequate way.

In addition, the same sorts of consideration that enable theory-laden observation to be a check and restraint on theory can operate to allow interpretations of particular passages to be checks and constraints on interpretations of whole texts. The interpretation of a passage in which Hamlet allegedly shows oedipal behavior O might be based on an alleged connection C between O and behavior B. Whether C is acceptable would depend on factors similar to those considered in natural science contexts: whether the background knowledge on which C is based is free from doubt; the length and complexity of C; and the specific nature of C, for example, whether it is unique and deterministic. The acceptability of C could also be based on two independent factors analogous to those that are relevant in natural science contexts. A reading of a particular passage, although based on some interpretation, might not be based on the particular interpretation that is being validated by this reading. If so, then this reading could serve as an independent check on the interpretation that is being validated. Or the connected properties that constitute a particular interpretation of the whole text might be based on a variety of independent and heterogeneous sources, such as letters by the author, literary works by other authors, literary conventions of the period whose chance convergence would be highly unlikely.

Everything said so far concerning literary interpretation applies to interpretation in the social sciences. Theoretical category influence will determine how one categorizes social scientific data but it does not entail that someone who accepts an interpretation will always construe the data in terms of the premises of the theory. On the other hand, there is no a priori reason to suppose that theoretical premise influence is always strong, or that, even when it is, one cannot overcome it. Furthermore, there is a posteriori reason to suppose that it is not always strong and that, when it is, one can sometimes overcome it. Social scientists no less than literary critics sometimes find evidence against their interpretations and as a result have to reject or modify them.[37]

Although Taylor is correct that there are no brute data in social science and that observations are based on interpretations, observation in the social sciences as in the natural sciences can sometimes function as a constraint and a check on theory. Suppose an archaeologist claims to observe that an artifact A belongs to culture C, a culture that existed ten thousand years ago. Let us admit that this observation is an interpretation and is based on an alleged connection N between a physical property of the artifact and a process used in making artifacts in C. The extent to which this interpretation can function to validate objectively another interpretation will depend on the same sorts of factors as those considered above.

The two aforementioned independent factors are also relevant. For example, suppose that the archaeologist's claim to have observed that an artifact A belongs to culture C is used to validate Theory T_1. If the archaeologist's observation is based entirely on Theory T_2 that is not under test in the present context, then her observation, although based on a theory, is independent of T_1, the theory under test. Suppose, however, that the archaeologist claims to have observed that a past culture C has properties P_1, P_2, ...P_n that make up a coherent and interconnected whole and her observation or interpretation is based on heterogeneous and independent sources of theory-laden evidence E_1, E_2,. . . .E_n. It would be improbable in the extreme that these independent sources would converge in this way if this coherent whole did not actually exist; that is, if her interpretation of C was not true.

This analogy between the objective testing of theories in natural science, despite the theory-laden nature of observation, and the objective validation of interpretations in hermeneutic disciplines, despite the hermeneutic circle, was drawn explicitly by two important methodologists of hermeneutics *before* the publication of Taylor's article. Taylor does not cite them, let alone attempt to rebut their arguments.

In 1962, Emilio Betti[38] argued that hermeneutic knowing involves public objects that are constructions of the human mind and that it is the job of the interpreter to grasp or reconstruct the ideas and intentions expressed in these objects. Consequently, he opposed what he called the subjective approach of Gadamer in which there is a "fusion of horizons" between the text and the interpreter.[39]

Also rejecting the subjective approach of Gadamer,[40] in 1967, E. D. Hirsch[41] maintained that the validation of an interpretation is simply an application of the hypothetico-deductive method.[42] Although one cannot validate any interpretation with certainty, one can often eliminate alternatives in light of the evidence. Starting with an initial hypothesis with low probability about the meaning of a text, the interpreter proposes and tests new hypotheses as more evidence is obtained. One determines probability judgments primarily used in this testing on the basis of three criteria: the narrowness of the class, the number of members of the class, and the frequency of the trait among those members. For example, suppose that the meaning of a particular phrase in a nineteenth-century English novel is unclear to an interpreter. He or she might argue that the dozen or so nineteenth-century English novelists so far examined used this phrase in a certain sense about 70 percent of the time. Consequently, it is probable that this novelist did so as well. This hypothesis could then be strengthened by narrowing the reference class. For instance, it might be possible to establish that this particular novelist always used the phrase in this particular sense in her other novels.

Hirsch argued that one can use genres to evaluate the probability of certain interpretations. For example, the conventions found in a particular literary genre might allow one to argue that it is likely that a symbol means one thing rather than something else. This judgment might, of course, be undermined by further evidence, e.g., that this author indicated in her correspondence with her sister that she was trying to break out of this genre and was attempting to use the symbol in a new way. But if one could not narrow the reference class in this or similar ways, an interpreter would indeed be justified in supposing that this symbol was used in the standard way found in the genre. This in turn would help the interpreter to eliminate alternative interpretations related to the symbol.

Hirsch linked the possibility of the objectivity of interpretations with the possibility of being able to discern the author's meaning,[43] but there is no necessity in this linkage. The possibility of the objectivity of interpretations should be understood in terms of the falsifiability of interpretations and the ability to support interpretations by probability judgments. Nothing Taylor says undermines the claims of objectivity of literary interpretation in this sense. But if one can use objective considerations in the interpretation of literary texts, as Betti and Hirsch have argued, and the interpretation of society and social practice is analogous to the interpretation of literary texts, as Taylor has suggested, then this seems to weaken still further Taylor's thesis of the fundamental difference between social and natural science. Both the social and the natural sciences can use objective criteria of interpretation.[44]

Nonsubjective Meanings

The alleged impossibility of objective interpretations affects Taylor's views on the ontology of social meaning. Taylor contrasts his interpretive approach to social science, and in particular his approach to political science, with the approach of "the empiricists." The empiricists' approach is based on verification in terms of "brute data"; that is, data "whose validity cannot be questioned by another interpretation or reading, data whose credibility cannot be founded or undermined by further reasoning."[45] However, unlike natural science which can be understood in terms of brute data, social science cannot.

Consider political science. According to Taylor, mainstream political science identifies political behavior with action that is "brute data identified"; that is, identified in terms of physical end states or of institutional rules that are closely tied to some physical end state, e.g., raising one's hand at an appropriate time when a vote is being taken. One determines the meaning of voting, in contrast to voting behavior, via ascertaining certain facts about the actors' subjective states by such techniques as opinion polls and content analysis. Thus, once political scientists know how people vote (which can be established by observing their behavior in certain institutional contexts), they can determine the subjective bases of their vote—their beliefs, attitudes, and values—by asking them questions and making inferences on the basis of their answers.

Taylor maintains that this construal wrongly makes the meaning of political behavior subjective, in that it construes meaning in terms of the beliefs, attitudes, and values of the social actors. This is to overlook intersubjective and common meanings. Consider the concept of bargaining. It is part of a field of concepts including entering into negotiations, bargaining in good (bad) faith, breaking off negotiations, which one uses to interpret social practices in this society but not in some other societies, e.g., the Japanese. It would be a complete misconstrual, according to Taylor, to suppose that the reality that this field of concepts refers to is something that is purely subjective. In fact, our language of bargaining is constitutive of our social reality—our social world. Just as one would not have chess without certain rules that govern the movement of the queen, so one would not have our social reality without certain bargaining rules.

For Taylor, then, there are meanings that are intersubjective, and the language used to express them is constitutive of social reality. But he holds that intersubjective meaning is not the only type of nonsubjective meaning that empiricists have overlooked with their reliance on brute facts. There are also common meanings which provide shared values that are part of our common world and supply the locus for our common aspirations and sense of community. For example, he says that "there is a common meaning in our civilization connected around a vision of the free society in which bargain has a central place."[46] Although this vision of a free society has been challenged from several quarters, it nevertheless furnishes a locus for debate.

Taylor's intersubjective meanings connect in interesting ways with the position of Verstehen theorists previously considered. Although none of these theorists explicitly draws Taylor's distinction between intersubjective and subjective meanings, one can make educated guesses on how they should be classified. One would suppose that Weber's explanatory Verstehen, Winch's social rules, Dray's principles of action, Schutz's life-world, and Popper's situtational logic rely on intersubjective meanings while Dilthey's reliving sense of Verstehen and Collingwood's rethinking assume subjective meaning. However, if this is true, it would not follow that these theorists would be committed to other aspects of Taylor's thesis. For example, neither Dilthey nor Collingwood would suppose that subjective states of actors could be understood just by asking them questions and making inferences on the basis of the answers. Reliving and rethinking are also necessary.

What can one say about Taylor's notions of intersubjective and common meaning? Let us suppose that his ontological thesis is correct: that one cannot explain these meanings as mere psychological projections of the social actors. It does not follow that other aspects of his claim are correct. As we have seen, Taylor maintains that the nonsubjective meaning that is made clear in an interpretation is always meaning *for* a subject or subjects. But what exactly does this involve? With respect to intersubjective meaning IM of practice P, does this mean that social actors in P would tend under questioning to agree that IM is constitutive of P? With respect to common meaning CM of P does this mean that they would tend under questioning to agree that CM provides a sense of shared values and community? Or is there a much more indirect relation between the intersubjective meaning and common meaning of a social practice and the reactions of the actors in the practice?

Whatever the relation between the reaction of social actors and the social meanings that one supposes is for social actors, one must question whether social meaning must always be for social actors. It is possible that the social actors of P might have no understanding or even awareness of the meaning of P that is postulated by a social -scientist. Certainly, theories of ideology and false consciousness seem to assume this possibility. In addition, the Weltanschauung of a society as formulated through historical research and understood by scholars might not be comprehensible to a typical member of that society.[47] Since the commonsense categories of the actor may be imprecise and muddled, a reformulation, an explication, or even a replacement of them would certainly seem to be in order as it is in other scientific fields. Furthermore, as we have seen in earlier chapters, many sociological explanations are couched in terms the actor would not understand.[48]

Another obvious difficulty with Taylor's theory is that of reconciling his insistence on an objective ontology of meaning and a subjective epistemology for determining such meaning. Taylor calls both common and intersubjective meanings "nonsubjective meaning" because on this view they exist as part of the objective fabric of the social world and not merely in the minds of the social actors. Nevertheless, he denies that one can establish any judgment about social meaning by objective rational procedures and maintains in the end that disagreements about meaning must come down to conflicting intuitions. Thus, he wants social meanings to have an objective ontological basis but at the same time he construes their epistemological basis as subjective. There is nothing inconsistent about this dualism but a recent historical analog does suggest some difficulties with it.

Although there are obvious differences,[49] early twentieth-century ethical intuitionism provides an analogy to Taylor's dualism of ontological objectivism and epistemological subjectivism. Intuitionists such as G. E. Moore claimed that ethical properties were part of the objective furniture of the world although they could only be discerned by intuition. However, since the intuitions of different people conflicted, there seemed to be no rational way of reconciling them. Given this problem, critics argued that there was no good reason to suppose that ethical properties existed in the objective world. It was much more plausible to suppose that the phenomenological objectivity of ethical experience, e.g., that the moral obligation which an action seems to impose on one from the outside, could be better explained as a psychological illusion than as an objective ontological fact. If human beings projected their values and subjective ethical views onto the world and wrongly read them as an objective part of it, this could explain why different people have conflicting intuitions about a supposedly objective ethical reality: different people are making different projections.

Can the phenomenological objectivity of the meaning of social institutions and practices be better explained as a psychological projection than as an objective ontological fact? It would seem that one could give the same argument against it as against ethical intuitionism: If human beings project their subjective beliefs and goals onto the world and wrongly read them as an objective part of it, this could explain why different people have conflicting intuitions about a supposedly objective realm of meaning: Different people are making different projections. In order to avoid the problem Taylor would have to maintain (as we have seen he should have maintained) that the interpretation of meaning is objectively discernible.

Taylor's Later Work in the Philosophy of Social Sciences

About a decade after "Interpretation and the Sciences of Man," appeared, Taylor published several more papers on the philosophy of the social sciences. These later papers—together with "Interpretation and the Sciences of Man" and another early paper—were reprinted in a collection entitled *Philosophy and the Human Sciences* and present a picture of Taylor's vision of the social sciences that differs from his earlier view in only a few respects.[50]

Taylor himself does not seem to see any significant differences between his earlier and later positions. In the introduction to this collection he maintains that the collected papers are the work of "a monomaniac" and a "tightly related agenda" underlies all of them[51] and makes it clear that this tightly related agenda is connected with a rejection of the naturalistic model in the social sciences. Taylor associates this model with behaviorism and other reductionistic views. Admitting that the views he opposes are diverse, he maintains that they nevertheless form a family. First, they have a common metaphysical motivation in that they oppose all anthropocentric properties, that is, properties that things have only with respect to the experience of agents of a certain kind. Second, the naturalistic view he rejects ignores a crucial feature of human agency, namely, self-interpretation: A fully competent human being "has some understanding (which may be also more or less *mis*-understanding) of himself, but is partly constituted by this understanding."[52] This self-interpretation involves considerations of values and worth. According to Taylor this means that there can be no absolute understanding of persons since persons can only be understood against a background of a distinction of worth and values. However, the language of science, he says, aspires to value neutrality.

All of Taylor's essays on the philosophy of social science are indeed opposed to naturalism in the social sciences. However, the notion of self-understanding plays a relatively minor role in his early essay[53] but takes on a crucial importance in some later ones and in his retrospective interpretation of all of his work. For example, in "Social Theory as Practice," Taylor's major thesis is that members of society have pretheoretical understanding of society.[54] Consequently, the framing of social scientific theories either makes implicit practice explicit or shows our implicit understanding wrong or shows that some practice has a significance that was not understood.[55] Thus, he argues that there is a disanalogy between the natural sciences and the social sciences. In the natural sciences the object of investigation is independent objects, but in the social sciences the objects of investigation are partly constituted by self-understanding. Consequently, he argues that the natural science model does not apply to social science except in economics where laws change very slowly and people operate according to instrumental rationality.

Here again one sees that, although Taylor does not use the term "Verstehen," his views are based on Verstehen ideas: understanding a social practice is at least indirectly related to the social actors' understanding and is impossible without it. His views differ from some Verstehen theorists such as Dilthey and Weber in that, although he admits that the actor's understanding may have to be corrected and refined, it cannot be ignored or bypassed. In this respect his view is closer to Winch's and Schutz's who also allow for social science theory to transcend the categories of the actors so long as it is indirectly based on these categories.

Moreover, unlike the rather subjective view of interpretation developed in "Interpretation and the Sciences of Man," Taylor later maintains that theories are validated in practice. Correct theories should be accepted if they make for a more effective practice—if they reform it, put it on firmer basis. On the other hand, practice informed by wrong theory is self-defeating. Good theory enables practice to be less stumbling and more clairvoyant. Sometimes this involves realizing a practice is in vain.

In Taylor's, "Understanding and Ethnocentricity," taking into account the self-understanding of the actors also plays an essential role.[56] Here he argues that objective social science is not merely the prediction of social patterns or historical events, but it must make sense of the agents. This does not mean that social science must show that the agent's action makes sense since it might be confused, and so on. Rather, by identifying the confusions we make sense of what the agents do. In order to do this we must grasp an agent's self-understanding. This is neither empathy nor taking the point of view of the actor since actors may be confused and mistaken. Self-descriptions of the actor (i.e., how the actor would describe the situation if more reflective) are essential for identifying the explananda. This use of self-description can be avoided only by not explaining the details of a social phenomenon, for example, the details of a particular religion in the society in terms of the agents' action, feeling, aspiration. Here again one sees sophisticated Verstehen ideas informing his views. Although rejecting the requirement that understanding must be in terms of the actors' point of view, the actors' reflective self-description must define what is to be understood. Again the similarity to Winch and Schutz should be noted.

There are problems with Taylor's more recent construal of interpretive social science. First, it is not true that the natural science model of social science opposes all anthropocentric properties. For example, the natural science model as interpreted by Carl Hempel and Ernest Nagel allows social science to explain behavior in terms of laws and initial conditions couched in anthropocentric language. Although the natural science model is compatible with behaviorism and physicalism, that is, the reduction of all sciences to physics, these positions are not entailed by this model. Second, whether it is true that human agency is constituted by self-understanding and that self-understanding is value-laden, is certainly not obvious. But even if it were, the crucial issue is whether social science should be restricted to this concept of agency. There is no good reason to believe that it should be since scientific understanding can transcend this self-understanding and take many different forms. Taylor's more recent views, like his previous one, put unacceptable limits on social scientific understanding.

Members of society may have no pretheoretical understanding of some aspects of society that social scientists are interested in investigating. For example, there may be certain patterns of population densities that are correlated with personality variables. Members of society might have no pretheoretic understanding of these patterns since they are completely unaware of them. So social scientists are not making a social practice explicit or showing that the implicit understanding is wrong or showing the practice has a significance that was not understood. They are trying to understand a social pattern that the social actors are completely unaware of.

Taylor makes an exception of economics. But there might be aspects in all social sciences including political science that are beyond self-understanding in the sense that social actors are unaware of them. To be sure, social actors can become aware of these aspects but it would be mistaken to say that they are implicit in their practice or their significance is misunderstood. Suppose investigation reveals the influence of birth order on voting behavior in some regions and not in others. In such a case, it is extremely unlikely that social actors have a pretheoretical understanding or even misunderstanding of this pattern since they would likely be unaware of it.

These theories do not have to take into consideeration the agent's self-understanding since the agent has none. Nor is the self-description of the actors if they were more self-reflective essential for identifying the explananda since it could be identified in terms of the theoretical interests of the social scientists. This self-description is not bypassed, as Taylor suggests, since there is nothing to bypass. Details of voting behavior might not be defined in terms of the agent's action, feeling, and aspirations but in terms of what is of theoretical interest to social scientists. For example, detailed statistical patterns of voter turn-out and distribution and how these relate to birth order may be of great significance to social scientists but be beyond the ken of the average voter.

The theories about birth order and voting and about personality and population density are not tested in practice in the way Taylor has in mind. They are tested in the ordinary way by proposing hypotheses that explain these patterns and seeing if these hypotheses have other confirmed implications. This is not to deny that some social scientific theories may sometimes be tested in practice in the sense that acting on certain theories may bring about more or less effective practice. But this way of testing is not so essential as Taylor thinks.

Conclusion

Despite the importance of Taylor's article, the interpretive approach that he presents has serious problems. First, the scope of the social sciences as Taylor conceives of it is too narrow and excludes important questions that social science has been and should be concerned with.

In particular, it excludes causal questions that any social science should deal with. Moreover, even if one limits one's concerns to the interpretation of meaning, causality is relevant since interpreting the meaning of a social practice often involves understanding the connections between causal notions. Second, despite what Taylor says, objective interpretations seem possible. Even if there is a hermeneutic circle, this does not rule out the use of evidence from either falsifying or supporting interpretations via probabilistic reasoning nor does it exclude the placing of objective constraints on interpretations. Third, Taylor's theory is restrictive in still another way: It requires that social scientists use theoretical concepts that at least indirectly relate to the understanding of the social actors. Finally, although Taylor's more recent work on the philosophy of the social sciences, differs in some respects from his earlier work, problems remain. Social science need not be based on the self-understanding or misunderstanding of social actors, and theories need not be tested in social practice in the way Taylor has in mind.

Notes

1. This chapter is based on my paper, "Taylor on Interpretation and the Sciences of Man," in *Readings in the Philosophy of Social Science,* ed., Michael Martin and Lee C. McIntyre (Cambridge, MA; The MIT Press, 1994), pp. 259-79.
2. This paper was originally published in *The Review of Metaphysics* 25, 1971, pp. 3-51.
3. See, for example, David Braybrooke, *Philosophy of Social Science* (Englewood Cliffs, NJ: Prentice-Hall, Inc., 1987), p. 3; David Thomas, *Naturalism and Social Science* (London and New York: Cambridge University Press, 1979), p. 23; Daniel Little, *Varieties of Social Explanation* (Boulder, CO: Westview Press, 1991), p. 68.
4. For example, Taylor's paper is reprinted in Paul Rabinow and William M. Sullivan eds., *Interpretive Social Science: A Second Look* (Berkeley and Los Angeles: University of California Press, 1987); Fred R. Dallmayr and Thomas A. McCarthy eds., *Understanding and Social Inquiry* (Notre Dame: Notre Dame University Press, 1977); and Eric Bredo and Walter Feinberg eds., *Knowledge and Values in Social and Educational Research* (Philadelphia: Temple University Press, 1982).
5. Braybooke, *Philosophy of Social Science.*
6. See Harold Kincaid, *Philosophical Foundations of the Social Sciences* (New York: Cambridge University Press, 1996), pp. 205-12. Kincaid's critique appeared two years after the paper on which this chapter is based and some of our criticisms overlap.
7. Taylor, "Interpretation and the Sciences of Man," *Interpretive Social Science: A Second Look* eds. Rabinow and Sullivan, p. 33.
8. Ibid., p.34.
9. Ibid., p. 41.
10. Ibid., p. 43.

11. Taylor seems to have exaggerated the importance of interpretation in another way. He seems to assume implicitly that understanding can only be achieved via interpretation. However, understanding is sometimes immediate and prereflective.
12. See, for example, Janice Delaney, *The Curse* (New York: E. P. Dutton, 1976).
13. Marla N. Powers, "Menstruation and Reproduction: An Oglala Case," *Signs* 6, 1980, pp. 54-65.
14. See Arnold Van Gennep, *The Rites of Passage* (Chicago: University of Chicago Press, 1960).
15. See Victor Turner, *The Ritual Process* (Chicago: Aldine Publishing Co.,S 1969).
16. Powers, "Menstruation and Reproduction," p. 65.
17. See, for example, H. G. Gough, "Personality factors related to reported severity of menstrual distress," *Journal of Abnormal Psychology* 84, 1975, pp. 59 -65; P. Slade and F. A. Jenner, "Attitudes to female roles, aspects of menstruation, and complaining about menstrual symptoms," *British Journal of Social and Clinical Psychology* 19, 1980, pp. 109–13.
18. See Paula Weideger, *Menstruation and Menopause* (New York: Alfred A. Knopf, 1976), chapter 4.
19. Taylor, "Interpretation and the Sciences of Man," p. 63.
20. In criticizing Taylor's apparent rejection of the function approach, I do not wish to deny that some functional explanations of social phenomena are problematic. However, which functional accounts are problematic cannot be determined a priori. See Daniel Little, *Varieties of Social Explanation* (Boulder, CO: Westview Press, 1991), pp. 91-102.
21. Taylor, "Interpretation and the Sciences of Man," p. 64.
22. Ibid., pp. 42–43.
23. See Sigmund Freud, "The Sexual Aberrations," in *The Basic Writings of Sigmund Freud*, ed. A. A. Brill (New York: The Modern Library, 1938).
24. Taylor, "Interpretation and the Sciences of Man," p. 75.
25. Ibid., p. 76.
26. Ibid., p. 77.
27. For a defense of the objectivity of interpretation along somewhat different lines, see James Bohman, *New Philosophy of Social Science* (Cambridge, MA: The MIT Press, 1991), chapter 3.
28. See Michael Martin, *Concepts of Science Education* (Chicago: Scott-Foresman, 1972), pp. 116-21. My argument here is based on the analysis of Israel Scheffler, *Science and Subjectivity* (Indianapolis: The Bobbs-Merrill, Co. Inc., 1967).
29. Jerome Bruner and Leo Postman, "On the Perception of Incongruity: A Paradigm," *Journal of Personality* 18, 1949, pp. 206-23.
30. I am indebted here to Alison Wylie's discussion in "Evidential Constraints: Pragmatic Empiricism in Archaeology," reprinted in eds. Martin and McIntyre, *Readings in the Philosophy of Social Science*.
31. On a similar point connected with theory-laden observation in the natural sciences, see Dudley Shapere, "Observation and the Scientific Enterprise," *Observation, Experiment and Hypothesis in Modern Physical Science*, ed. P. Achinstein and O. Hannaway (Cambridge, MA: The MIT Press, 1985), p. 29, cited by Wylie, op. cit.
32. On a similar point connected with the natural sciences, see Peter Kosso, "Dimensions of Observability," *British Journal for the Philosophy of Science* 39, 1988, p. 445, cited by Wylie, "Evidential Constraints."
33. On an analogous consideration in the natural sciences, see Ian Hacking, *Representing and Intervening* (Cambridge, MA: Cambridge University Press, 1983), pp. 183–85, and Kosso, "Dimensions of Observability," p. 456, cited by Wylie, "Evidential Constraints."

34. See Peter Kosso, "Science and Objectivity," *Journal of Philosophy* 86, 1989, p. 247, or for a similar point in the natural sciences, see Wylie, "Evidential Constraints."
35. For a defense of the thesis that hermeneutics is simply the application of the method of hypothesis applied to meaningful material, see Dagfinn Føllesdal, "Hermeneutics and the hypothetico-deductive method," *Dialectica* 33, 1979, pp. 319-36.
36. See Ernest Jones, *Hamlet and Oedipus* (Garden City, NY: Doubleday and Co., Inc., 1955).
37. For an example from social science literature where an interpretation is objectively confirmed, see Kincaid, *Philosophical Foundations of the Social Sciences,* pp. 212-15.
38. Emilio Betti, "Hermeneutics as the General Methodology of the Gestewissentschaften" (1962); reprinted and trans. in Josef Bleicher, *Contemporary Hermeneutics* (London: Routledge and Kegan Paul, 1980), pp. 51-94.
39. Betti, "Hermeneutics," p. 79.
40. See E. D. Hirsch, Jr., "Gadamer's Theory of Interpretation," *Review of Metaphysics*, March, 1965; reprinted in Hirsch, *Validation in Interpretation*, (New Haven: Yale University Press, 1967), appendix 2.
41. E. D. Hirsch, Jr., *Validation in Interpretation.*
42. Ibid., p. 264.
43. See the critique of Hirsch's appeal to the author's intention by David Couzens Hoy in *The Critical Circle* (Los Angeles: University of California Press, 1982), pp. 11-40.
44. For a recent attempt to defend the objectivity of the social sciences, see Brian Fay, *Contemporary Philosophy of Social Science* (Cambridge, MA: Blackwell, 1996), chapter 10.
45. Taylor, "Interpretation and the Sciences of Man," p. 38.
46. Ibid., p. 61.
47. See Thomas, *Naturalism and Social Science*, pp. 96–97.
48. Several examples of sociological explanations not in terms of the commonsense categories of the actor are given in chapters 4 and 5.
49. There are, of course, two basic differences between Taylor's position and the intuitionists. First, ethical intuitionists claimed that ethical properties were not culturally relative. Taylor claims that meanings are relative and vary from culture to culture. Second, Taylor advocates intuition when interpretation in its usual sense fails to convince someone who does not accept your interpretation. Ethical intuitionists relied on intuition right from the start.
50. Richard Taylor, *Philosophy and the Human Sciences, Philosophical Papers* 2 (Cambridge: Cambridge University Press, 1985).
51. Ibid., p. 1.
52. Ibid., p. 3.
53. As far as one can determine this idea is mentioned only once. See "Interpretation and the Sciences of Man," p. 46.
54. Taylor, "Social Theory as Practice," *Philosophy and the Human Sciences,* pp. 91-115.
55. Whether Taylor is committed here to emancipatory goals of the critical social sciences and the Critical Theory of the Frankfurt School is uncertain. See David Ingram, *Critical Theory and Philosophy* (New York: Paragon House, 1990), chapter 1; Brian Fay, *Critical Social Science* (Ithaca, NY: Cornell University Press, 1987).
56. Taylor, "Understanding and Ethnocentricity," *Philosophy and the Human Sciences,* pp. 116-33.

8

Verstehen and Anthropology

We have seen how a Verstehen approach can be developed within different well-articulated philosophical backgrounds. A Verstehen approach can be cultivated also in particular social sciences. In this chapter[1] its use by the anthropologist Clifford Geertz will be considered. Although Geertz, like Taylor, uses the term "interpretation" rather than "Verstehen," the basic problems of his approach are very similar to those of Verstehen theorists already considered: He restricts the task of the social sciences to giving interpretations and he restricts interpretations to ones that are related to the subjective meanings of the actors.

In contemporary thought Geertz's name has become closely associated with an interpretive approach not only to his own field of anthropology but to the social sciences generally and even to history.[2] Although Peter Winch, Charles Taylor, Alfred Schutz, Paul Ricoeur, Hans-Georg Gadamer, and Jürgen Habermas are also advocates of interpretivism, Geertz is perhaps unique in being a social scientist who uses his theory in his empirical investigations of other cultures. Thus, while other advocates of Verstehen have provided it with a philosophical rationale, Geertz's theoretical papers taken together with his anthropological fieldwork provide both a rationale and a concrete model of what the results of an interpretive approach would look like. Although the philosophical influences on Winch and Schutz are clear and unambiguous, those on Geertz are more eclectic. We know that from Max Weber Geertz developed the idea that culture is a web of meanings created by human beings; from the French hermeneutic phenomenologist, Paul Ricoeur, he took the notion that culture is like a text that must be interpreted; from the British ordinary language analyst, Gilbert Ryle, he borrowed the idea of thick descriptions, arguing that cultural interpretations must be in terms of such descriptions. While helping to revive the holistic and humanistic approaches to culture of Alfred Kroeber and Franz Boas in American anthropology, Geertz's interpretive approach challenged his colleagues to reject the natural science approach that tends to dominate the profession.[3] As Paul Shankman has noted,

> Geertz has proposed that social scientists study meaning rather than behavior, seek understanding rather than causal laws, and reject mechanistic explanations of the natural science variety in favor of interpretive explanations. He has invited his colleagues to take seriously the possibilities of analogy and metaphor, to consider human activity as text and symbolic action as drama. In other words, he has asked social scientists to rework, if not abandon, their traditional assumptions about the nature of their intellectual enterprise.[4]

Despite Geertz's importance and the critical response to his work that has been generated in the anthropological literature, however, philosophers of the social sciences have not given his theories the critical attention they deserve.[5] In this chapter I will elucidate and then critically evaluate Geertz's interpretive approach. In particular, I will show that one of the root problems with his theory is the dependence on the analogy of interpreting a text. This analogy leads him to exclude important questions from the purview of social science, to underestimate the significance of causality in social science, and to propose an inadequate account of the validation of social scientific interpretations.

Geertz's Theory

Interpretive Anthropology

What is interpretivism?[6] Geertz's answer, given in his paper "Thick Descriptions: Toward an Interpretive Theory of Culture,"[7] is that in order to understand culture ethnographers should give detailed microscopic descriptions which are based on a complex web of interpretations. Although generalizations are not precluded, these descriptions make theorizing difficult.

Geertz assumes that one of the primary aims of anthropology is to understand culture. "The concept of culture I espouse," he says,

> is essentially a semiotic one. Believing with Max Weber that man is an animal suspended in webs of significance he himself has spun, I take culture to be those webs, and the analysis of it to be therefore not an experimental science in search of laws but an interpretive one in search of meaning.[8]

In order to find this meaning he believes it is necessary for ethnographers to provide what he calls "thick descriptions":

What the ethnographer is in fact faced with . . . . is the multiplicity of complex conceptual structures, many of them superimposed upon or knotted into one another, which are at once strange, irregular, inexplicit, and which he contrives somehow first to grasp and then to render. And this is true at the most down-to-earth, jungle fieldwork levels of his activity: interviewing, informants, observing rituals, eliciting kin terms, tracing property lines, censuring households . . . . writing his journal. Doing ethnography is like trying to read (in the sense of "construct a reading of") a manuscript—foreign, faded, full of ellipses, incoherences, suspicious emendations, and tendentious commentaries, but written not in conventional graphs of sound but in transient examples of shaped behavior.[9]

Geertz acknowledges that ethnographers' thick descriptions are interpretations. Indeed, these descriptions are based in part on the interpretations of informants which, in turn, are interpretations of what informants think they are doing. In other words, "anthropological writings are themselves interpretations and second and third order ones to boot."[10] However, he stresses that anthropologists in their interpretations are seeking neither to become natives nor to mimic them[11] and he emphasizes elsewhere that it is not necessary to empathize or sympathize with the natives to provide these interpretations.[12] In this respect, Geertz's views resemble all of the Verstehen theories examined so far except Dilthey on the reliving interpretation.

What is not completely clear, however, is whether the interpretations Geertz seeks are supposed to stick with the meanings assumed by the natives or whether they can go beyond them. On the one hand, his reliance on Weber, his statement that "man is an animal suspended in webs of significance he himself has spun," his claim that an analysis of culture is a search for these webs of significance, all suggest that interpretation is restricted to those meanings assumed by the natives. If so, his view is similar not only to Weber's, but to Dilthey's (on the reconstruction interpretation), Popper's, and Dray's. On the other hand, some of the interpretations of meaning of culture Geertz gives seem to go beyond what one would expect a native to have. However, Winch, Schutz, and Taylor allow social scientists' theories to go beyond the categories of the actors *so long as* they are indirectly related to these categories. A plausible hypothesis is that Geertz does the same thing. In support of this construal of Geertz, recall that he maintains that the interpretations of anthropologists are interpretations of natives' interpretations. So although some interpretations transcend the native understanding, they are indirectly based on natives' interpretation.

One important characteristic of thick descriptions is that they are microscopic, that is, they are interpretations of cultural details. This is not to say that there can be no broad interpretations: "It is merely to say that the anthropologist characteristically approaches such broader interpretations and more abstract analyses from the direction of extremely extended acquaintances with extremely small matters."[13] The important thing about "anthropological findings is their complex specificness, their circumstantiality."[14] Geertz, however, rejects the idea that ethnographic descriptions can be regarded on a "microcosmic model"; that is, he rejects the view that the subject of such a description is a miniature version of the larger society of which it is a part.

The Refiguration of Social Thought

In his later writings Geertz generalizes his program for cultural anthropology to a "refiguration of social thought" which links the social sciences and the humanities. Thus, he opens his essay "Blurred Genres" by saying, "A number of things, I think, are true." One is that there has been a great amount of genre mixing in intellectual life. Social scientists, he says, have turned away from explanations in terms of laws. They are

> looking less for the sort of thing that connects planets and pendulums and more for the sort that connects chrysanthemums and swords. Yet another is that analogies drawn from the humanities are coming to play the kind of role in sociological understanding that analogies drawn from the crafts and technology have played in physical understanding. Further, I not only think these things are true, I think they are true together; and it is the culture shift that makes them so that is my subject: the refiguration of social thought. [15]

Geertz goes on to argue that one implication of this is that it is harder to think of the social sciences as either "underdeveloped natural sciences" or "ignorant and pretentious usurpers of the mission of the humanities" or "comprising a clearly distinctive enterprise, a third culture to Snow's canonical two."

He says that the interpretive movement in the social sciences has grown tremendously:

> [T]he move toward conceiving of social life as organized in terms of symbols (signs, representations, *significants, Darstellungen* . . . . the terminology varies) whose meaning (sense, import, *signification, Bedeutung...*) we must grasp if we are to understand that organization and formulate its principles, has grown by now to formidable proportions. The woods are full of eager interpreters.
>
> Interpretive explanation—and it is a form of explanation, not just exalted glossography—trains its attention on what institutions, actions, images, utterances, events, customs, all the usual objects of social-scientific interest, mean to those

whose institutions, actions, customs, and so on they are. As a result, it issues not laws like Boyle's, or forces like Volta's, or mechanisms like Darwin's but in constructions like Burckhardt's, Weber's or Freud's systematic unpacking of the conceptual world in which *condotiere*, Calvinists, or paranoids live.[17]

Science, Geertz maintains, conceives of things in terms of analogies. New analogies are needed in the social sciences to give them new life. In particular, mechanistic analogies from natural science and engineering should be replaced by ones derived from "cultural performance." Nonreductive social sciences have borrowed analogies "from theater, painting, literature, law, play. What the lever did for physics, the chess move promises to do for sociology."[18]

Like interpretive theorists such as Taylor, Geertz draws an analogy between interpreting a text and interpreting a culture. Following Ricoeur, he argues that the key to the transition from text (a written document) to text analog (a culture) is the concept of inscription, that is, the fixation of meaning by means of language. The meaning of utterances as well as actions in a culture persists and can be recorded. To see social institutions as readable, Geertz says, is to change our sense of what sociological interpretation is and to "shift it toward modes of thought rather more familiar to the translator, the exegete, or inconographer than to the test giver, the factor analyst, or the pollster."[19]

After explaining "cultural performance" analogies such as the game and the drama that are now used in social science, Geertz concludes:

Matters are neither stable nor consensual, and they are not likely to become so. The interesting question is not how all this muddle is going to come magnificently together, but what does all this ferment mean.

One thing it means is that, however raggedly, a challenge is being mounted to some of the central assumptions of mainstream social science. The strict separation of theory and data, the "brute fact" idea; the effort to create a formal vocabulary of analysis purged of all subjective references, the "ideal language" idea; and the claim to moral neutrality and Olympian view, the "God's truth" idea—none of these ideas can prosper when explanation comes to be regarded as a matter of connecting action to its sense rather than behavior to its determinants. The refiguration of social theory represents, or will if it continues, a sea change in our notion not so much of what knowledge is but what it is we want to know. Social events do have causes and social institutions effects; it just may be that the road to discovering what we assert in asserting this lies less through postulating forces and measuring them than through noting expressions and inspecting them.[20]

Interpretive Social Science in Action: The Balinese Cockfight

In order to see Geertz's interpretive approach in action, let us consider one of his best-known cultural interpretations: "Deep Play: Notes on the Balinese Cockfight."[21] In what has been called an "elegant and revelatory essay,"[22] he describes the sport of cockfighting in Bali which, he says, may appear to be a superficial social practice but in fact is related to deep elements of the Balinese culture, self -concept, and world-view.

Balinese men spend a enormous amount of time on the various activities involved in cockfighting: they groom and train the cocks, they feed them with special diets, they watch them fight, they bet on them, they talk endlessly about them. Geertz describes these activities in detail in the context of a Balinese village. He also describes the jokes and language that are related to cockfighting and explains the special social and cultural significance the sport has by situating it within the broader Balinese culture.

For all the detail he gives us, however, Geertz's interpretation of the Balinese cockfights remains somewhat elusive. Indeed, different scholars, apparently focusing on different things that Geertz says, have come up with what seem to be different readings. Whether these can be reconciled is not clear. For example, Paul Rabinow and William M. Sullivan understand Geertz as providing what might be called a therapeutic interpretation. They say that on his view the cockfight domesticates and organizes violence:

> As Geertz presents it, the Balinese cockfight ritualizes violent conflict and thereby orders and to an extent domesticates it. Cultural form plays a therapeutic role by organizing and thereby making comprehensible violence and inequality.[23]

This rendering of the main thrust of Geertz's interpretation should be contrasted with Daniel Little's. Reading Geertz as saying that the cockfight is a surrogate for the struggle between good and evil, Little argues that Geertz gives what might be called a symbolic struggle interpretation:

> He interprets the pattern of large-scale betting on cockfights as emblemizing social relations in local society—kinship, village, and status relationships. And he construes the cockfight itself as an emblem—positive or negative—for elements in Balinese life . . . Particularly important, in Geertz's account, is the Balinese distaste for animal-like behavior in human beings; animals represent the "Powers of Darkness." Geertz construes the fascination with cockfighting as a surrogate for the struggle between good and evil.[24]

William Roseberry, stressing yet a different aspect of Geertz's paper, arrives at a different reading. According to him, Geertz presents what might be called a status organization and commentary interpretation. Geertz, he says, maintains that the cockfight is a stimulation of the social matrix, while at the same time providing a commentary on this matrix:

Geertz then looks to two aspects of significance in the cockfight. Both are related to the hierarchical organization of the Balinese society. He first observes that the cockfight is a "simulation of the social matrix," or following Goffman, a "status bloodbath . . ." As Geertz moves toward the second aspect of significance, although he has not yet referred to the cockfight as a text, he begins to refer to it as "an art form." As an art form display, it "displays" fundamental passions in Balinese society that are hidden from view in ordinary daily life and comportment. As an atomistic inversion of the way Balinese normally present themselves to themselves, the cockfight relates to the status hierarchy in another sense—no longer as a status-based organization of the cockfight but as a commentary on the existence of the status difference in the first place.[25]

Little's symbolic struggle reading of Geertz finds support in the text of Geertz's paper:

> The connection of cocks and cockfighting with such powers [of darkness], with the animalistic demons that threaten constantly to invade the small cleared off space in which the Balinese have so carefully built their lives and devour its inhabitants, is quite explicit. A cockfight, any cockfight, is in the first instance a blood sacrifice offered, with the appropriate chants and oblations, to the demons in order to pacify their ravenous, cannibal hunger . . . In the cockfight man and beast, good and evil, ego and id, the creative powers of aroused masculinity and destructive power of loosened animality fuse in a bloody drama of hatred, cruelty, violence, and death.[26]

However, Roseberry's social organization and commentary interpretation also find support there for Geertz does maintain that the cockfight is "a simulation of the social matrix":[27]

> The cocks may be surrogates for their owners' personalities, animal mirrors of psychic forms, but the cockfight is—more exactly, deliberately is made to be—a simulation of the social matrix, the involved system of cross-cut, overlapping, highly corporate groups—village, kingroups, irrigation societies, temple congregations, "castes"—in which the devotees live. And the prestige, the necessity to affirm it, defend it, celebrate it, justify it, and just plain bask in it . . . is perhaps the central force in any society, so also . . . is it of the cockfight.[28]

And Geertz also argues that the cockfight is "a Balinese reading of Balinese experience, a story they tell themselves about themselves":[29]

> What the cockfight says it says in a vocabulary of sentiment—the thrill of risk, the despair of loss, the pleasure of triumph. . . . Attending a cockfight and participating in them is, for the Balinese, a kind of sentimental education. What he learns there is what his culture's ethos and his private sensibility (or, anyway, certain aspects of them) look like when spelled out externally in a collective text.

Moreover, he says that in the cockfight, "the Balinese forms and discovers his temperament and his society's temperament at the same time."[31]

The therapeutic interpretation suggested by Rabinow and Sullivan is not stated explicitly in Geertz's article but it can be argued that it is implicit in some of the things he says. If the cockfight is symbolic of the struggle of good and evil, then one might suppose it has the function of ritualizing violence and domesticating it.

Geertz's Theory Evaluated

The Scope of Interpretive Anthropology

Conceiving the task of anthropologist as analogous to the interpreter of a text and likening culture to a text, Geertz maintains culture must be interpreted, its meaning deciphered. But he does not stop here. In Geertz's conception of social science the text analogy takes over, dictating how the discipline is defined, how it cuts off, even to the extent of excluding, noninterpretive questions and approaches. Even those anthropologists who believe that interpretation has a place in their discipline might believe that it is not the whole story, that noninterpretive questions can and should be asked. For Geertz, however, interpretation is all important. In "Thick Descriptions" he does not allow for any tasks besides interpretation[32] for he assumes that since culture consists of complex structures of meanings, anthropologists must limit themselves to making sense of these.

Yet even if one accepts the text analogy, there are more jobs for social scientists to do than just interpretation. The text analogy need not be so restrictive. A reader of a text might ask not only what the text means but why the text was produced in the first place, why it takes this form rather than some other, what functions the text has, what psychological effects a given interpretation has on readers who accept it. Just as a reader might want to know how a text developed, a social scientist might want to know how a culture developed. Just as he or she might wonder why one text has a particular form while a similar text has a different one, a social scientist might wonder why one culture has a particular form while another culture has a different one. Just as a reader might be interested in what function a certain part of a text has (given a certain interpretation), a social scientist might be interested in what function a social practice has (given a certain interpretation). Just as a reader desires to find out what psychological effects an interpretation has on someone who accepts it, a social scientist might desire to find out what psychological effects a social practice (interpreted in a certain way) has on a social actor who participates in it.

Geertz does not ask noninterpretive questions such as these in either "Thick Descriptions" or "Deep Play." In the former he gives no indication that such questions are legitimate and in the latter he almost entirely avoids them in his discussion of the Balinese cockfight. Thus, after reading Geertz's study one has no idea why there is the practice of cockfighting in Bali, why males engage in it, why cockfighting takes this form in Bali and different forms in other cultures. Presumably the answers to these questions will involve causal factors—psychological, sociological, geographical—that go beyond the purview of the interpretive approach.[33]

Moreover, it is not clear if Geertz allows the question of what function or dysfunction cockfighting has in Bali. He certainly does not use function language in his paper. Does he implicitly attribute a function to cockfighting, however? Rabinow and Sullivan maintain that Geertz says that cockfighting domesticates and organizes violence. One way to understand this is as a functional thesis; however, this reading of Geertz seems strained. It is not justified by any direct quotations from the text.[34] Furthermore, the whole spirit of Geertz's philosophy of anthropology is opposed to a functional approach.[35]

Although Geertz makes remarks throughout "Deep Play" that might well be interpreted as psychological statements about the effects of cockfighting on Balinese males, the issue of the psychological effects on those participating in cockfighting is not explicitly posed and answered in any systematic way. Insofar as he cites the psychological effects of cockfighting—for example, that the person who eats the losing cock experiences aesthetic disgust as well as cannibalistic joy[36]—it is to justify his interpretation. He makes no effort to explore the question in its own right, perhaps because to do so would be to investigate causal matters and would involve using psychological theories and laws. However, this is exactly what Geertz considers suspect.

As a result of Geertz's disinterest in the issue of the psychological effects of cockfighting, important questions are not asked, let alone answered. For example, one would like to know whether men who raise and fight cocks have a different personality or psychological profile from those who don't; what Balinese women think of cockfighting and how their attitudes towards it affect their relations with men; whether the psychology of men has changed because of the recent tougher governmental policy on cockfighting; how men's psychological attitudes towards cockfighting are affected by their formal education, by religious conversion, by the influx of Western ideas and values.

In sum, questions about origins, functions, and psychological effects go well beyond the scope of interpretive social science. Since they are legitimate and important, any approach that excludes them has serious limitations.

In addition, even if one allows that the only task of the social sciences is interpretation, Geertz wrongly restricts this task. To be sure, he does not restrict interpretations to those adopted by the natives. This is shown by some of the interpretations of the meaning of the cockfight considered earlier. They are not interpretations that participants have of their own activity. For example, it is unlikely that the participants actually understand cockfighting as a surrogate struggle between good and evil. Nevertheless, Geertz seems to restrict anthropologists' interpretations that transcend those of the participants to those that are somehow based on the participants' own interpretations: They are interpretations of the natives' own interpretations. Unfortunately, Geertz does not specify which interpretation of the participants is the basis for the anthropologist's good-evil struggle interpretation.

In any case, Geertz's restriction is unjustified. There is no good reason why anthropologists' interpretations must be based on the natives' own interpretations. Geertz's restriction is unwarranted in the same way Winch's, Schutz's, and Taylor's restrictions were: They prevent social scientists from theorizing in ways that are not at least indirectly tied to categories and understanding of the social actors.

Interpretation and Causality

There is good reason to suppose that Geertz's theory like Taylor's represses causal considerations. Geertz forsakes appeals to causal laws in the social sciences, rejects the natural science approach to the social sciences in which causal attribution is central, fails to list "cause" or "causality" in the indexes of *The Interpretation of Cultures* and *Local Knowledge*, and refrains from using explicit causal language in his interpretative work. This repression of causality is to be expected if one lets the text analogy dominate one's thought since causality plays no role in the interpretation of texts. Geertz's position, however, would find no sympathy with Weber or Popper, both of whose theories of Verstehen were closely linked with causal explanations. On the other hand, a neglect of causal explanation characterizes the theories of Winch, Dray, Schutz, and perhaps Dilthey.

However, Geertz's repression of causality is not complete. In "Blurred Genres," he acknowledges that there are causal considerations in the social sciences and only rejects the way the analysis of causality is approached: "Social events do have causes and social institutions effects; it just may be that the road to discovering what we assert in asserting this lies less through postulating forces and measuring them than through noting expressions and inspecting them."[37] Apparently, then, interpretative anthropology is concerned with causes after all, although, it is not clear how.[38]

It is worth noting that all three readings of Geertz's interpretation of Balinese cockfighting cited above implicitly have a causal dimension. When Rabinow and Sullivan understand Geertz as offering a therapeutic interpretation according to which the cockfight domesticates and organizes violence, they do not speak in causal terms. However, they are surely saying that cockfighting—the psychology of the participants, the social practice and its implications, and so on—causally affects people, albeit in some unspecified manner, in such a way that their violent behavior is controlled and tamed.[39] The symbolic struggle reading of Geertz suggested by Little also has a causal aspect. Males presumably have an unconscious belief connected with the symbolic struggle between good and evil. Under certain unspecified circumstances this belief causes them to be obsessed with cocks and to be ambivalent about eating a dead cock and so on. Causal considerations also apply to the social organization and commentary reading of Geertz suggested by Roseberry. On this interpretation, the views and attitudes that Balinese men have of the social matrix of their society get transformed by some unspecified psychological and sociological process into the institution of the cockfight. This institution, in turn, stimulates this social matrix and provides a commentary on it. The way this transformation works and what causal mechanisms are involved is not made clear by Geertz.

In short, causal considerations and mechanisms are implicit in Geertz's interpretation of the Balinese cockfight. However, the text analogy tends to obscure their presence.

The Validation of Interpretations

What is the epistemological status of cultural interpretations? Are some interpretations true and others false? If one cannot speak of "true" and "false" interpretations, are some interpretations better than others? If interpretations in social science are true or false, how can their truth or falsehood be validated? If some are better or worse than others, what criteria of "better" or "worse" should be used?

Unfortunately, Geertz is not very helpful in answering these questions. Again one suspects that the text analogy adversely affects his account, leading him to suppose that cultural interpretations are either like subjective literary interpretations[40] or else are based on considerations that have nothing to do with the validation of scientific hypotheses. In "Thick Descriptions," he seems to suggest that interpretations are subjective and that therefore there are no objective criteria for evaluating them.[41] Here his view is similar to Taylor's in that they both reject the possibility of objective interpretations.

Explicitly rejecting accurate prediction as a criterion of the validity of interpretation—at least in "the strict meaning of the term" prediction[42]—Geertz indicates that the verification of interpretations is problematic:

> The besetting sin of interpretive approaches to anything—literature, dreams, symptoms, culture—is that they tend to resist, or to be permitted to resist, conceptual articulation and thus to escape systematic modes of assessment. You either grasp an interpretation or you do not, see the point of it or you do not, accept it or you do not. Imprisoned in the immediacy of its own detail, it is presented as self validation, or, worse, as validated by the supposedly developed sensitivities of the person who presents it; any attempt to cast what it says in terms other than its own is regarded as a travesty—as the anthropologist's severest term of moral abuse, ethnocentric. For a field of study which, however timidly (though I, myself, am not timid about the matter at all), asserts itself to be a science, this just will not do. There is no reason why the conceptual structure of a cultural interpretation should be any less formulable, and thus less susceptible to explicit canons of appraisal, than that of, say, a biological observation or a physical experiment—no reason except that the terms in which such a formulation can be cast are, if not wholly nonexistent, very nearly so. We are reduced to insinuating theories because we lack the power to state them.[43]

In this passage, Geertz links the difficulty of verifying interpretations in social science with the lack of a well-articulated theoretic language. However, it is unclear why one needs well-articulated theories in order to verify cultural interpretations. In the natural sciences it is possible to verify ill-articulated theories. Indeed, verifying theories that lack precise articulation is often necessary to develop the theory in more rigorous ways. Geertz, in fact, seems to have things backwards. Far from well-developed theories being necessary for verification, verification is often necessary for developing well-articulated theories.

However, Geertz never explicitly advocated a relativistic anything-goes approach. Indeed, some of his own disciples maintain that he did not go far enough in the rejection of objectivity.[44] In places, he argues that some interpretations are better than others. However, the criteria he uses in making such assessments are unclear. He says,

A good interpretation of anything—a poem, a person, a history, a ritual, an institution, a society—takes us into the heart of that of which it is the interpretation.
When it does not do that, but leads us instead somewhere else—into an admiration
of its own elegance, of its author's cleverness, of the beauties of Euclidean order—it may have intrinsic charms; but it is something else than what the task at
hand...calls for.[45]

One supposes that Geertz is saying here that good interpretations take
one to the heart of the matter whereas bad ones do not. However, he
does not explicate what exactly this involves; in particular, he does not
explain how one tells what the heart of the matter is.[46] Elsewhere in
"Thick Descriptions," he says that "a study is an advance if it is more
incisive—whatever that means—than those that preceded it."[47] Could
this be an attempt to explicate what it means for "an interpretation that
goes to the heart of the matter"? If so, it does not help since the criterion of being more incisive is no clearer than the criterion of going to
the heart of the matter.

Suppose one anthropologist argues that interpretation X is more incisive than interpretation Y while another maintains the opposite. How
can one tell which anthropologist is correct? Geertz suggests it is very
difficult to do so:

The claim to attention of an ethnographic account does not rest on its author's
ability to capture primitive facts in faraway places...but on the degree to which he
is able to clarify what goes on in such places, to reduce the puzzlement—what
manner of men are these?—to which unfamiliar acts emerging out of unknown backgrounds naturally give rise.

This raises some serious problems of verification, all right—or, if "verification"
is too strong a word for too soft a science (I, myself, would prefer "appraisal"), of how
you can tell a better account from a worse one. But this is precisely the virtue in it.[48]

This "virtue" would imply that one has no rational reason to believe
Geertz's interpretations over alternatives.[49] One cannot be certain that
he completely realizes this implication. In any case, he goes on to say
that interpretations cannot be judged against uninterpreted data and
that "we must measure the cogency of our explications, but against the
power of the scientific imagination to bring us into touch with lives of
strangers."[50] Unfortunately, this new criterion—bringing anthropologists into touch with the lives of natives—is not very helpful and is not
clearly compatible with the criterion of incisiveness. How can one tell
which of two conflicting interpretations brings us in better touch with
the lives of natives? Furthermore, why should one suppose that the
more incisive interpretation will bring anthropologists into close touch

with the lives of the natives? After all, the more incisive interpretation may be couched in language that is divorced from the natives' experiences and their concepts while the interpretation that brings us close to the lives of natives may not be.

Furthermore, why this criterion is to be preferred over many others that might be suggested is not specified. For example, one might judge alternative interpretations in terms of traditional scientific criteria such as explanatory power and simplicity. The text analogy seems to obscure this obvious point.

The epistemological problems connected with Geertz's general approach to interpretation certainly affect his reading of the Balinese cockfight. Following Little, let us suppose that Geertz is giving the symbolic struggle interpretation of Balinese cockfighting. Is it justified? One can understand Geertz as appealing to the following sorts of considerations to justify this interpretation:

(1) Balinese males identify with their birds. Geertz bases this on the things that Balinese males say. He admits that he has no "unconscious material either to confirm or disconfirm this intriguing notion."[51] Nevertheless, he argues that it is universally recognized by the Balinese that cocks are the masculine symbol par excellence.

(2) The moral language of Bali has roosterish imagery. Geertz bases this on examples. The Balinese word for cock is used metaphorically to mean "hero," "warrior," "tough guy"; court trials, wars, etc. are compared to cockfights, and so on.

(3) Men are obsessed with cocks and cockfights. Geertz bases this on the vast amount of time men spend tending, feeding, grooming, and training their birds and on the way they describe their activities.

(4) The Balinese are revolted by any behavior regarded as animal. Geertz cites examples such as eating and defecation which are regarded as almost obscene activities because of their association with animals.

(5) When the owner of the winning cock takes the carcass of the losing cock "home to eat, he does so with a mixture of social embarrassment, moral satisfaction, aesthetic disgust, and cannibal joy."[52] This is presumably based on his personal observations on the culture and his conversations with Balinese.

(6) A man who "has lost an important [cock]fight is sometimes driven to wreck his family shrines and curse the gods, an act of metaphysical (and social) suicide."[53] This is based on the same evidence as (5) above.

(7) Balinese compare heaven with the mood of a man whose cock has just won and hell with the mood of a man whose cock has just lost. This is based on the same evidence as (5) above.

Are (1)- (7) true? At best Geertz offers impressionistic and anecdotal evidence to support these claims, some of which involve statistical inferences. For example, (1) is supported by appealing to a few examples and by Geertz's impression of what is universally recognized, and (2) is also supported by a few examples. However, we have no reason to suppose that these examples are representative or that Geertz's impressions are reliable. Thus, one would like to know *how* widespread roosterish imagery is in Balinese moral language in comparison with imagery that might indicate a different interpretation. Although we know from Geertz's paper that there is "roosterish imagery" in Balinese moral language, it perhaps appears rarely while other imagery appears frequently.

However, let us suppose that (1)-(7) are well-established propositions about the Balinese culture and society. One wonders how Geertz might use (1)-(7) to support:

(8) Cockfighting is a surrogate for the struggle between good and evil.

(8) is obviously not entailed by (1)-(7). It might, however, be justified on inductive grounds. For example, (8) might be an "inference to the best possible explanation." That is to say, this hypothesis might be the best explanation of the evidence. Is (8) the best explanation of (1)-(7)? Viewed in this way, a possible line of inductive reasoning leading from (1)-(7) to (8) can be reconstructed[54]:

(a) The symbolic struggle hypothesis (8) has a nonnegligible prior probability.

(b) If the symbolic struggle hypothesis (8) is true, then the evidence statements [(1)-(7)] used to support it are probably true.

(c) No other hypothesis is as strongly confirmed by the evidence statements; that is, any other hypothesis H such that if H is true, then (1)-(7) are probably true has a lower prior probability than (8).

Given (1)- (7), and (a)-(c), (8) is well supported.

When it is reconstructed along these lines, the symbolic struggle interpretation is simply a hypothesis that should be evaluated by the usual criteria. One would then ask if it is better confirmed than rival hypotheses, if (c) is met, if rival hypotheses are initially less plausible than (8) and in consequence have less prior probability than (8). Unfortunately, Geertz does not consider rival interpretations and does not attempt to determine if (c) has been met.

One obvious rival hypothesis that is simpler than (8) is that cockfighting is regarded with great ambivalence by Balinese males. They are attracted to its macho quality and yet at a deep level are repelled by its animalistic dimensions. On this interpretation, cockfighting need not have cosmic moral significance, as it does on the symbolic struggle interpretation. The ambivalence hypothesis might, of course, be entailed by the symbolic struggle hypothesis but it certainly would not entail it. Is this hypothesis initially more plausible than (8)? Given the usual understanding that, other things being equal, the simplest hypothesis is the most plausible one, it is. If Geertz rejects this connection between simplicity with plausibility, he owes us an explanation.

Would the ambivalence hypothesis explain everything the symbol struggle hypothesis explains? It does not appear to explain (6) above: that a person who loses a cockfight sometimes wrecks his family shrine and curses the gods. However, Geertz gives such incidents cosmic meaning by saying that the loser in so acting commits "metaphysical suicide." This reading of the action might well attribute more significance to it than is warranted. One wants to know how common such actions are and what significance the frustrated Balinese losers give to them.

It is certainly not obvious that (b) is true. For example, if the symbolic struggle interpretation is true, then would men be so openly obsessed with cocks and cockfighting as they are pictured by Geertz? One would suppose that the male obsession with cock fighting would be more subtle, less obvious, and more conflicted than Geertz describes. The mixed-emotions connected with eating the loser's cock that Geertz describes—social embarrassment, moral satisfaction, aesthetic disgust, cannibal joy—seem strangely absent from the daily activities of training and fighting the cocks.

Conclusion

Although Geertz is a leading advocate of the interpretative approach to the social sciences, providing a rationale as well as a concrete model of what the results of such an approach would entail, his account has serious limitations. He is not only vague about what constitutes a valid interpretation in his theoretical writings, but his interpretation of the Balinese cockfight leaves many questions unanswered. In particular, it is ambiguous what his interpretation of the Balinese cockfight amounts to, whether it is supported by the evidence, and why it should be preferred to alternatives. In addition, in Geertz's view, social science is arbitrarily limited to providing interpretations—thick descriptions—and no other tasks are permissible. Moreover, he arbitrarily limits such interpretations to those based on the interpretations of the natives. Finally, causality has a much more important role to play in the social sciences than Geertz allows. Even if one restricts social science to the giving of interpretations, causal considerations enter into the specification of the web of meanings of social practices and institutions. If the job of social science is conceived of as including more than merely interpreting the culture as it surely does, then causality plays an even more important role.

Notes

1. This chapter is based on my paper, "Geertz and the Interpretive Approach in Anthropology," *Synthèse* 97, 1993, pp. 267-86.
2. See Ronald Walters, "Signs of the Times: Clifford Geertz and Historians," *Social Research* 47, 1980, pp. 537-56.
3. James Peacock, "The Third Stream: Weber, Parsons, and Geertz," *The Anthropological Society of Oxford* 7, 1981, pp. 122–23.
4. Paul Shankman, "The Thick and the Thin: On the Interpretive Program of Clifford Geertz," *Current Anthropology* 25, 1984, p. 261.
5. For example, in standard texts such as David Braybrooke, *Philosophy of Social Science* (Englewood Cliffs, NJ: Prentice-Hall, 1987), and Alexander Rosenberg, *Philosophy of the Social Sciences* (Englewood Cliffs, NJ: Prentice-Hall, 1988), Geertz is not mentioned at all. While Daniel Little, *Varieties of Social Explanation* (Boulder, CO: Westview Press, 1991), considers Geertz's view, Little's critical comments are rather brief.
6. I have relied heavily on Shankman, "The Thick and the Thin," in my exposition of Geertz.

7. Clifford Geertz, "Thick Descriptions: Toward an Interpretive Theory of Culture," *Interpretation of Cultures* (New York: Basic Books, 1973), pp. 3-30.

8. Ibid., p. 5. This view of culture is expressed in his most recent book, *After the Fact* (Cambridge, MA: Harvard University Press, 1995), p. 43, p. 115.

9. Geertz, "Thick Descriptions: Toward an Interpretive Theory of Culture," p. 10.

10. Ibid., p. 14. In *After the Fact*, Geertz says (p. 62) that the anthropologist tells "stories about stories."

11. Geertz, "Thick Descriptions: Toward an Interpretive Theory of Culture," p. 13.

12. See Geertz, "Blurred Genres: The Refiguration of Social Thought," *Local Knowledge* (New York: Basic Books, 1983), pp. 55-59.

13. Ibid., p. 21.

14. Ibid., p. 23.

15. Ibid., p. 19.

16. Ibid., p. 21.

17. Ibid., pp. 21-22.

18. Ibid., p. 20.

19. Ibid., p. 31.

20. Ibid., p. 34.

21. Clifford Geertz, "Deep Play: Notes on the Balinese Cockfight," *Interpretation of Cultures*, pp. 421-53.

22. Paul Rabinow and William M. Sullivan, "The Interpretive Turn," in Paul Rabinow and William M. Sullivan, eds., *Interpretative Social Science: A Second Look* (Berkeley and Los Angeles: University of California Press, 1987), p. 26.

23. Ibid.

24. Little, *Varieties of Social Explanation*, pp. 69-70.

25. William Roseberry, "Balinese Cockfights and the Seduction of 'Anthropology,'" *Social Research* 49, 1982, p. 1018.

26. Geertz, "Deep Play," pp. 420-21.

27. Ibid., p. 436.

28. Ibid.

29. Ibid., p. 448.

30. Ibid., p. 449.

31. Ibid., p. 451.

32. I do not wish to claim that Geertz is completely consistent. Some of his research belies the restrictions he imposes on social science in this paper. On this point see Little, *Varieties of Social Explanation*, p. 238n. 4.

33. It might be replied that questions of origins might be addressed in terms of narrative explanations. Assuming such explanations are interpretive, the question still remains of whether all legitimate questions of origins can be addressed by narrative accounts. This is surely an open question.

34. Indeed, the terms "function" or "functionalism" are not listed in the index of Geertz, *Interpretation of Cultures*. In Geertz, *Local Knowledge*, p. 99, he mentions functionalism only to reject one of the implications of holding it.

35. If Geertz is implicitly appealing to function in this case, he provides no evidence that cockfighting has this function. The function of a culture practice is ordinarily understood in terms of the causal consequences of practice, and he provides no evidence that cockfighting has the causal consequences of organizing and domesticating violence.

36. Geertz, *Interpretation of Cultures*, p. 421.

37. Geertz, *Local Knowledge*, p. 34.

38. Kincaid points out that Geertz's interpretive ideology is inconsistent with his practice where he makes standard naturalist judgments about causal structure.

See Harold Kincaid, *Philosophical Foundations of the Social Sciences* (New York: Cambridge University Press, 1996), p. 208.

39. Perhaps Rabinow and Sullivan, strong advocates of interpretative social science, would reject this causal interpretation. However, they provide no alternative account and it is hard to see what other is available.

40. However, there is no good reason to suppose that literary interpretation cannot be based on objective considerations. See for example, Føllesdal, "Hermeneutics and the hypothetico-deductive method," *Dialectica* 33, 1979, pp. 319-36, and E. D. Hirsch, *Validation in Interpretation* (New Haven: Yale University Press, 1967).

41. He express skepticism about objectivity in his latest book, *After the Fact*, pp. 3, 18-19. On the other hand, he does not believe that problems about objectivity completely undermine the possibility of doing comparative ethnography. See Geertz, *After the Fact*, p. 129.

42. Geertz, *The Interpretation of Culture*, p. 26.

43. Ibid., p. 24.

44. See David Berreby, "Unabsolute Truths," *New York Times Magazine*, April 9, 1995, pp. 44-48; Peter Novick, *That Nobel Dream* (Cambridge, MA: Cambridge University Press, 1988), pp. 551-54.

45. Geertz, *The Interpretation of Culture*, p. 18.

46. See Shankman, "The Thick and the Thin, p. 263.

47. Geertz, *The Interpretation of Culture*, p. 25. Cf. Geertz, *After the Fact*, p. 19.

48. Geertz, *The Interpretation of Culture*, p. 16.

49. In chapter 9, I argue that interpretations can be objective. See also Michael Martin, "Taylor on Interpretation and the Sciences of Man," *Readings in the Philosophy of Social Science*, ed. Michael Martin and Lee McIntyre (Cambridge, MA: The MIT Press, 1994), pp. 259-79.

50. Geertz, *The Interpretation of Culture*, p. 16.

51. Ibid., p. 420.

52. Ibid., p. 421.

53. Ibid.

54. For this sort of analysis of confirmation, see Merrilee Salmon, *Philosophy and Archaeology* (New York: Academic Press, 1982), pp. 49-51.

9

Verstehen and Critical Theory

From the point of view of critical social science, social science should expose the hidden biases and ideologies in our thinking, even in our social scientific thinking. The advocates of this critical social science maintain that deep unconscious prejudices about class, race, and gender influence our thinking and that the social sciences should raise them to consciousness so that we can escape their influence and become liberated.[1] Unlike the naturalistic or the antinaturalistic (interpretive) social science approaches, critical social science has as its direct goal human emancipation: liberation from prejudice, ignorance, and oppression. Influenced by the Enlightenment idea that knowledge is liberating, perhaps the two main sources of critical social science are the theories of Marx and Freud. Combining Marx's theory of ideology that moral, religious, and political doctrines are nothing but reflections of the interests of powerful elites with Freud's theory in which deference to these doctrines is based on deep-seated rationalizations, critical social science argued that social science should expose these interests and these rationalizations.

This approach to social science methodology combined with a substantive neo-Marxist theory of advanced capitalism has come to be known as Critical Theory and is closely connected with the Frankfurt School. In turn this school of thought is principally associated with the social theorists, Max Horkheimer, Herbert Marcuse, Theodor Adorno, and Jürgen Habermas. However, two qualifications are necessary. Many examples of critical social scientific theories are found outside the context of the Critical Theory of the Frankfurt School.[2] Moreover, some members of the Frankfurt School became skeptical of the liberating potential of social science and abandoned it.[3] One reason for their skepticism was their belief that scientific reasoning had to be instrumental, that is, a means to some end. However, they maintained that there was no way to reason about the end.

Jürgen Habermas, the most influential second-generation member of the Frankfurt School, rejected this skepticism and argued that genuine social critique was still possible. Critical of the modern tendency to identify reason with instrumental reason in which the determination of ends is outside of reason's scope, Habermas has argued against the "scientization" of politics where political questions are reduced to problems of technical control and public discussion over social goals is impaired. His solution to this problem is to shift the philosophical emphasis from subject-object relations to the process of intersubjective communication. In his early work, *Knowledge and Human Interest*,[4] Habermas distinguished two forms of action: instrumental and communicative. These correspond to two distinct types of interest which are the basis of two types of inquiries. Thus, instrumental action gives rise to empirical-analytic inquiries that aim to predict and control objective processes, while communicative action leads to interpretative and critical inquiries that aim to understand others and uncover unconscious biases.[5]

In his later work, Habermas developed "a universal pragmatics" in which he attempted to show that there are normative assumptions implicit in linguistic communication. Thus, he maintained that when speakers attempt to reach consensus through discussion they tacitly assume the presence of conditions of unrestrained communication such as equality and reciprocity of participation. These implicit assumptions of communication make possible a criticism of inequities of social and political power that is not based merely on personal values. This "ethics of communication" plays a pivotal role in Habermas's massive treatise on social theory, *The Theory of Communicative Action*.[6] There he maintained that the problems of contemporary society can be traced to the colonization of the lifeworld, that is, the taking over of the world of everyday life by economic and administrative systems that undermine participatory democracy and unfettered communication.[7]

As with other members of the Frankfurt School, Habermas has maintained that an essential part of a program of emancipation is an interpretive approach to social sciences. David Ingram, a Critical Theory and Habermas scholar, has put the general position of the members of the school in this way:

A sociology restricted to causal explanations, they realized, can only *describe* social behavior as a necessary and predictable outcome of the existing system. It cannot *criticize* such behavior as the result of *false* consciousness. It cannot, in other words, regard the behavior of social actors as historically conditioned and changing through efforts of the enlightenment. This would require an *understanding* of subjective ideas and objective cultural ideals motivating action as well as their *evaluation* in terms of furthering an *objectively* rational (anticipatory) potential.[8]

Habermas's interpretivism is more moderate than Peter Winch's or Charles Taylor's. In *On the Logic of the Social Sciences,* Habermas spoke with approval of a "functionalism that is hermeneutically enlightened and historically oriented,"[9] and commentators point out that he combines interpretive and causal analysis.[10] In addition, in a 1983 paper entitled "Interpretive Social Science vs. Hermeneuticism," Habermas argued that the "main arguments for philosophical hermeneutics have become more or less accepted. . . as a research program *within* social science, within anthropology, sociology, and social psychology."[11] This seems to suggest that nonhermeneutic approaches would also be legitimate research programs within the social sciences.

However, this moderate appearance is to some extent deceptive. Concentrating on what follows in *On the Logic of the Social Sciences* (1967) and his discussion of understanding and rationality in *The Theory of Communicative Action,* vol. 1 (1984), I will show that Habermas is so strongly committed to the interpretive model that his approach, if adopted, would unduly restrict social scientific inquiry and rule out purely noninterpretive approaches. In this chapter, I will demonstrate that Habermas's theory has other serious problems as well.

The Interpretive Orientation of *On the Logic of the Social Sciences*

Rejecting the positivists' doctrine expounded by methodologists such as Theodore Abel that Verstehen is simply a heuristic device useful in the context of discovery,[12] in *On the Logic of the Social Sciences* Habermas defends a broadly conceived interpretive approach to the social sciences. Recall that, according to Abel, Verstehen enables one to understand why there is an observed connection between an external stimulus such as a drop in temperature and an external response such as building a fire. By means of introspection of one's own experience one can understand why these two factors are connected by postulating a subjective state connecting the external stimulus and response:

The person who built the fire did so because he was cold due to the drop in temperature. Abel argued that Verstehen is not sufficient to verify that this explanation is correct but is only useful as a means of generating the hypothesis.

Abel also argued that one understands the connection between the success of a harvest and the frequency of marriage in rural communities by postulating that the loss of income brings about anxiety. According to Habermas, this example is not based on introspection but "requires a controlled appropriation through the hermeneutic understanding of meaning."[13] In fact, Habermas suggests that Abel's interpretation of the connection between the success of a harvest and the frequency of marriage is problematic. Marriage does not need to be evaluated primarily as an economic burden and depends on "traditional notions of values and institutional roles."[14] In any case, Abel is incorrect, according to Habermas, to suppose that advocates of Verstehen believed that it was a means of verifying the motivation of social actors. Verifying the validity of an interpretation is not achieved by Verstehen itself but is "subjected to test in the usual manner."[15]

Habermas concludes that only a critique that "challenged the very need for subjective access to social facts would call into question the methodological principle of Verstehen."[16] However, he believes this cannot be called into question without accepting a problematic behaviorism. Thomas McCarthy in his commentary on *On the Logic of the Social Sciences* has put Habermas's views in this way: "Behavior in society is mediated through the interpretive scheme of the actors themselves. Consequently the attempt to grasp social reality independently of the participant's own 'definition of the situation,' to pursue the tasks of concept and theory formation in abstraction from the prior categorical formation of the object domain, is condemned to failure."[17]

However, as Habermas makes clear in other parts of *On the Logic of the Social Sciences*, the subjective interpretive schemes of the actors are only part of an adequate social science. He rejects the subjectivism of phenomenology and ethnomethodology and argues that the meaning of social norms extends beyond the limits of the subjectively intended meanings of individuals acting according to norms.[18] Habermas also rejects Winch's Wittgensteinian approach to social understanding in terms of language games and forms of life as relativistic and ahistorical. In the Winchian approach, as Habermas sees it, one is socialized into a form of life that constitutes a linguistic totality, a closed perspective for viewing the world.[19]

Habermas is more sympathetic to Gadamer's hermeneutical approach with its emphasis on history and tradition in which a language user is never locked into a single language. Instead of Winch's stress on socialization into a particular language, Gadamer emphasizes translation and dialogue in which the interpreter-translator gradually becomes cognizant of his own form of bias in the course of her interpretive operation. In this translation and dialogue the interpreter must preserve the foreignness of the material and yet at the same time bring it into a meaningful relation with his own life-world, relating the text to her situation.[20]

Habermas accepts Gadamer's thesis that the interpreter necessarily relates what is to be understood to her own situation. However, Habermas has serious reservations about that relation and what he sees as the conservative implications that Gadamer draws from it. Gadamer's identification of hermeneutic investigation with the prolongation of tradition places a one-sided emphasis on participation and dialogue over critical reflection. According to Habermas, "Gadamer fails to recognize the power of reflection that unfolds in Verstehen."[21] The reflection that is part of the understanding of social meaning, he claims, can profoundly alter the tradition from which it grows and develops. Habermas maintains that hermeneutic interpretation must be conjoined with a critique of ideology, an analysis of social systems in terms of the empirical condition under which a tradition develops, and a philosophy of history that attempts to anticipate the future as a practical enterprise and not in a purely contemplative way.[22]

It seems clear from this summary of Habermas's earlier work on philosophy of the social sciences that the interpretation of meaning in terms of the subjective categories of social actors is for him a necessary condition—but not a sufficient condition—of understanding. Although Habermas believes that much more is needed in social science—ideological critique and an analysis of social systems, for example—and although interpretation must be historically sensitive to tradition and yet be able to critically revise this tradition, utilization of the subjective categories of the actor is indispensable for understanding.

In short, in *On the Logic of the Social Sciences*, Habermas advocated the following Interpretive Thesis:

(IT) In order to understand a human action it is necessary to interpret this action in terms of the subjective categories of the social actors.

The Restrictive Nature of Habermas's Construal

Although Habermas's construal of the interpretive approach is certainly much more liberal and moderate than theories which view interpretation in terms of the subjective categories of the actor as exhausting the scope of social inquiry, it still is not liberal or moderate enough. There is no good reason why, depending on the purpose of inquiry and the description of the phenomena, subjective categories of the actor have to be utilized at all. Habermas tends to forget two essential and related aspects of social scientific understanding.[23] First, there are different ways of understanding social reality—some appropriate for some purposes and not for others. There is no more reason to think that utilizing the subjective categories of an actor is relevant for *all* purposes than to suppose that utilizing causal analysis is. Second, we always understand social phenomena under a particular description. A description in terms of the subjective categories of the actor is one kind of description that *might* be relevant and appropriate under certain circumstances. But given other circumstances, it might not be.

As we have seen, any given thing can be understood internally or externally. Moreover, both external and internal understanding can take many different forms. Habermas arbitrarily requires that understanding must include one type of internal understanding, namely that based on the descriptive terms used by the social agents. The position put forth in (IT) above in effect claims that external understanding is inapplicable to human action *unless* it is combined with internal understanding of a certain kind. However, understanding an action in terms of the categories of the agent is not the only way to understand an action. We also find it enlightening to be shown the connection between an action and some antecedent event, e.g., a childhood experience, or some standing condition, e.g., a state of society, or to be shown that an action fits into a larger context such as a historical trend or falls under some interesting and surprising category.[24] Furthermore, this enlightenment and illumination can be had independently of internal understanding.

This is not to say that in such a situation one has complete understanding. However, complete understanding usually is not what is sought. Obviously there is further understanding that could be achieved. But this further illumination might not be relevant to purposes at hand. One can go on to ask, for example, how a childhood experience led to some particular action. Here internal understanding may be relevant. But it might not be. It will depend on the purposes and context.

According to McCarthy, Habermas maintains that since social behavior is mediated through the interpretive scheme of the actors themselves, the attempt to understand social reality independently of the participant's own construal of the situation "is condemned to failure." However, this ignores the points raised above. Just because social behavior is mediated through the interpretive schemes of social actors, it does not follow that one must understand social behavior in these terms. After all, social behavior is mediated in some sense through the brain states of the actors, yet no one supposes that the actors' brain states must be utilized in understanding social reality. For certain purposes one might understand social behavior externally, for example, in terms of prevailing social conditions. For example, a revolution might be understood in terms of the repression by the authorities and the poverty of the people. Given a certain context, there need be no recourse to the interpretive scheme of the social actors.

Although internal understanding might be appropriate in a given context, it need not be in terms of actors' interpretive schemes. Thus, a social action might be understood in terms of unconscious desires and repression: for example, the strong attraction of "defense intellectuals" to weapons of mass destruction such as nuclear missiles, and the sexual imagery used in talking about such weapons, has been understood in terms of unconscious sexual desires.[25] This construal entails describing the nuclear missiles in different terms from those used by the actors, for example, as phallic symbols. However, given the context, there might be no need to mention the subjective interpretive scheme of the actors.

In opposition to my arguments it might be said that Habermas holds the position of critical social science. As the above quotation from Ingram attempts to demonstrate, in order to have emancipatory goals Verstehen is necessary. Let us call this the Emancipation-Verstehen Thesis and formulate it as follows:

> (EVT) In order to emancipate the members of a society by exposing their biases, prejudices, etc., it is necessary to use Verstehen.

Now if EVT is true, this would not effect a major thesis of this book: There are different types of understanding relevant to different pur-

poses and contexts. Understanding in terms of the subjective categories of the actor is only one kind. This type of understanding may well
be necessary for the purposes of critical social science.

Unfortunately, although Habermas certainly accepts EVT, he goes
beyond it. As previously noted, Habermas supposes that the only alternative to an unacceptable behaviorism is the acceptance of Verstehen,
and McCarthy, following Habermas, maintains that all attempts to understand without utilizing the subjective meaning of the actors is condemned to failure. Obviously these claims are not entailed by EVT.

But is EVT true? In so far as emancipation involves exposing the false
beliefs of the social actors one must know what the beliefs of the actors are. Verstehen in a narrow sense involves knowing the beliefs
and other subjective states of the actors. So, in this sense, EVT is
trivially true. However, in a broader sense and more common sense
of Verstehen, EVT is false. For in this sense, Verstehen involves knowing the beliefs and other subjective states of the actors *and* using
these to interpret the actors' behavior. But it is not true that in order
to know the beliefs of the actors it is not necessary to interpret their
behavior in these terms.[26]

Moreover, even if one supposes that EVT is true in the broader sense
of Verstehen, in the above quotation Ingram draws unwarranted inferences from this supposition.

1. Ingram supposes that the only alternative to *not* providing understanding in terms of the subjective categories of the actor is providing
causal explanations. However, this is a false dichotomy. There are not
just two alternatives. For example, one could understand the actors'
behavior in terms of categories of cognitive psychology or psychoanalysis, and causal laws need not be involved. Moreover, as Weber's
and Popper's construal of Verstehen show, causal explanations can be
in terms of the subjective categories of the agent. There need be no
opposition between causal explanations and Verstehen.

2. Ingram believes that unless we interpret the actors' action in terms
of their subjective categories we cannot regard them as historically
conditioned and as being able to change. However, it is unclear why
this is so. Change in social behavior can be understood in many ways,
not just in terms of the subjective categories of the actors.

One must conclude that Habermas has not shown that Verstehen is
necessary for understanding human action. Even if emancipation is a
goal of the social sciences, Verstehen is not necessary for all contexts
where understanding is sought. However, except in a trivial sense,

Verstehen does not seem to be necessary even for emancipation and the admission that it is necessary in this sense does not have the implications that are sometimes drawn from this.

Interpretivism in *The Theory of Communicative Action*

In his massive *The Theory of Communicative Action* (1981),[27] Habermas's broadly interpretive approach is again evident. As in his earlier discussion of interpretivism, although he does not restrict the scope of the social sciences to interpretation, he sees interpretation as essential to all social understanding. Thus, his later work, as his earlier work, can be understood as advocating:

> (IT) In order to understand human action it is necessary to interpret this action in terms of subjective categories of the social actors.

However, his later views are more sophisticated than his earlier ones. Tied to different concepts of rational action and a theory of understanding the meaning of action, they require separate treatment.

Rational Understanding and Four Sociological Concepts of Action

Habermas distinguishes four sociological concepts of action—teleological, normatively regulative, dramaturgical, and communicative—and argues that one interprets and thus understands social action in terms of these concepts.

In teleological action the actor brings "about the occurrence of a desired state by choosing means that have promise of being successful in the given situation and applying them in a suitable manner."[28] This concept can be expanded into a strategic model "when there can enter into the agent's calculations of success the anticipation of decisions on the part of at least one additional goal-directed actor."[29] This strategic concept is often interpreted in utilitarian terms whereby the actor maximizes his or her utility and it is the basis of decision-theoretic and game-theoretic approaches in social sciences such as economics.

Normatively regulated action refers to "members of a social group who orient their action to common values."[30] A social actor is expected to comply with a certain norm, not in the sense that it is predicted that the actor will comply, but in the normative sense that members of the social group are entitled to expect. Dramaturgical action, in turn, refers primarily to "participants in interaction constituting a public for one another, before whom they present themselves. The actor evokes in his public a certain image, an impression of himself, by more or less purposely disclosing his subjectivity."[31] And communicative action "refers to the interaction of at least two subjects capable of speech and action who establish interpersonal relations (whether by verbal or by extraverbal means). The actors seek to reach an understanding about the action situation and their plans of action in order to coordinate their action by means of agreement."[32]

Habermas relates social scientific understanding of the meaning of social action to all four concepts. For example, utilizing Max Weber's view, he maintains that in teleological action an interpreter understands the action in terms of an ideal type of purposive-rational action that specifies the standard of "the rationality of objective correctness" for interpreting this kind of action. He says, "The more clearly an action corresponds to the objectively purposive rational action, the less we need additional *psychological* considerations to explain it."[33]

In normatively regulated action an interpreter can rationally understand the social actor's action, not just in terms of the actor's conformity to social norms, but also in terms of the correctness of the norms. The actor "challenges the interpreter to examine not only the actual norm-*conformity* of his action, or the de facto currency of the norm in question, but the rightness of the norm itself."[34] Habermas maintains that an interpreter can accept this challenge or, from the points of view of value skepticism and noncognitive ethics, reject it as senseless.

Dramaturgical action can also be interpreted rationally. An interpreter can "interpret an action rationally in such a way that he thereby captures elements of self-deception or deception. . . . He can expose the latently strategic character of a self-presentation by comparing the manifest content of the utterance, that is, what the actor says, with what the actor means."[35]

Although Habermas admits that rational interpretation in social sciences enjoys a "questionable status," he says he will not attempt to demonstrate the possibility of rational interpretations since he will show that such interpretations are *"unavoidable.* Communicative action always requires an interpretation that is rational in approach."[36] However, he makes it clear that rational interpretations are not unavoidable with respect to other types of action. Thus, in the case of teleological, normative, and dramaturgical action, interpreters have a choice of interpreting the action in rational terms or giving a descriptive account.[37] Although what exactly a descriptive account of some action would be is not completely clear, one assumes that it is any description of the action in which instrumental, normative, and dramaturgical considerations are not at issue. For example, one could describe Jones's action as walking across the road without interpreting it instrumentally as the most efficient way get to the other side. One could interpret Smith's action as mailing the check to the Internal Revenue Service without interpreting it normatively as fulfilling her obligation of paying her income tax.

With respect to communicative action, however, rational interpretation is necessary since, according to Habermas, there is no separation between understanding the meaning of a communicative action, such as an utterance, and understanding the validity of the utterance. For example, an ordinary person who understands the meaning of Jones's assertion "The cat is on the mat" would have to know under what conditions one could justifiably assert that this was true. A social science interpreter of Jones's utterance would be basically in the same position as the ordinary person who would also have to understand under what conditions this utterance is true in order to understand the meaning of the utterance.

However, just because Habermas maintains that one has the option of using either a purely a descriptive account or instrumental, normative, or dramaturgical interpretations, it does not follow that he believes that some human actions can be understood without Verstehen. His position seems to be this: First, purely descriptive accounts such as "Smith crossed the road" do not provide any understanding of the action. Although we have four options, the description cannot provide any understanding of the action.[38] Second, in order to apply the instrumental, normative, or dramaturgical models, Verstehen is presupposed. Thus, to apply the instrumental model of rationality one has to interpret the action partly in terms of the subjective categories of the agent: For example, the subjective intent of the actor is judged against the ideal type of instrumental action, and deviations of the action from this ideal type are explained by referring to the actor's subjective state, for example, mental lapses, confusions, false beliefs.[39]

Given that rational interpretation is unavoidable with respect to communicative action and, if understanding is to be had at all in instrumental, normative, or dramaturgical contexts, rational interpretation is always necessary for understanding. In sum, Habermas advocates the following rational interpretive thesis:

(RIT) With respect to communicative action it is necessary to interpret this action in rational terms.

Given Habermas's four models of action, RIT becomes

(RIT^1) In order to understand human action it is necessary to interpret this action in rational terms in one of the four models of rational action.

RIT and RIT^1 might be considered special cases of IT, that is, in order to understand social action one must interpret a human action in terms of the subjective categories of the actor where this involves considerations of the actor's rationality.

The Ambiguity of This Conception

In order to evaluate RIT^1 one must first clarify what it means. First, in its strongest sense it might means that insofar as one understands human action, one must interpret humans as always acting in a rational manner according to one or the other of the four models. Any interpretation of an action that renders it irrational is a misinterpretation. For example, in interpreting actions teleologically one must always interpret humans as choosing the means that have the most promise of being successful in a given situation and applying them in a suitable manner. This lends itself to two readings. On the subjective and more plausible readings this would mean that the actor always brings about the occurrence of a desired state by choosing the means that have the promise of success and applying them in a suitable manner *in terms of the agent's information and knowledge.* On the objective meaning, it would entail that the actor bring about the occurrence of a desired state by choosing means that have the best promise of success and applying them in a suitable manner *in terms of the objectively warranted information and knowledge.*

In a second, less strong sense, (RIT^1) might mean that there is always a rebuttable presumption that in order to understand human action it is necessary to interpret humans as acting in a rational manner in one or the other of the four models.[40] By a rebuttable presumption of rationality I mean an assumption that a human action is rational that could be defeated only by strong contrary evidence. This presumption could be understood in terms of the subjective reading or objective reading of "rational" mentioned above.

In a third, still weaker sense, (RIT^1) might mean that in understanding human beings it is relevant and illuminating to interpret social action in rational terms. This would mean, for example, that it would always be relevant and illuminating to judge whether humans choose the means that have the most promise of being successful in a given situation and apply them in a suitable way. Less than completely rational action would be understood in terms of deviations from an ideal of rational action which could be specified in either subjective or objective terms. This third sense of RIT^1 seems to come the closest to Habermas's meaning with respect to instrumental action since he relates his instrumental rationality to Max Weber's ideal type of purposive rational explanation that explains deviations from this ideal.

In the weakest sense, (RIT^1) could mean that it is always possible to judge human action in terms of the rational model. Thus, in teleological context one could always judge whether humans choose the means that have the most promise of being successful in a given situation and apply them in a suitable way in either the subjective or the objective sense of rationality.

Must Instrumental Action Be Interpreted in Rational Terms?

Using instrumental action as an example one can show that it is possible to understand such action without assuming the action is rational in any of the senses considered above. It seems clear that the strongest and weakest senses will not do. On the one hand, there is good reason to suppose that the strongest thesis is false: Not all instrumental action can be construed as rational in either the subjective or the objective sense. To suppose otherwise is to rule out irrational instrumental action a priori. However, there are such actions and one can understand them, for example, in causal terms: A person's irrational instrumental action can be understood in terms of the psychological factors that cause it. On the one hand, the weakest thesis seems trivial and uninteresting. No matter what the instrumental action being investigated, it is possible to judge it by the rational standards of the instrumental model in either the subjective or objective sense. But this judgment may provide no understanding in this context since it may be pointless and unhelpful. It may be pointless since the instrumental rationality or irrationality of the action may never have been in doubt. It may be unhelpful since the judgment that some action is rational might provide no insight into the question being asked in this context about the instrumental action, for example, why are these social actors acting so irrationally or why is this social actor rational when others in the same context are obviously not? Further, considerations of rationality or irrationality in some instrumental contexts might not even be directly relevant. The relevant question might be how the action of this group inhibits the present trend or how this minority group action is related to the action of the dominant majority. In order to answer these questions a judgment of whether or not the actors chose the means that have the most promise of being successful would not be useful. In short, instrumental action can be understood but not in the rational terms specified in the first and last meaning of rational.

This last example suggests that the third meaning—that it is always relevant and illuminating to judge instrumental action in terms appropriate to this model, that is, how much the action deviated from some ideal of instrumental action. However, one might not care how much the actors' behavior deviates from the standards of the instrumental model. The question that interests the investigator might be how the actors' behavior fits into a larger social trend or how it compares with the behavior of a group of ethnically related social actors who were previously studied. The application of the instrumental rational model might well be irrelevant to this task. However, the rejection of this model would not prevent the action in question from being understood.

What about the second sense that there is a presumption to interpret human instrumental action as rational? There is no good reason to suppose that this is true either. Indeed, our background knowledge might indicate that instrumental rationality is unlikely in a given context. Given this knowledge there might be a presumption that human action is *not* instrumentally rational in this context. This would not mean that this action could not be understood. Suppose that, according to our psychological background knowledge, members of a particular society tend to be irrational in both the subjective and objective senses considered above. We might know this because we know that most members of the society ingest a drug as part of their religious ritual that adversely affects their reasoning powers. Although their behavior would not be understandable in terms of rational categories, it would be explicable in terms of our knowledge of the psychological effects of the drug. Moreover, this irrational action would still be instrumental in the sense that it is aimed to achieve some specific end. Given this background knowledge, it surely would be incorrect to say that there is presumption of rationality.

Suppose, however, that we are starting without any background knowledge or that the background knowledge indicates no systematic instrumental irrationality among the people being investigated. In such a case, there might well be a presumption of rationality. As David Henderson has argued, this presumption would be useful in the initial stage of inquiry and could be rejected later as we learned more about the irrationality of the society under investigation.[41] Furthermore, this presumption would be a special case of a more general presumption: All instrumental action is explicable in some way or other. However, this result would hardly show that a rationality assumption is the only way to provide understanding in the context of instrumental action.

It seems clear that similar considerations can be adduced to show that normatively regulative and dramaturgical rationality are not the only ways to provide understanding in contexts where Habermas thinks they are relevant. But what about communicative action? Since this type of action is given special treatment by Habermas, I will consider it separately here.

Communicative Action and the Alleged Methodological Difference between Natural and Social Science

The Alleged Difference

Habermas sees the necessity of a rational approach to communicative action as crucial to the methodological difference between the natural and the social sciences. Although he notes important similarities between the two kinds of sciences, he maintains that the social sciences are significantly different from the natural sciences. The crucial difference, he argues, is the sort of interpretation that defines the social sciences.

Unlike Taylor, Habermas is well aware of the theory-laden nature of the language of the natural sciences. Citing Mary Hesse he says that one cannot argue for a fundamental methodological difference between social and natural science based on the alleged fact that the phenomena of the nature science consist of uninterpreted facts while the phenomena of the social science do not. He emphasizes that the phenomena of the natural sciences are also interpreted. He says that Hesse infers from this that "theory formation in the natural sciences is no less dependent on interpretation than it is in the social sciences—interpretations that can be analyzed in terms of the hermeneutic model of *Verstehen*."[42] However, despite what Hesse says, Habermas maintains that there is still a crucial difference between the natural and social sciences. Utilizing Anthony Giddens' work, Habermas maintains that the social sciences have a "*double* hermeneutic task."[43] By this Giddens means that social sciences deal with "a preinterpreted world where the creation and reproduction of meaning-frames is a very condition of that which it seeks to analyze, namely human social conduct. . . ."[44] "The *specific Verstehen problematic*," Habermas says, "lies in the fact that social science cannot 'use' this language 'found' in the object domain as a neutral instrument." A social scientist cannot "'enter into' this language without having recourse to the pretheoretical knowledge of a member of the life-world—indeed of his own—which he has intuitively mastered and now brings unanalyzed into every process of achieving understanding."[45] Habermas argues that

> The problem of *Verstehen* is of methodological importance in the humanities and social science primarily because the scientist cannot gain access to a symbolically prestructured reality through *observation* alone, and because *understanding meaning* [*Sinnverstehen*] cannot be methodically brought under control in the same way as can observation in the course of experimentation. The social scientist basically has no other access to the lifeworld than the social-scientific layman does. He must already belong in a certain way to the lifeworld whose elements he wishes to describe. In order to describe them, he must understand them; in order to understand them, he must be able in principle to participate in their production, and participation presupposes that one belongs.[46]

There is no doubt that Habermas is correct in that social scientists often must give interpretations of interpretations, that is, they must interpret the social actors' interpretations of their situations. But in the above quotations, Habermas implies much more than this. First, he implies that the social scientist must give interpretations of interpretations. Second, he implies that natural scientists never give interpretations of interpretations, that is, that they never have a doubly hermeneutic task. Third, he implies that observation cannot be used to understand social reality. Presumably this is because one cannot understand the interpreted elements of social reality, that is, the elements of the social world as interpreted by social actors, via mere observation. And fourth, he implies that one understands these interpreted elements only by belonging and participating. This third point is crucial to understanding what is involved in the other two.

Critique of the Alleged Difference[47]

(1) Although it is true that social scientists often give interpretations of the actors' interpretations, this is by no means necessary. Habermas

makes it seem as if there are only two alternatives for social scientists: use uninterpreted data or interpret the interpretations of the actors. Since the first alternative is impossible, only the second remains. However, there is a third alternative. Social scientists can ignore the actors' interpretations and directly interpret the data in terms of social scientific theories. Such an approach to theorizing may have disadvantages but it cannot be ignored and may well be useful for certain purposes and contexts.

(2) Now, in one obvious sense, natural scientists sometimes *do* have a double hermeneutic task. A natural scientist might interpret a prior theory of the phenomenon before giving an interpretation of it in terms of his or her own theory. For example, Einstein interpreted Newton's theory in order to discover its problems and how it could be improved on. In an obvious sense, Einstein's theory is dependent on a reading of Newton's theory—indeed, it is built on correcting this reading. Sometimes the interpretation that a natural scientist interprets is not based on a well-articulated theory but on an implicit theory embedded in common sense. For example, commonsense interpretations of the weather in *The Farmers' Almanac* are reinterpreted and corrected by modern meteorology in its own terms.

These examples might suggest that natural science never gives an interpretation of human beings' interpretation of themselves. But if medical science is a natural science—which it certainly seems to be—this is not so. Sick people interpret their own symptoms and other behavior. ("Well, Doc, I got the pain in my stomach from eating parsnips.") Medical doctors often interpret these patients' interpretations of their problems, trying to make sense out them in terms of the latest medical knowledge and theory.

Now it may be argued that in many instances, social science has a triple hermeneutic task. Thus, a sociologist might give an interpretation of Parsons' interpretations of the social actors' interpretations of their own actions. So, it might be said, there is still a crucial difference between the social and natural sciences. Now it is true that this triple hermeneutic task is seldom found in the natural sciences, but it is not unknown. A medical doctor might give an interpretation of a medical theory's interpretation of a patient's interpretation of his or her problem. Moreover, it is unclear how often interpretations of interpretations of interpretations are found in the social sciences. In any case, it is important not to exaggerate their frequency. Habermas, it should be noted, is claiming only a doubly hermeneutic task for the social sciences. But even if it turned out that there is a significant difference in the frequency of multiple hermeneutic tasks in the social and natural sciences, the above examples would show that this difference is only a matter of degree rather than of kind. In any event, it is uncertain what methodological implications this difference of frequency would have.

One suspects that the double hermeneutical aspect of social scientific inquiry would not be important for Habermas if it were not for the *type* of hermeneutic understanding Habermas believes that this entails: the participation—in a sense yet to be specified—of the social scientist in the life-world of the social actors. Even when natural scientists have double or even triple hermeneutic tasks, Habermas might argue that there is no participation in the relevant sense.

(3) At first blush it is unclear why Habermas believes that observation cannot be used to understand social reality—especially when he admits that observation is theory-laden. After all, it might be said that observation can be laden with the theories about the meaning of the actors' actions. Thus, a social scientist with the right training and theoretical background can *observe* that a social actor is performing some social action pregnant with social significance. One might suspect that Habermas's scruples here are based on too limited a view of what theory-laden observation can do or too exalted a view of what interpretation consists of. Indeed, one might even suppose that Habermas rejects observation as a means of acquiring understanding because he supposes that interpretation must always be consciously inferential rather than immediate and direct. A critic might remind us that Max Weber long ago recognized that Verstehen could be based on observation. In what he called direct observational Verstehen[48] Weber argued that one immediately categorizes some piece of behavior as an action in terms which the actor himself or herself uses to categorize his or her action. For example, one has observational Verstehen, when one immediately sees the arm-moving behavior of a man as chopping wood and this is indeed how the man categorizes his own behavior. Weber did not categorize the understanding one has of the man's action when set in a larger context as observational Verstehen. When his reasons and motives are known and we learn that he is chopping wood in order to earn money for his family Weber called this explanatory Verstehen. But there is no a priori reason why under certain circumstances this knowledge could not be immediate and hence classified as observational Verstehen. Given certain background and training, one could be said to see that the man was

chopping wood in order to earn money for his family. To a knowledgeable observer this could be just as immediate as the fact that his arm movements were chopping wood. Thus, it might be said, once one accepts theory-laden observation there is no reason to suppose that observation cannot be used to understand social reality.

However, Habermas could accept much of this reasoning and it would not affect his main point which rests on his notion of participation. Observation *alone* cannot be used to understand social action for observation does not involve participation. Were it not for the necessity of participation one could understand human action directly and noninferentially by theory-laden observation. But since participation is involved, this is impossible. The key again is the notion of participation.

(4) Habermas seems to maintain that one can understand communicative action only by participating in the life-world of the social actor one is trying to understand. Indeed, he says that the social scientist must already belong to the life-world of the actor in order to understand the actor. But interpreted literally this is surely false. Historians cannot literally participate in the life-world of many people that they study yet this does not prevent them from understanding them. Although some anthropologists use participant observation methods to understand living societies and cultures, this method is not used to study dying societies or ancient cultures. Informants and inferences from archaeological remains provide ways of understanding when participation in the life-world is impossible.[49]

Examples could be multiplied, but it seems fairly clear that Habermas should not be taken literally. He says that a social scientist must be able "in principle" to participate in the actors' life-world; he also says that the social scientist must belong "in a certain way" to this life-world in order to understand it. The crucial question is what he means by these qualifying expressions. The key to understanding Habermas is his notion of *virtual* participation. This notion enables him to argue for the *unique* features of the double hermeneutic aspect of social inquiry and maintain the impossibility of theory-laden observation alone as a way of understanding social phenomena.

Problems with Virtual Participation

In order to understand the society or culture they are studying, social scientists, according to Habermas, must be "virtual participants"[50] in this society or culture. By this he means two closely related things.

First, social scientists in order to understand the meaning of a claim must know the conditions under which a claim made by a social actor is accepted as valid by the actor. Second, in order to understand the meaning of a claim the social scientist must either evaluate the reasons given by the social actor to support a claim or know why such an evaluation is not yet possible. What being a virtual participant does not mean is that the social scientist must act as a member of the society or culture—living, working, etc., in it.

> Those immediately involved in the communicative practice of everyday life are pursuing aims of *action*; their participation in cooperative processes of interpretation serves to establish a consensus on the basis of which they can coordinate their plans of action and achieve their aims. The social-scientific interpreter does not pursue aims of action *of this kind*. He participates in processes of reaching understanding for the sake of understanding and not for the sake of an end that requires coordinating the goal-oriented action of the interpreter with the goal-oriented action of those immediately involved . . . . In concentrating, as a speaker and hearer, exclusively on the process of reaching understanding, the social scientist takes part in the observed action system *subject to the withdrawal*, as it were, *of his qualities as an actor.*[51]

A virtual participant must be familiar with the conditions of validity of the actors' speech. "In order to understand an utterance in the paradigm case of a speech act oriented to reaching understanding, the interpreter has to be familiar with the conditions of its validity; he has to know under what conditions the validity claim with it is acceptable, that is, would have been acknowledged by a hearer."[52] Thus, in order to understand an expression, "the interpreter must *bring to mind the reasons* with which a speaker would if necessary and under suitable conditions defend its validity, he is *himself* drawn into the process of assessing validity claims."[53] He goes on to say,

> One can understand reasons only to the extent that one understands *why* they are or are not sound, or why in a given case a decision as to whether reasons are good or bad is not (yet) possible. An interpreter cannot, therefore, interpret expressions connected through criticizable validity claims with a potential of reasons (and thus represent knowledge) without taking a position on them.[54]

According to Habermas, there are three basic kinds of validity claims: the claim to be true, the claim to be right or proper or acceptable according to the prevailing social norms, and the claim to be authentic, that is, sincerely expressive of the speaker's subjective state.[55] For example, in order to understand the meaning of the actor's utterance, "Wise people kill snakes before sunset," the social scientist must know under what conditions this claim is held to be true by the speaker. Or if the social actor says, "Abu ought to be given the death penalty for murdering his father," the social scientist must know under what prevailing social conditions the death penalty is appropriate punishment and, in particular, whether it is the right punishment for murder. Again, if a social actor complains bitterly about the treatment he has received from his employer, the social scientist must know under what conditions such a complaint is sincere.

In addition, Habermas claims that in order to understand what the social actor says, the social scientist must be drawn into the evaluation of these claims, that is, he or she must assess the claims. Thus in order to understand the meaning of the utterance about killing snakes before sunset, the social scientist must either determine the validity of conditions under which the speaker would defend its truth or determine why the claim cannot yet be assessed. In a similar manner, in order to understand the meaning of the utterance about the death penalty it would be necessary to assess the appropriateness of this penalty for patricide or determine why the claim cannot yet be established.

One can distinguish two theses Habermas maintains about virtual participation—the Validity Condition Thesis and the Assessment Thesis:

(VCT) In order to understand the meaning of an utterance one must know the validity conditions of the utterance, that is, the conditions under which a speaker would defend its validity.

(AT) In order to understand the meaning of an utterance one must either assess the reasons for it or understand why it is not yet possible to assess it.

The question remains, however, what Habermas means by "the meaning of an utterance."[56] Two possibilities suggest themselves. Habermas may have in mind the *linguistic* meaning, that is, what the utterance says (semantic content). Or he could have in mind, the *pragmatic* meaning, that is, what is going on when an utterance is being made. Associated with these two senses of meaning are two senses of "understanding an utterance," namely, understanding what is being said and understanding what is going on in its being said.[57]

However, there is good reason to reject Habermas's claims about virtual participation and consequently the restricted claims concerning understanding that are associated with it.[58] It seems clear, however, that in whatever way one construes meaning that (VCT) and (AT) are unwarranted. There is no good reason to suppose that the *meaning* of an utterance is internally connected with either its validity condition or its assessment. One general consideration that seems to tell against both (VCT) and (AT) is a variant of the "open question" argument. If Habermas was correct, the following sorts of questions would make no sense:

> (Q1) I know what the speaker meant when she said, "The cat is on the mat," but under what conditions would she accept this statement as either true or false?

> (Q2) I know what the speaker meant when she said, "Bill should get a reward for returning the ring," but should Bill be so rewarded and does this sort of action ever deserve a reward?

They would make no sense since one could not understand the meaning of the respective utterances without knowing the conditions of validity and making an assessment. However, both of these questions make perfect sense.

Indeed, one can imagine particular circumstances in anthropological contexts that would seem to serve as counterexamples to (VCT) and (AT). With respect to pragmatic meaning (VCT) becomes:

> (VCTa) In order to understand what is going on in what is being said (the pragmatic meaning of an utterance), one must know the validity conditions of the utterance, that is, the conditions under which that speaker would defend its validity.

Suppose a native says, "Wise people kill snakes before sunset." By saying this, let us suppose, the native is expressing one of his beliefs about wise people and urging others to hold a similar belief. This is what is going on by this being said. This pragmatic meaning might well be known by an anthropologist. For the reasons suggested below, however, the anthropologist might not know under what conditions this statement is accepted as true or false by the community.

With respect to linguistic meaning (VCT) becomes:

> (VCTb) In order to understand what is being said (the linguistic meaning of an utterance), one must know the validity conditions of

the utterance, that is, the conditions under which that speaker would defend its validity.

However, it seems possible that an anthropologist could understand what is being said without knowing under what conditions this statement is accepted as true or false by the native's community. In the community someone might accept an utterance about snakes as true only if it was accompanied by a secret handshake and otherwise reject it as false. An anthropologist who does not know the handshake will not know the validity conditions and, consequently, will not know the conditions that are relevant in this community for accepting the native's statement as either true or false. However, there seems to be no good reason why the anthropologist could not know what is being said. He or she might use a reliable native informant who clarifies the meaning of the utterance but who refuses to reveal the condition of validity, namely, the presence of the secret handshake.

With respect to pragmatic meaning (AT), becomes (ATa):

(ATa) In order to understand what is going on in what is being said (the pragmatic meaning of an utterance), one must either assess the reasons for accepting it or understand why it is not yet possible to assess them.

Let us suppose that a native says "Abu should get the death penalty for murdering his father." Suppose the speaker is expressing his belief about the appropriateness of the death penalty for Abu's action and urging others to hold a similar view. It would seem that an anthropologist can know this and yet not know whether patricide is a capital offense in this community or else know that it is and yet not know if it would be justified in the case of Abu. It would also seem that an anthropologist could understand what is going on when this is being said, yet not assess whether it is an appropriate offense for patricide in any community, or if it is, whether it would be justified in this case.

With respect to linguistic meaning, (AT) becomes:

(ATb) In order to understand what is being said (the linguistic meaning of an utterance), one must either assess the reasons for accepting it or understand why it is not yet possible to assess them.

When a native says "Abu should get the death penalty for murdering his father," an anthropologist could understand what is being said without knowing whether patricide is a capital offense in this community. Moreover, even if the anthropologist knew that patricide is a capital offense, he could know what is being said *without* knowing if the death penalty would be justified in the case of Abu. Suppose in this community the crimes punishable by death penalty are not made public by the tribal elders. One can only tell what is a capital offense from observing when in the past the death penalty was administered. Since prior to Abu's action no one had killed his or her father, there would be no way of knowing the appropriate punishment for patricide. Thus, a reliable native informant could interpret the linguistic meaning of what Abu said but not be able to inform him or her whether patricide was a capital offense in this community.

Moreover, it also seems possible that an anthropologist could understand what is being said without assessing either whether patricide should ever be a capital offense or whether or not it should be so in the case of Abu. An anthropologist who believed that in certain circumstances the death penalty was justified for patricide, might not know enough of the details of the case of Abu to know whether he should receive the penalty. But this need not affect his understanding of what is being said. It would seem possible that his native informant could interpret the meaning of the actor's statement to the anthropologist and yet not be able to provide the information to help him decide in terms of his own considered moral principles whether or not the death penalty applies in Abu's case.

Moreover, it certainly seems possible that an anthropologist could know what is being said and yet not be able to make a judgment about whether patricide is a capital offense in relation to his or her own moral principles. For one thing, the anthropologist might have a strong psychological aversion to considering difficult moral issues and, believing this is such an issue, might not be able to face it. For another, on some metaethical views, questions about the death penalty are impossible to answer. But then, it would be impossible for an anthropologist to assess the reasons for imposing the death penalty.[59] Again, the anthropologist might correctly believe that he does not have enough time or competence to answer moral questions about the death penalty and therefore refrain from trying to do so. Indeed, Habermas's thesis of an internal relation between meaning and assessment seems completely gratuitous.[60]

Would it be possible for Habermas to escape the difficulties pertaining to (ATa) and (ATb) by claiming that the examples cited are not genuine counterexamples? He might argue that the examples cited only show that one can understand the linguistic or pragmatic meaning of an utterance without assessing the reasons for it, without showing that one can understand the meaning of an utterance but not understand why it is not yet possible to assess these reasons. Recall that (AT) reads, "In order to understand the meaning of an utterance one must either assess the reasons for it or *understand why it is not yet possible to assess it.*"

The phrase "yet possible" perhaps suggests that the assessment of the reasons for the utterance will be possible in the fullness of time. However, in some of the counterexamples cited above, the assessment of reasons would be impossible in some clear senses of "impossible." For example, for a person with a strong psychological aversion to difficult moral issues assessing reasons for the death penalty would be psychologically impossible. For a person with no time or competence such an assessment would be impossible in an even stronger sense. If a metaethical view in which reasoned ethical assessment is unrealizable is correct, then assessment of ethical reasons is impossible in a still stronger sense.

Even if one waives the implied requirement of its being possible to assess the reasons at some future time, one wonders why it is necessary to *understand* why it is impossible to assess the reasons. The anthropologist who relies on a native informant to interpret the utterance "Wise people kill snakes before sunset" might have no idea why it is impossible to know a key validity condition of the utterance. He or she may have been misinformed by the native informant and have a completely mistaken idea of why he cannot find out the conditions of the validation. But there is no reason to suppose that this lack of understanding would prevent the anthropologist from understanding what is being said.

Again, in the case of the death penalty, the anthropologist might be completely mistaken about why it was impossible for him to know whether or not death was an appropriate punishment for patricide in this community. However, this would seem unrelated to the anthropologist's ability to understand what is being said when a native makes the utterance "Abu should get the death penalty for murdering his father." For example, he might wrongly believe that the native informant knows whether it is an appropriate punishment and does not tell him because this knowledge is forbidden to outsiders.

With respect to the impossibility of the anthropologist's assessment of the death penalty for patricide in terms of his own considered principles, the anthropologist could surely fail to understand why this assessment is impossible and yet understand what is being said when a native says "Abu should get the death penalty for murdering his father." For example, an anthropologist might wrongly believe that it is impossible for him to assess whether or not the death penalty is justified in the case of Abu because of a metaethical theory he holds that entails that the assessment of ethical reasoning is impossible whereas in fact, he is unable to make the assessment because he lacks relevant factual information.

Admitting that Habermas's claim that to understand something is necessarily to evaluate it "seems clearly false," James Bohman has suggested a weaker interpretation of Habermas. According to Bohman the scope of Habermas's claim should be restricted to validity claims, "a claim that the action is justifiable relative to some form of shared knowledge. Interpreters bring their own cognitive resources and well-justified knowledge claims to bear on the claims to others . . . . If understanding an action or expression requires taking justification into account, then its interpretation requires the employment of the interpreter's knowledge qua participant, not to do so is to set the interpretation adrift in 'some view from nowhere.' But this does not mean that all interpretation is evaluative, since the interpreter may not be in a position to identify the expressions of others as recognizably justified at all."[61]

Obviously Bohman's restrictions considerably weaken Habermas's thesis. But is the weakened thesis true? Bohman's Restricted Assessment Thesis would seem to amount to this:

(RAT) In order to understand the meaning of a validity claim one must either assess the reasons for it or understand why it is not yet possible to assess it.

A validity claim (VC) is a claim with roughly the form, "X is justified relative to knowledge K." Let's interpret "the meaning" as linguistic meaning. However, in order to understand the linguistic meaning of (VC) an anthropologist does not have to evaluate the reasons for (VC). Indeed, he might have no idea if (VC) is true and yet understand its linguistic meaning perfectly well. For example, from native informants he might know that a prediction of disaster is justified relative to a native's knowledge of magic. But the anthropologist need not assess the reasons for this claim to understand it. Nor need the anthropologists understand why it not possible yet to assess these reasons. In fact, he might know that it is now possible to assess them but has not bothered to do so. Similar points can be made against (RAT) when it is interpreted in terms of pragmatic meaning.

There is yet another possible way that Habermas might try to escape the criticism raised here. My criticism has assumed that his account of understanding the meaning of an utterance is descriptive. Although this assumption is a natural one to make, it may be mistaken. It is possible that Habermas is not attempting to describe what understanding means but to *prescribe* what it means. Thus, perhaps (VCT) and (AT) are to be construed as *proposals* and are to be read in the following way:

> (VCT^1) Let us define "understand" in such a way that in order to understand the meaning of an utterance one must know the validity conditions of the utterance, that is, the conditions under which the speaker would defend its validity.

> (AT^1) Let us define "understand" in such a way that in order to understand the meaning of an utterance one must either assess the reasons for it or understand why it is not yet possible to assess it.

Construed in this way what Habermas says is trivially true by definition, and I have raised no genuine counterexamples against his theory. But the question now is why we should accept these proposals. Habermas offers no good reasons for their acceptance and there seems to be good reason to resist them. For one thing, accepting these proposals would severely limit those cases in which we could claim to understand an utterance. For example, there are surely many cases in which we do not know the validity conditions of an expression but in which it seems natural to say we understand the meaning of the expression. For another, we would have to invent another term to say what we wanted to say. For example, although we could no longer say that we understand (comprehend? grasp?) the meaning of an utterance such as "Abu should get the death penalty for killing his father" unless in some sense we appraise it, could we say that we *know* the meaning without this appraisal? Presumably not, since "knowing the meaning of utterance" and "understanding the meaning of an utterance" seem to be virtually synonymous expressions. What then could we say? Perhaps only a neologism could be used to replace the work that is ordinarily done by "understand" and related expressions. However, this move seems necessary only if we accept these proposals. A much simpler solution is to note that Habermas's use of the term "understanding" is extraordinary and confusing, reject these proposals, and suggest that *he* adopt a new term.

Conclusion

Habermas's views on Verstehen contrast in interesting ways with the theorists considered earlier. Explicitly critical of the Verstehen theories of Weber, Abel, Winch, and Schutz and more moderate in his approach than Dray, Geertz, and Taylor, Habermas combines his Verstehen theory with causal and functional analysis, and the emancipatory goals of critical social science. For example, rejecting Winch's theory as relativistic and ahistorical and going beyond Geertz's theory in having emancipatory goals, like Winch and Geertz, Habermas constructs his interpretivism on the interpretation of the actors. Nevertheless, despite these differences and despite his allegiance to critical social science, Habermas, like the other Verstehen theorists, has too restricted a view of social scientific understanding. Insensitive to the contextual nature of understanding, Habermas apparently assumes that Verstehen is necessary for social scientific understanding in all contexts.

In his earlier work, *On the Logic of the Social Sciences,* Habermas ruled out any approach to social understanding in which the subjective categories of the social actor were not utilized. However, the contextual nature of social scientific inquiry as well as the relativity of social understanding to the description of social phenomena makes even Habermas's modest interpretivism unacceptable. In *The Theory of Communicative Action,* Habermas again argues for a moderate interpretivism and his theory has similar problems. In addition, his attempt to distinguish natural and social science in terms of the double hermeneutical approach of the latter fails. However, Habermas's main contribution is linking his elaborate theory of rational social action to understanding. But there is little reason to suppose that human action has to be understood in rational terms and no good grounds to believe that it is unavoidable that communicative action in particular be rationally comprehended.

The lesson to be learned from this examination of Habermas' views on Verstehen in *On the Logic of the Social Sciences* and *The Theory of Communicative Action* is that even a complex and sophisticated theory such as Habermas's can go wrong in closing off certain approaches to social scientific understanding.[62]

Notes

1. See David Ingram, *Critical Theory and Philosophy* (New York: Paragon House, 1990), chapter 1; Brian Fay, *Critical Social Science* (Ithaca, NY: Cornell University Press, 1987).
2. Fay, *Critical Social Science*, pp. 3-4.
3. For example, Marcuse in *One Dimensional Man* (1964) and Horkheimer and Adorno, *The Dialectic of the Enlightenment* (1947). See Fay, *Critical Social Science*, p. 4.
4. Jürgen Habermas, *Knowledge and Human Interest*, trans. Jeremy J. Shapiro (Boston, MA: Beacon Press, 1971).
5. "Jürgen Habermas," *Concise Encyclopedia of Western Philosophy and Philosophers*, ed. J. O. Urmson and Jonathan Rée (London: Unwin, 1989), pp. 122-23.
6. Jürgen Habermas, *The Theory of Communicative Action*, vols. 1 and 2, trans. Thomas McCarthy (Boston, MA: Beacon Press, 1984, 1987).
7. "Jürgen Habermas," *Concise Encyclopedia of Western Philosophy and Philosophers*, pp. 122-23.
8. Ingram, *Critical Theory and Philosophy*, p. 52.
9. Jürgen Habermas, *On the Logic of the Social Sciences,* trans. Shierry Weber Nicholsen and Jerry A. Stark (Cambridge, MA: The MIT Press, 1988), p. 187.
10. See Kenneth Baynes, "Rational Reconstruction and Social Criticism: Habermas's Model of Interpretive Social Science," *The Philosophical Forum* 20, 1989-90, p. 122, and Thomas McCarthy, *The Critical Theory of Jürgen Habermas* (Cambridge, MA: The MIT Press, 1978), p. 140.
11. Jürgen Habermas, "Interpretive Social Science vs. Hermeneuticism," *Social Science as Moral Inquiry*, Norma Haan et al. (New York: Columbia University Press, 1983), p. 252. For further ideas about Critical Theory as a research program, see John S. Dryzek, "Critical Theory as a Research Program," *The Cambridge Companion to Habermas*, ed. Stephen K. White (Cambridge, MA: Cambridge University Press, 1995), pp. 97-119.
12. According to McCarthy, The Critical Theory of Jürgen Habermas, p. 147, such positivists' reflections "do not cut deeply enough."
13. Habermas, *On the Logic of the Social Sciences,* p. 57.
14. Ibid.
15. Ibid., p. 59.
16. Ibid., p. 60.
17. McCarthy, The Critical Theory of Jürgen Habermas, pp. 155-56.
18. Habermas, *On the Logic of the Social Sciences*, pp. 92 -116.
19. Ibid., pp. 117-43.
20. Ibid., pp. 143-70.
21. Ibid., p. 168.
22. Ibid., p. 172. See also Jürgen Habermas, "A Review of Gadamer's *Truth and Method*," in Fred R. Dallmayr and Thomas A. McCarthy, eds., *Understanding*

and Social Inquiry (Notre Dame, IN: University of Notre Dame Press, 1977), pp. 335-63, and McCarthy, The Critical Theory of Jürgen Habermas, pp. 162-93; Charles A. Pressler and Fabio B. Dasilva, *Sociology and Interpretation*(Albany, NY: SUNY Press, 1996), chapter 8.

23. I am indebted in what follows to Jane Roland Martin, "Another Look at the Doctrine of Verstehen," in M. Martin and Lee C. McIntyre, eds. *Readings in the Philosophy of Social Science* (Cambridge, MA: The MIT Press, 1994), pp. 247-58. This paper was first published in *The British Journal for the Philosophy of Science*, 20 1969, pp. 53–67.

24. Ibid., p. 251.

25. Carol Cohn, "Sex and Death in the Rational World of Defense Intellectuals," *Signs* 12, 1987, pp. 687-718.

26. Cf. James Bohman, *New Philosophy of Social Science* (Cambridge: The MIT Press, 1991), p. 191.

27. Habermas, *The Theory of Communicative Action*, vol. 1, chapter 4.

28. Ibid., p. 85.

29. Ibid.

30. Ibid.

31. Ibid., p. 86.

32. Ibid.

33. Ibid., p. 103.

34. Ibid., p. 104.

35. Ibid., p. 105.

36. Ibid., p. 106.

37. Ibid.,p. 119. See William Outwaithe, *Habermas: A Critical Introduction* (Stanford: CA: Stanford University Press, 1994), p. 73.

38. Although I cannot find Habermas saying this explicitly, this seem to be the import of his discussion in ibid., pp. 102-19.

39. Ibid., p. 103.

40. Habermas says that the interpreter "proceeds from the presumption of rationality of the questionable expression in order, if necessary, to assure himself step by step of its irrationality." Ibid., p. 55.

41. See David K. Henderson, *Interpretation and Explanation in the Human Sciences* (Albany, NY: SUNY Press, 1993) .

42. Habermas, *The Theory of Communicative Action*, vol. 1, p. 109.

43. Ibid., p. 110.

44. Anthony Gidden, *New Rules of Sociological Method* (London: 1976); quoted by Habermas, *The Theory of Communicative Action*, vol. 1, p. 109.

45. Habermas, *The Theory of Communicative Action*, vol. I, p. 101.

46. Ibid., p. 108.

47. For a different criticism of Habermas's attempt to distinguish the methodologies of the social and natural sciences, see Joseph Rouse, *Knowledge and Power* (Ithaca, NY: Cornell University Press, 1987).

48. Max Weber, "The Fundamental Concepts of Sociology," in *The Theory of Social and Economic Organization,* trans. A. M. Henderson and Talcott Parsons (London: The Free Press of Glencoe, 1947), p. 94.

49. See Michael Martin, "Understanding and Participant Observation in Cultural and Social Anthropology," in Michael Martin, *Social Science and Philosophical Analysis* (Washington, D.C.: University Press of America, 1978), pp. 343-49.

50. See Habermas, *The Theory of Communicative Action*, vol. I, pp. 114-15.

51. Ibid., pp. 113-14.

52. Ibid., p. 115.

53. Ibid.
54. Ibid., p. 116.
55. Ibid., pp. 306-307.
56. Habermas seems to switch back and forth between linguistic and pragmatic meaning. See Habermas, *Theory of Communicative Action*, vol. 1, pp. 102, 106, 107, 113, 115, 135. See also Theodore R. Schatzki, "The Rationalization of Meaning and Understanding: Davidson and Habermas," *Synthèse* 69, 1986, pp. 65–66.
57. Schatzki, "The Rationalization of Meaning and Understanding: Davidson and Habermas," p. 65.
58. I am indebted in what follows to Theodore R. Schatzki, "The Rationalization of Meaning and Understanding: Davidson and Habermas," pp. 51-79, for many of my critical insights.
59. Habermas seems to admit that one could *hold* such a metaethical view. (See Theory of Communicative Action, vol. 1, p. 104.) But he does not consider the possibility that such a view could be true.
60. Even McCarthy rejects Habermas's position on this point. See Thomas McCarthy, "Reflections on Rationalization in *The Theory of Communicative Action*," *Habermas and Modernity*, ed. Richard J. Bernstein (Cambridge, MA: The MIT Press, 1985), pp. 183-85. See also Stephen K. White, *The Recent Work of Jürgen Habermas* (New York: Cambridge University Press, 1988), pp. 41-42.
61. Bohman, *New Philosophy of Social Science*, p. 138.
62. I am uncertain whether Bohman is making a similar point. See ibid., pp. 142-45.

Conclusion:
Towards a Theory of Methodological Pluralism

Introduction

Neither the classical Verstehen position nor more recent interpretive versions of it are defensible because they presuppose too narrow a view of the social sciences. Verstehen is necessary to scientific understanding only in certain contexts and for certain purposes. One can understand social scientific phenomena in different ways, some appropriate for some contexts and some for others. In this concluding chapter, a flexible pluralistic approach to understanding that is sensitive to context and purpose will be developed further and will be related to three theories of methodological pluralism in the social sciences.

In general, methodological pluralism attempts to reconcile different methodological approaches to the social sciences. Believing that different methodologies have important insights that will be neglected by concentrating exclusively on one methodology, different methodological pluralists try to allow for these insights in different ways.[1] Some argue that different methodologies are appropriate in different areas of science, others that different methodologies are relevant for different purposes and contexts, and still others that different methodologies should be combined in any inquiry.

Two recent philosophical precedents for methodological pluralism in the social sciences come to mind. Although the analogy between philosophical precedents and methodological pluralism in the social sciences is far from perfect, there is Carnap's principle of tolerance that one should be free to develop different linguistic forms according to one's purposes.[2] Although Carnap did not apply his principle to methodologies, the spirit of this principle seems applicable to more things than linguistic forms. The second precedent is the epistemological anarchy advocated by Paul Feyerabend who maintained that "knowledge is obtained from the proliferation of views rather than from the determined application of a preferred ideology."[3] However, as we shall see, methodological pluralists in the social sciences are much more conservative than Feyerabend who advocated the proliferation of nonscientific theories such as magic and witchcraft as well as scientific ones and also the application of inductive as well as counterinductive procedures. Nevertheless, Feyerabend's rationale for his extreme pluralism is relevant to the narrower context of social scientific methodologies: Different methodologies complement each other and help to mutually correct their respective problems.

The Different Areas Account

On what I will call the Different Areas account of methodological pluralism, because different methodological approaches are appropriate in different areas of social science, it is a mistake to suppose that one approach is uniquely adequate in all areas. Such a position is advocated by Daniel Little in *Varieties of Social Explanation*.[4] Little's rationale is based on what he takes to be the failures of the two main methodological positions in the philosophy of social science: naturalism and antinaturalism.

On the one hand, Little considers what he calls *strong reform naturalism*. This is the position that

(a) all social sciences should attempt to provide causal explanations of social phenomena; [5]

(b) the explanations should be grounded on analyses of the circumstances of agency of the participants;[6]

(c) social theories should be supported by a rigorous use of empirical evidence in order to rule out alternative explanations.

Little rejects this view as too comprehensive on the grounds that there are areas of the social sciences that do not involve causal explanations. He contrasts strong reform naturalism, however, with what he considers to be the more acceptable position of *weak reform naturalism*. This is the view that there are many good examples of social science that conform to strong reform naturalism. A prime example, according to Little, are those cases where rational choice theory is used. In such cases, social phenomena are explained in terms of the aggregate consequences of the rational choices of individual actors. This theory depends on what Little calls a thin theory of human action, that is, an account of abstract descriptions of goals, utilities, and simple modes of reasoning.

On the other hand, Little would have us consider what might be called *strong antinaturalism.*[7] This is the view that

(a) social phenomena—behavior, social practices, and social institutions—are inherently meaningful in that they are constituted by meanings that participants attach to them;

(b) social phenomena can only be explained through a hermeneutical unpacking of the meaning that constitutes them;

(c) interpretations of social phenomena can only be evaluated in terms of internal coherence and their fit with the behavior and avowals of the participants;

(d) causal explanations have no legitimate place in the social sciences; and

(e) inductive regularities and prediction have no legitimate role in social science.

Little says this position, which resembles some of the Verstehen and interpretive theories considered in earlier chapters, is also too comprehensive. Arguing that since there are examples of legitimate causal explanation[8] in the social sciences this account will not do, he puts forward a more acceptable position that he calls *weak antinaturalism.* According to weak antinaturalism, *some* social sciences depend on the interpretative method where thick descriptions are used. Thick descriptions are detailed descriptions of norms, cultural assumptions, metaphors, religious beliefs and practices. Little maintains the use of thick descriptions in interpretations is neither explanatory nor causal. Consequently, their use is radically different from the methods of the natural sciences. Little cites Geertz's interpretation of the Balinese cockfight as an example of an interpretation where thick description is used that is not explanatory. He also considers noncausal the explanation that Navajo speakers find the sentence "the horse was kicked by the man" amusing because they believe that horses cannot "control" men.[9]

Since, according to Little, neither strong naturalism nor strong antinaturalism constitutes a comprehensive account of social science, he opts for their weak counterparts. The combination of weak naturalism and weak antinaturalism that he endorses entails a particular form of methodological pluralism, one in which interpretative methods are appropriate in some areas and natural sciences methods are appropriate in others.

Evaluation of the Different Areas Account

The Different Areas version of methodological pluralism has three significant strengths. In allowing alternative methodological approaches it gives naturalism and antinaturalism their due. In addition, it confirms the intuitions shared by many social scientists that naturalism and antinaturalism are appropriate in different areas of the social sciences. Finally, it explicitly allows for the possibility of noncausal understanding and interpretations that are not merely preliminary to explanation.

However, the Different Areas account also has important problems. One is that it neglects the contextual and purposeful aspects of social scientific understanding and assumes there are certain areas in the social sciences where understanding should take on one form and not some other. In particular, it takes it for granted that in certain areas of social science understanding must be in terms of the agent's point of view where this involves thick descriptions and no causal understanding while in other areas understanding must be in terms of thin descriptions and causal understanding. But this account puts too much faith in the correctness of actual practice. Why, for example, should we assume that just because Clifford Geertz has given an interpretation of the Balinese cockfight in terms of thick descriptions that seem to preclude causal understanding, other social scientists cannot understand such a practice in causal terms.[10] In general, there is no reason why, depending on one's purpose and questions, both thick and thin descriptions cannot be given on the same phenomenon.

Another problem with Little's version of the Different Areas approach is that it assumes that naturalistic understanding must be from the perspective of the social actor. This is suggested by Little's requirement that naturalistic causal explanations should be grounded in the analyses of the circumstances of agency.[11] But, as we have repeatedly seen, in certain contexts and for certain purposes, understanding can be achieved without taking the point of view of the actor.

Yet another problem with the Different Areas version of methodological pluralism concerns the limitations it places on causal understanding. Maintaining that although human action described by a thick theory cannot be causally understood, action in terms of a thin theory can be, Little seems to exclude from this category, understanding in terms of a thick theory of action.[12] However, he provides no good reason why actions that are thinly described can be causally understood while actions that are thickly described cannot be. Nevertheless, a clear rationale is important for Little's position since one of the main reasons for weak antinaturalism is that there are noncausal explanations in terms of thick description that are neglected by strong naturalism.

Still another limitation of Little's account has to do with the methodological positions it excludes. Little confines his discussion to naturalism and antinaturalism, but there is a least one other position to be considered, namely critical social science. As we have seen in our discussion of Habermas, according to critical social science, the social sciences should expose the hidden biases and ideologies that lie behind our social thinking. The advocates of critical social science maintain that the deep unconscious prejudices we hold about class, race, and gender influence our research, and that the social sciences should raise these to consciousness so that we can escape their influence and become liberated.[13] Thus, for instance, arguing that the social sciences display a deep bias towards women, feminist scholars have attempted to bring this to the surface in social scientific research. Unlike the naturalist and antinaturalist approaches, critical social science has as its direct goal human emancipation: liberation from prejudice, ignorance, and actual oppression.

An inclusive pluralism should be able to embrace the methodology of critical social science. However, it is difficult for Little's Different Areas account to do so. In order for critical social science to be assimilated to the Different Areas approach, criticism would have to be appropriate only in certain areas of social science. But this is not the case. Practically all areas of social science have theories, explanations, and information that can be used as criticism depending on the circumstances. As James Bohman has argued, explanations from ethnomethodology to rational choice theory, from economics to anthropology can be used with a critical purpose although some explanations are more adequate than others.[14]

The Synthesis Account

The pluralistic methodology that Brian Fay and J. Donald Moon developed in their paper, "What Would an Adequate Philosophy of Social Science Look Like?"[15] represents a sharp contrast to Little's Different Areas version of methodological pluralism. According to their Synthesis Account, methodological pluralism[16] involves a synthesis of different methodological points of view in order to overcome the weaknesses of each one considered in isolation.

Fay and Moon maintain that neither the naturalistic nor the antinaturalistic position can answer three questions that any adequate philosophy of the social sciences must address: What is the relation between interpretation and explanation? What is the nature of scientific theory? What is the role of critique?

Interpreting human action is essential to social science, they argue, for descriptions in terms of human action can neither be reduced to behavior nor eliminated. In this respect they believe the interpretative position to be right and naturalism wrong. In their view, however, it does not follow from the necessity of interpretation that social science *only* consists in the interpretation of human actions, as the interpretative position claims. Noting that social scientists give causal explanations of actions and of many other phenomena, they conclude that neither naturalism nor antinaturalism provides an adequate account of the relation between interpretation and explanation. Nor, according to these authors, does either position give an adequate account of social scientific theory. The interpretative position neglects the topic entirely, they say, while the naturalistic position wrongly assimilates social scientific theories to naturalistic ones. Further, Fay and Moon hold that neither position gives an explanation of the role of critique. Whereas the interpretative position is unable to transcend the limited and perhaps false and irrational perspective of social actors and show that their outlook is mistaken, the naturalistic position is unable to assess the rationality of the actors' beliefs since it is not concerned with the rationality of belief systems.

Are the two versions of methodological pluralism so far compatible? It seems on the face of it that they are not. Whereas Little's Different Areas account entails that there are areas in which causal explanation is inappropriate or impossible, Fay and Moon's Synthesis Account seems to assume that *every* explanation of human action involves *both* causal and interpretative aspects. Fay and Moon's account seems to rule out both noncausal explanations, that is, interpretations that are not the first step towards explanation. In addition, Little assumes that naturalism is compatible with both the development of social scientific theories and a concern with rational belief. For instance, he argues that rational choice theory is compatible with naturalism. Arguing that naturalism cannot develop theories appropriate to the social phenomena, Fay and Moon deny this.

Are any of the Verstehen theorists considered in the previous chapters a methodological pluralist in the synthesis sense? Perhaps the closest candidate is Habermas who, according to his interpreters, combines interpretative, causal, and critical aspects in his overall philosophy of social science.[17] However, it is difficult to find any specific causal theses in Habermas's text[18] and the index to *The Theory of Communicative Action* contains no references to causality.

Evaluation of the Synthesis Account

Fay and Moon's Synthesis Account has two important strengths. First of all, this version of methodological pluralism recognizes that interpretation and causal understanding, far from being incompatible, might work in tandem. In addition, it acknowledges both the importance of critical social science and the relevance of naturalistic and antinaturalistic methodologies to critical social science. However, like the Different Areas version, it has significant problems.

As we have seen, the Synthesis Account seems to assume that causal explanations of human action are always appropriate and that there is no room for autonomous nonexplanatory interpretations of human action. Fay and Moon provide no justification for these contentions. One cannot rule out a priori the possibility that there are interpretations of action that are not preliminary to causal explanations, yet this is what the Synthesis Account does. In some contexts and relative to some purposes, understanding might consist in giving an interpretation of what has happened without this being preliminary to a causal explanation.

Another problem with Fay and Moon's account is that they seem to assume that interpretation is always necessary in the social sciences, and in fact seem to identify giving an interpretation with understanding human behavior as human action. However, it is not obvious that interpretation is always necessary.[19] Moreover, one can interpret human behavior as, for example, part of a social movement or a historical trend rather than as a human action.

The Pragmatic Account

A third version of methodological pluralism has been developed by Paul A. Roth.[20] On this Pragmatic Account, multiple theoretical approaches are to be encouraged in the social sciences on both moral and scientific grounds.Roth opposes what he calls methodological exclusivism, that is, the view that there is just one proper method for the social sciences. Thus, he opposes both the view expounded by Richard Rudner, among others, that there is a unity of method between the natural and social sciences, and the view of those such as Peter Winch and others that there is a fundamental difference between the methodologies of the social and the natural sciences.

Methodological pluralism, according to Roth, is the denial of methodological exclusivism. His major argument against the latter is that it wrongly assumes that there is one proper set of rules that defines the study of human behavior. Roth maintains that no sense can be made out of "one proper set of rules." Basing his position on the theories of Quine, Feyerabend, and Rorty, he argues that there is a parallel between the defense of a pluralistic methodology and J. S. Mill's defense of liberty. We should be methodological pluralists, he says, because it is "in the interests of both freedom and knowledge to do so."[21]

Methodological pluralism in the social sciences, Roth says, maximizes the opportunities of freedom of thought and the growth of scientific knowledge. It does not mean that anything goes, however. On the contrary, one can evaluate different approaches pragmatically, that is, in terms of whether they further our goals. This idea is made clear in his discussion of the doctrine of Verstehen. According to advocates of Verstehen, one must understand human beings on their own terms: that is, the action must be comprehensible in human terms. However, critics of Verstehen maintain that understanding social phenomena in human terms is not necessary. Roth agrees with Rorty that whether one uses Verstehen or not "is a moral decision—a question of how one chooses to view one's fellow humans, or a question of the purpose for which one is studying them. The method is a function of the interest of the researcher and not the essence of the object studied."[22]

This brand of methodological pluralism is to be contrasted with the two previously considered. First of all, although the scope of Roth's pluralism is somewhat vague it seems to be broader than either Little's or Fay and Moon's. While Little's theory encompasses only naturalism and antinaturalism and Fay and Moon's includes only naturalism, antinaturalism, and critical social science, Roth's pluralism can include alternative approaches to inquiry.[23] A more important difference, however, is that Little believes that naturalism and antinaturalism are appropriate in different areas of social science whereas Roth maintains that the approach one uses is dependent on one's goals and interests. This pragmatic aspect of Roth's methodological pluralism also contrasts with the position of Fay and Moon that both naturalism and antinaturalism are intrinsically limited and require synthesis in every case.

Evaluation of the Pragmatic Account

Roth's Pragmatic Account has two major strengths. It recognizes explicitly that different methodological positions are appropriate or inappropriate relative to certain purposes and questions. In this respect it is closer than the other types to the kind of methodological pluralism advocated here. Moreover, it acknowledges that not "everything goes" and that methodologies can and should be evaluated in terms of contextual purposes and questions.

However, this version also has an important problem. Although it emphasizes the pragmatic dimension of methodologies in the social sciences and the need for empirical evaluation, it neglects to supply the needed evidence to justify its overall claims. Why should we suppose that the use of multiple methodologies in the social sciences will maximize the growth of social scientific knowledge, as Roth assumes? Presumably his claim for the virtues of methodological pluralism is in part empirical and thus requires empirical support which he does not supply.

The only argument Roth adduces in support of his thesis that methodological pluralism maximizes social scientific knowledge is a vague analogical one. He maintains that "my effort is, like John Stuart Mill's defense of liberty which I greatly admire, to show that we are most likely to do best (in the pursuit of knowledge) by adopting a nonrestricted view of what is to count as a form of rational inquiry."[24] However, this parallel is hardly convincing. Even if freedom of thought and unrestricted self-regarding action is better for the pursuit of knowledge than restricted thought and self-regarding action, it is by no means clear that methodological pluralism in the social sciences is better than its alternatives for the pursuit of social scientific knowledge. For one thing, the problem arises of how to decide when social scientific knowledge has increased, since what counts as increased knowledge may be relative to the methodology pursued. For example, an increase in nomological generalizations that provide warranted predictions would be counted as increased knowledge for naturalism but not antinaturalism, while an increase in justified thick descriptions would be considered as an increase in knowledge for antinaturalism but not for naturalism unless these descriptions were preliminary to causal explanations.

Furthermore, whether freedom of thought and unrestricted self-regarding action is more conducive to the pursuit of knowledge than its alternative is not proven. After all, science has progressed in many different times and many different cultures, including one in which freedom has been greatly restricted relative to our standards.[25] It is uncertain whether its progress in these times and cultures would have been greater had freedom been less restricted.

Roth's basic mistake, as I see it, is to commit himself to providing a general rationale for his type of methodological pluralism in terms of the overall growth of science. Although it may be possible to provide such a rationale, Roth is not close to doing so and, more important, such a rationale is not necessary. Whether or not the use of a plurality of ways of understanding contributes to the overall growth of scientific knowledge—whatever that might mean—it does enable us to ask and answer different questions about social phenomena. Surely this is enough of a rationale.

In previous chapters, the question at issue was not whether the restrictions that Verstehenists put on social inquiry would undermine the overall growth of scientific knowledge. The issue was that these restrictions block important questions and lines of inquiry. The question of whether these restrictions would tend to contribute to the overall growth of social science is too unclear to be of much interest.

Conclusion

Although Little's Different Areas approach and Fay and Moon's Synthesis Approach are improvements over methodological exclusivism, these positions still entail unacceptable restrictions on scientific understanding. Roth's Pragmatic Approach to methodological pluralism is correct in principle. However, Roth goes astray in trying to produce a general rationale in terms of the growth of science. Such a rationale is neither successful nor necessary.

Above all, what needs to be grasped is the contextual aspects of social inquiry and how this affects understanding. Understanding social phenomena is dependent upon at least three interrelated factors: the interests of the social scientist who is trying to understand, the questions being asked by the social scientist, the description of the phenomena given by the social scientist. Any approach that prevents diverse interests of social inquiry from being fulfilled, that blocks different questions from being asked, and that is insensitive to the different descriptions of the phenomena under investigation is unwarranted.

First of all, understanding is dependent on the interest of the social scientist. If a social scientist is interested in the social conditions that are relevant to causally explaining a social revolution, then citing causally relevant social conditions would provide understanding, and citing the beliefs and aspirations of the actors would not. However, if one is concerned about the psychological factors that induce some people to take part in the revolution and some people not to, then relating their beliefs and aspirations to their actions is appropriate, and citing social conditions is not. But, even in this case, Verstehen may be irrelevant for understanding if the social scientist is interested in the deep unconscious motives that lead to revolution, and thus understanding action in terms of subjective categories of the actor would not be suitable to this purpose.

Closely related to the interest of the social scientist is the question being asked. For example, an answer to a question concerning what function a social revolution serves provides different understanding from an answer to a question about the origin of the institution. In either case Verstehen may or may not be relevant depending on what other questions are being asked. With respect to the function of an institution, suppose the question at issue is how the institution of Mormon polygamy functions to keep women subservient to men. One type of answer could be in terms of the effects of the beliefs about polygamy on male dominance and female submissive behavior. Verstehen in terms of the subjective understanding of the actors might well be relevant. On the other hand, suppose the question at issue is the function of polygamy in the control of sexually transmitted diseases among Mormons. Here it is less obvious that subjective understanding of the actor would be relevant and knowledge of causal relations between objective variables may serve well enough.

Moreover, closely related to the interests of the social actors and the questions being asked in terms of these interests are the descriptions of the phenomena under investigation. On the one hand, if human behavior is described in action terms, then understanding in terms of the subjective categories of the actors is appropriate. On the other hand, if the technical terms of cognitive psychology are used, understanding would not be in these terms. What descriptive categories are used would in turn be in terms of the social scientists' interests and goals and the questions the scientists are being asked.

These considerations indicate the grains of truth in the Different Areas account and the Synthesis Account. With respect to the Different Areas account, it is true that in certain areas of social scientific inquiry, a certain purpose, specific questions, and descriptions may be so common and ingrained that it is difficult to imagine these areas being approached in a different way. Consequently, it is easy to suppose that a single methodology is appropriate to these area. However, this is an illusion caused by not looking beyond the dominant methodology to the interests, questions, and descriptions that motivate and characterize it. With respect to the Synthesis Account, it is true that in relation to certain purposes a synthesis of different methodological approaches is needed. However, this special case need not set the standard for the entire field. Thus, even supposing Moon and Fay are correct that critical social science needs to be synthesized with naturalist and interpretive elements, social critique is not relevant in all contexts.

I believe that it is possible to formulate a more adequate account of methodological pluralism based on these insights. The type of methodological pluralism I will now suggest is borrowed from the other versions. I formulate Complex Methodological Pluralism as a set of maxims to guide action.

The Fundamental Maxim (FM) of Complex Methodological Pluralism is:

(FM): Develop and use alternative methodologies and theoretical approaches that are relevant to the goals pursued and questions being asked!

A special case of (FM) is M1 that urges the pursuit of naturalism, antinaturalism, and critical social science methodologies in the social sciences. It can be formulated in this way:

M1: Develop and use the methodologies of naturalism, antinaturalism, and critical social science when these are appropriate to the goals pursued and to the questions being asked!

Giving Different Areas Methodological Pluralism its due, M_1^{I} is a special case of M_1^{I}:

M_1^{I}: Develop and use the methodologies of naturalism, antinaturalism, and critical social science in different areas of social science so long as these are appropriate to the goals pursued and the questions being asked in these areas!

Giving the Synthesis Account recognition, M_1^{II} is also a special case of M_1^{II}:

M_1^{II}: Synthesize the methodologies of naturalism, antinaturalism, and critical social science so long as this is appropriate to the goals pursued and questions being asked in different areas of social science!

I make no claims about whether following these maxims will maximize social scientific knowledge. What I do believe is that following these maxims will result in a less restrictive social science and enable social scientists to answer more questions. However, it should be clear that problems remain with respect to all of the methodologies at issue. For example, with respect to Verstehen's progeny—interpretive social science—the question of the testing of conflicting interpretations is a continuing problem. This problem will have to be solved before interpretation can provide understanding of social behavior in appropriate contexts of inquiry.

Notes

1. I would argue that there are alternative methodologies in the natural sciences and a pluralistic approach to methodology is advisable in the natural sciences. But I will not have time to develop this thesis here. The question of whether methodological pluralism is a viable approach in the natural sciences should not be confused with whether pluralistic *theories*, rather than methodologies, should be used in the natural sciences. Arne Naess, for example, has advocated pluralistic theorizing in the natural sciences and philosophy. See Arne Naess, "Pluralistic Theorizing in Physics and Philosophy," *Danish Year Book of Philosophy*, vol. 1964, pp. 101-11. However, it seems clear that Naess would be sympathetic to methodological pluralism.

2. See, for example, Rudolf Carnap, *Introduction to Semantics* (Cambridge, MA: Harvard University Press, 1948), p. 247.

3. Paul Feyerabend, *Against Method: Outline of an Anarchist Theory of Knowledge* (London: New Left Books, 1975), p. 52.

4. Daniel Little, *Varieties of Social Explanation* (Boulder, CO: Westview Books, 1991), chapter 11.

5. Little seems to assume that the main goal of the natural sciences is to provide causal explanations; consequently, a naturalistic approach to the social sciences should have the same goal. Elsewhere I have argued that this account of the natural sciences is incorrect. See Michael Martin, *Concepts of Science Education* (Chicago: Scott-Foresman, 1972).

6. By this Little means that, although social concepts are not reducible to individual concepts and social explanations need not be derivable from laws of individual-level phenomena, social phenomena supervene on the actions of individuals. This means that it must be possible to indicate at least schematically "the mechanism at the level of local individual behavior through which the aggregate phenomena emerge." According to Little, these mechanisms involve individual choice and decision and thus seem to presuppose the point of view of the actor. See Little, *Varieties of Social Explanation*, p. 200.

7. Little does not explicitly use this term but it is in keeping with the spirit of his terminology.

8. Causal explanations for Little are closely connected with causal mechanisms. A causal explanation of E in terms of C in terms of a causal mechanism would specify a series of events leading from C to E in which the transition between these events is governed by one or more laws. This account should be contrasted with the covering-law account of explanation. See Carl Hempel, "The Function of General Laws in History," in *Aspects of Scientific Explanation* (New York: The Free Press, 1965).

9. Little does not explicitly say that this explanation is not causal, but unless one assumes that it is a noncausal explanation it is difficult to make sense of his thesis. See *Varieties of Social Explanations*, pp. 233-34. On p. 233, Little argues that according to antinaturalism causal explanations have no legitimate role to play and only interpretative explanations are permissible. On p. 234, Little gives examples of social science explanations, some of which involve interpretation and some of which do not. This example is cited as one involving interpretation and as conforming to the antinaturalist restrictions. One naturally assumes from this that it is a noncausal explanation.

10. This is especially true when there is good reason to think that causal notions are presupposed in Geertz's own interpretation despite his rejection of them. See chapter 8.

11. See note 6.

12. See Little, *Varieties of Social Explanation*, chapters 2-4.

13. See David Braybrooke, *Philosophy of Social Science* (Englewood Cliffs, NJ: Prentice-Hall, 1987), chapters 1 and 4; see also Brian Fay, *Critical Social Science* (Ithaca, NY: Cornell University Press, 1987).

14. James Bohman, *New Philosophy of Social Science* (Cambridge, MA: The MIT Press, 1991), p. 227.

15. Brian Fay and J. Donald Moon, "What Would an Adequate Philosophy of Social Science Look Like?" Michael Martin and Lee McIntyre, eds., *Readings in the Philosophy of Social Science* (Cambridge, MA: The MIT Press, 1994), pp. 21-35; originally published in *Philosophy of Social Science* 7, 1977, pp. 209-27. David

Braybrooke develops a pluralistic methodology to the philosophy of social science that is based on the approach of Fay and Moon. See Braybrooke, op. cit.

16. Fay and Moon do not call their approach methodological pluralism but it is clear that this is, in fact, what it is.

17. See Kenneth Baynes, "Rational Reconstruction and Social Criticism: Habermas's Model of Interpretive Social Science," *The Philosophical Forum* 20, 1989-90, p. 122, and Thomas McCarthy, *The Critical Theory of Jürgen Habermas* (Cambridge, MA: The MIT Press, 1978), p. 140.

18. See Braybrooke, *Philosophy of Social Science* (Englewood Cliffs, NJ: Prentice-Hall, Inc., 1987), p. 87.

19. Sometimes understanding does not involve interpretation since we can understand something immediately and prereflectively. On this point, see Richard Shusterman, "Beneath Interpretation," *The Interpretive Turn*, eds. David R. Hiley, James F. Bohman, and Richard Shusterman (Ithaca, NY: Cornell University Press, 1991), pp. 102-28.

20. Paul A. Roth, *Meaning and Method in the Social Sciences: A Case of Methodological Pluralism* (Ithaca, NY: Cornell University Press, 1987).

21. Ibid., p. 74.

22. Ibid., p. 110.

23. Unfortunately, Roth is unclear on what these alternative approaches would be.

24. Ibid., p. 6.

25. For an argument that there is a correlation between science and democracy, see Joseph Needham, "Science and Democracy: A Fundamental Correlation," *The Radical Economy of Science*, ed. Sandra Harding (Bloomington, Indiana University Press, 1993), pp. 434-39. However, also see Sandra Harding's skeptical comments on this paper, p. 432.

Index

meaning of, 189
Transfer Verstehen
    examples of, 54
    intuitive insight Verstehen, 53-54
Turner, Victor, 146

Utterance meaning
    assessment making, 228
    meaning of, 227
    validity conditions, 228

Validity Condition Thesis (VCT)
    defined, 227
    linguistic meaning of, 228
    open question arguments, 228
    pragmatic meaning of, 228
    as proposals, 233
Verification
    anti-verification criticism, 43
    background, 41-43
    conclusions, 65-67
    criticisms of, 44-49
    positivism and, 41-43
    Verstehen defense methods, 49-65
Verification Thesis (VT)
    Abel's criticism, 45-46
    AVC and, 43
    Rudner's criticism, 47-49
    Scriven's criticism of, 59
Verstehen
    antipositivists and, 3
    classical theory analysis, 3
    contemporary varieties of, 3-4
    defined, 1, 2, 4
    as interpretation, 187
    methodological pluralism and, 4
    positivism and, 2
    positivists analysis, 3
    preliminary account of, 2-3
    social science use, 2
    theorists claims of, 4-5
    theorists views on, 1
Verstehen classic position
    Collingwood and, 25-35
    conclusions on, 35-36
    Dilthey and, 8-16
    social science approaches, 7
    uses of, 7
    Weber and, 16-25
Verstehen defenses
    AVC interpretations, 57
    historical inquiry and, 63

hypothesis verifying, 61-62
intersubjective verification, 59-60
intersubjective verifying, 60-61
intuitive insights, 62
knowledge without observations, 58-59
natural and social science tools, 54-56
nonempathetic methods, 56-57
reliability establishing, 60
social scientific techniques, 64-65
transfer sense of, 53-54
validating hypothesis validating, 49-50
verification methods and, 49
vs Abel's example, 50-51
vs Abel's thesis, 51-52
Warren Commission Report, 63-64
Verstehen interpretation
    epistemological problems of, 139-140
    life-world understanding and, 139
    social actors meaning, 140
    social reality inconsistency, 140
    social science methodology, 140-141
    subjective meaning experiencing, 141
Virtual participation
    actor's speech familiarity, 226
    claims assessments, 227
    prescribing understanding, 233-234
    RAT, 232-233
    "seems clearly false" assessments, 232
    social scientists as, 225-226
    thesis about, 227
    understanding vs assessing meaning, 229-231
    utterance meaning, 227
    validity claims types, 226-227
    "yet possible" assessments, 231
    See also Assessment Thesis; Validity Condition Thesis

Warren Commission Report, 63-64
Wax, Murray
    explanatory Verstehen, 82
    interpersonal intuition Verstehen, 81-82
    intercultural Verstehen, 81
    pattern recognition and interpretation, 81
    social scientific research and, 82
    Verstehen defending, 81
    vs Able, 81-82